UXBRIDGE College Learning Centre
Coldharbour Lane, Hayes, Middlesex UB3 3BB
Telephone: 01895 853740

Please return this item to the Learning Centre
on or before the last date stamped below:

1 0 NOV 2005		
1 2 DEC 2005		
		616.928

Aspergeris syndrome in young people

of related interest

Asperger's Syndrome
A Guide for Parents and Professionals
Tony Attwood
ISBN 1 85302 577 1

Relationship Development Intervention with Young Children
Social and Emotional Development Activities for Asperger
Syndrome, Autism, PDD and NLD
Steven E. Gutstein and Rachelle K. Sheely
ISBN 1 84310 714 7

Understanding Autism Spectrum Disorders
Frequently Asked Questions
Diane Yapko
ISBN 1 84310 756 2

Parenting a Child with Asperger Syndrome
200 Tips and Strategies
Brenda Boyd
ISBN 1 84310 137 8

Asperger Syndrome – What Teachers Need to Know
Matt Winter
Written for Cloud 9 Children's Foundation
ISBN 1 84310 143 2 pb

My Social Stories Book
Carol Gray and Abbie Leigh White
Illustrated by Sean McAndrew
ISBN 1 85302 950 5

Giggle Time – Establishing the Social Connection
A Program to Develop the Communication Skills of Children
with Autism, Asperger Syndrome and PDD
Susan Aud Sonders
ISBN 1 84310 716 3

Asperger's Syndrome in Young Children

A Developmental Guide for Parents and Professionals

Laurie Leventhal-Belfer and Cassandra Coe

Jessica Kingsley Publishers
London and New York

First published in the United Kingdom in 2004
by Jessica Kingsley Publishers Ltd
116 Pentonville Road
London N1 9JB, England
and
29 West 35th Street, 10th fl.
New York, NY 10001-2299, USA

www.jkp.com

Copyright © 2004 Laurie Leventhal-Belfer and Cassandra Coe

Library of Congress Cataloging in Publication Data
A CIP catalog record for this book is available from the Library of Congress

British Library Cataloguing in Publication Data
A CIP catalogue record for this book is available from the British Library

ISBN 1 84310 748 1

Printed and Bound in Great Britain by
Athenaeum Press, Gateshead, Tyne and Wear

Contents

ACKNOWLEDGMENTS   7

PREFACE   9

Part One: Understanding Asperger's Syndrome in Young Children

Chapter 1.   The World of the Young Child   17

Chapter 2.   The World of the Young Child with Asperger's
             Syndrome   32

Chapter 3.   The Diagnosis   53

Chapter 4.   The Many Faces of Young Children with
             Asperger's Syndrome   81

Chapter 5.   The Parents' Journey   105

Part Two: Interventions

Chapter 6.   Paths of Intervention: From Traditional to
             Alternative   131

Chapter 7.   Parent–Child Therapy: An Intervention for
             Building Relationships   144
             Lori Bond

Chapter 8.   Building Connections with Peers: Therapeutic
             Groups   160

Chapter 9.   Enhancing Relationships through Speech
             and Language Intervention   190
             Christine Bate

Chapter 10. Building Connections through Sensory and
             Motor Pathways: Occupational Therapy   211
             Teri Wiss

Chapter 11. Building Connections with the Child's School   238

Chapter 12. The Ongoing Journey   262

APPENDIX I   DIAGNOSTIC CRITERIA   270

APPENDIX II   BEHAVIORAL STRATEGIES CHART FOR GROUP
                 SETTINGS   274

APPENDIX III   ELIGIBILITY CRITERIA FOR SPECIAL EDUCATION
                 SERVICES IN THE UNITED STATES   280

APPENDIX IV   ASPERGER'S SYNDROME WEB SITES   284

THE CONTRIBUTORS   285

REFERENCES   286

SUBJECT INDEX   296

AUTHOR INDEX   301

Acknowledgments

The book is dedicated to the parents in the Friends' Program, a play-centered therapy group for young children with Asperger's Syndrome (AS) and their families, which we directed at the Palo Alto Children's Health Council. The parents have given us the opportunity to learn from them and learn what it means to have a child with AS. They have shared with us the dreams they have for their children, the barriers they have sometimes faced in seeking help, and the pleasures and rewards they have experienced with their children. Each and every parent's journey has informed us and educated us on how to be better clinicians working with young children with Asperger's Syndrome. We are also indebted to the children who have shown us that they, like all other children, love to play, have strong feelings, treasure having others interested in their ideas, and yearn for friends. What they have taught us informs and shapes the core of this work and reminds us how unique and individual children are.

We would also like to thank our husbands, without whose endless support, editing, childcare, and encouragement this book would never have been written. And our thanks to our children for providing us with the front row tickets to observe and engage in hours of play at the playground, birthday parties, play dates, and at their schools. And to Isaac, the oldest, we would like to express our thanks for his patient assistance on the computer, a tool he seems able to use as easily as we use the pen.

Preface

It seems as if a month does not pass without an article appearing in the lay press about the subject of Asperger's Syndrome or Autistic Spectrum Disorders. Since Asperger's Syndrome was officially recognized in the United States in the fourth edition of the *Diagnostic and Statistical Manual of Mental Disorders* (DSM-IV: American Psychiatric Association 1994) and in the tenth revision of the *International Classification of Diseases* (ICD-10: World Health Organization 1993) there has been a dramatic increase in the number of children diagnosed with this condition. This has been accompanied by an increase in the number of books and papers written about its history, diagnosis, etiology, and intervention approaches (Klin, Volkmar and Sparrow 2000). Historically the diagnosis was not made until the child was in elementary school. However, earlier identification is now occurring, due in part to the increase in the number of young children participating in group programs (e.g. childcare, preschool, and full-day kindergarten) and the consequent identification of children who have difficulty adapting to the social demands of these settings. Additionally, with the increase in the number of school age children being diagnosed with Asperger's Syndrome, there has been a growing awareness of the disorder and much interest in how it might present in younger children.

Our experiences in working with young children with Asperger's Syndrome and their families over the past 15 years have underscored the need for a book that provides parents and professionals with a working under-standing of the Syndrome in young children and models for intervention. This book was developed with these goals in mind.

The history of Asperger's Syndrome

The Syndrome is named after the Viennese pediatrician Dr. Hans Asperger who coined the term "autistic psychopathy" in 1944 to describe four boys, ages 6–11, who displayed problems adapting to social situations despite having good language and cognitive skills. The children were not thought to be unique but rather representative of a much larger set of children in his practice. In addition to having social problems the children were also described as being preoccupied by topics such as the weather or trains that dominated much of their lives and interfered with their work and play. He also observed that they were awkward and clumsy in group sports activities. They had difficulty understanding and being empathic to other children's feelings and social cues. Asperger described these children as being like "little professors" who could talk endlessly about their area of special interest but were oblivious to the nonverbal and verbal cues of others. These qualities often led to noncompliance and negativism towards teachers and peers who were not interested in their views, and resulted in aggression or withdrawal if they felt insulted. Still, Asperger viewed these children as having a relatively positive outcome since their parents often had similar qualities and were relatively well adapted (Klin, Volkmar and Sparrow 2000).

When Asperger wrote this paper he was not aware of Leo Kanner's original writing on childhood autism. Asperger's paper did not receive much attention until it was translated into English by Dr. Uta Frith in 1994 and applied in a clinical setting by the British psychiatrist Dr. Lorna Wing. Dr. Wing described a group of children who fit Dr. Asperger's original description. She elaborated on the diagnosis by presenting them as children who were bright and curious, but had a triad of challenges in the areas of social interaction, communication, and imagination. She went on to describe them as rigid, having a narrow range of interests, and repetitive patterns of activities. In contrast to autism these children did not show impairments in cognitive and language abilities early in life. Dr. Wing also dispelled an earlier belief that these children's difficulties were caused by poor parenting, asserting instead that Autistic Spectrum Disorders are caused by atypical development. Although Dr. Wing moved the conceptual framework of Asperger's Syndrome closer to autism there is still an ongoing debate as to whether it should be viewed totally apart from autism, as Dr. Asperger originally thought, or within the same classification system.

Overview of the book

How does one begin to understand the world of these children as described initially by Hans Asperger and later by Lorna Wing? Part One is devoted to answering this question.

We will begin in Chapter 1 by exploring the world of the young child and the developmental tasks of children between the ages of three and six. We feel that it is important to have knowledge of this stage of early childhood in order to understand how a young child with Asperger's Syndrome copes with the developmental undertakings of this period. The second chapter will look at these same developmental areas and the various ways that they may differ for a young child with Asperger's Syndrome. Chapter 3 will take a closer look at what a developmentally based assessment for a young child with Asperger's Syndrome entails, the different diagnostic criteria and diagnoses that may be considered, and how they are pertinent to young children. Because we are taking a multidisciplinary approach, the chapter will describe components of a mental health and cognitive evaluation, as well as evaluations in speech and language (Christine Bate) and occupational therapy (Teri Wiss). Chapter 4 presents a detailed description of three different young boys with Asperger's Syndrome. The case studies provide a rich example of how varied the children can be, each having different strengths, degrees of adaptation, and challenges. Chapter 5 will examine the developmental shifts that many parents go through as their understanding of their child grows.

Part Two of the book is devoted to interventions for children with Asperger's Syndrome. As we have emphasized, the young child's capacity to interact, communicate, and play with his peers plays a central role in his development. For this reason we have chosen to review interventions that we believe are best suited to understanding and facilitating the young child's social interactions, communication, imagination, and flexibility. Chapter 6 provides an overview of interventions that may help both the child and his parents utilize a range of services. Dr. Lori Bond writes the next chapter in this part, Chapter 7, on parent–child therapy. Dr. Bond is the director of a diagnostic and treatment program for young children with Autistic Spectrum Disorders. In this chapter her emphasis is on helping parents understand the diagnosis, and what it means to them and to their relationship with their child, and techniques for intervention. Chapter 8 describes a therapeutic group program for young children with Asperger's Syndrome and their parents. We see this type of program as a natural step for parents to take as they move from viewing their child solely within the context of their relationship to seeing their child within a peer group. The chapter explores the "nuts and bolts" of a group program as well as the therapeutic processes. The next two chapters are written by invited authors because of their expertise in the areas of speech and language intervention and occupational therapy. Christine Bate, in Chapter 9, explores the important role that speech and language intervention can play in expanding the young child's capacity to engage in social interactions, reciprocal communication, and imaginary play. In Chapter 10, Teri Wiss examines the valuable role that occupational therapy can play in helping us understand the motor and sensory challenges often experienced by young children with Asperger's Syndrome. From the perspective of an occupational therapist, people need to know how to connect with their own bodies before they can easily connect with their environment and other people. Chapter 11 is devoted to school-based interventions and emphasizes the importance of having collaborative relationships between the child's parents and teachers. The last chapter will provide an update on the children we first presented in Chapter 4 as well as a reflection of what we have learned about AS from working with these children and their families for the past 15 years.

To the parents of young children with Asperger's Syndrome

For many of the parents reading this book, perhaps because the diagnosis is so new, there is a very good chance that different professionals have offered different diagnoses and/or varying recommendations for interventions. Some may have said that your child has a serious developmental problem, others that all your child needs is better limit setting, and still others that nothing is wrong with your child. We hope that this book will provide you with a model for understanding normal development, Asperger's Syndrome in general, and what it means specifically for you and your child. We believe that reading this book will make you more empowered to ask professionals about your child and determine with them the best path of intervention to take. We realize that both your understanding of your child and the intervention choices that you make can change over time depending on the needs of your child and the resources available to you through your schools and community. Our goal is that the book leaves you with a feeling of hope. Our wish is that with early diagnosis and developmentally guided intervention the journey you travel with your child will be less stressful and more rewarding for everyone involved.

To the teachers and childcare providers

For many of you the term Asperger's Syndrome may have been first heard from a parent or a friend whose child had this disorder. This book was written to provide insight into how these children present themselves, experience the world, and turn to you for support. They pose a special challenge because there can be many apparently conflicting aspects to their presentation; they may appear so bright and have so much to say, yet surprise you when they grab things from another child or demand your full attention. We hope to provide you with a framework for understanding their behavior and models for intervention that can be easily integrated into your classrooms. Lastly, we hope that this book leaves you feeling supported for the important and challenging work you do with these children on a daily basis. In our opinion you are an invaluable resource for the family and professionals involved in the care of a young child with Asperger's Syndrome and deserve to be seen as a valued member of the child's treatment team.

To the medical and mental health community

We hope that the book provides you with insight into the world of young children with Asperger's Syndrome, the diverse ways they may present, the challenges that they pose for their parents, and paths parents may want to explore for intervention. Parents treasure a clinician who they feel is interested in learning about their child with them and supports them in this process.

Part One

Understanding Asperger's Syndrome in Young Children

CHAPTER 1

The World of the Young Child

Parents of a young child with Asperger's Syndrome often question if their child's behavior is within the "normal" range. The world of the young child is a rich and complicated place with so many things happening developmentally that this can be a difficult question to answer. Given the complexities of the world of the young child, we feel that it is important to develop a shared understanding of the developmental tasks salient at this age. This chapter will provide an overview of the areas of developmental growth that characterize the young child. What can make this time period both rewarding and challenging for parents, teachers, and children is that the children are undergoing major changes at varying rates in differing areas of development. With this in mind we will examine the developmental tasks which are characteristic of the young child in the areas of sensory-motor development, communication, cognition, play, emotional and social functioning, relationships with caregivers and peers, and the child's capacity to cope with stressful events.

Due to the fact that Asperger's Syndrome is much more prevalent in boys than girls, we have chosen to use the male pronoun "he" throughout the book, recognizing that the diagnosis also applies to girls. We also strongly encourage all readers to consider the impact that culture plays in our understanding and interpretation of behavior. All families have their own cultural framework from which they perceive and respond to the world around them. When interpretations of behavior are being made, sensitivity to this cultural lens is important for working with the family in a culturally respectful manner. Similarly, professionals working with these families (e.g. teachers, pediatricians, mental health professionals, and other clinicians) also wear their own cultural lens. The awareness of each other's cultural background and potential biases will help one gain a better understanding of the developmental tasks of the young child.

Let us now take a step into the young child's world by describing a common scene from the playground and invite you to think about the play, communication, and socialization of the children in this vignette.

A story common to many four-year-olds

As soon as John and Ben were let out of the car they ran to the large climbing structure and headed to the driver's wheel at the top of the climbing structure. Ben climbed to the top and announced, "All aboard, the ship is taking off for the sea." John quickly got on the "bridge" and pointed out the approaching pirate ships that he could see through his binoculars (fists). He told another boy who was digging in the sand that he better get on board or he would be attacked by a killer whale. John told him that he was the captain and that he could join the crew. Sam accepted the invitation, took hold of his shovel and joined John and Ben on the top of the structure. The boys looked out into the ocean announcing what they saw, warning the crew of dangers, and testing how far they could lean away from the boat's poles (the poles surrounding the slide) without falling off. With authority in their voices John and Ben informed each adult and child who approached the slide that they were on their ship in dangerous waters. A battle almost erupted as a toddler tried to take hold of the captain's steering wheel, leading to a confrontation between John, the "captain," and the toddler's mother. The crew decided to abandon the boat rather than include the group of pirates (toddlers) climbing on board.

As soon as they landed on the ground Ben pointed out that there was gold in the sand, and they quickly became a group of pirates, searching for the buried treasure. The two girls who were playing quietly under the structure watched with a look of disgust and found another place on the playground to have their private discussions. The boys, looking pleased with the girls' decision, continued digging as they announced their discovery of dinosaur bones and a "treasure map" (an old flattened paper cup) which John used to lead the crew on a rambunctious run across the park searching for the buried treasure. Ben's father, noticing that the boys were getting very excited and overheated, suggested that the "pirates" take a break and have some juice and snack. The boys seemed to alternate between eating the dinosaur cookies which Ben's father provided and moving them across the sand as they talked enthusiastically about which type of dinosaur was the most powerful, the fastest, and the smartest of them all. When the snack was finished they were told that they had ten more minutes before they had to go home. Ben announced a race to the tire swing where they stayed until it was time to go. The boys asked Ben's father to spin the swing around and they giggled with delight as they turned rapidly in the air and dared each other to jump off the swing, a dare which none accepted.

This vignette of these four-year-old boys visiting their neighborhood playground is just a snapshot of the rich, complex, and fast-paced play that characterizes the interactions between these children on a regular basis at the neighborhood park. The vignette illustrates many aspects of development so pertinent to the young child. As we have pointed out, their world is full of imagination, movement, social interactions, and problem solving. We will now look more closely at each area to fully appreciate all that is evolving in the young child. The first area we will examine is motor and sensory development.

Sensory and motor development

The park and school playgrounds are the best places to observe the dramatic leaps in the young child's *gross motor* development skills. In one section of the preschool you can see the two-year-olds tentatively climbing up ladders step by step and going down the slide with a teacher's assistance. In the next play yard there are the three- and four-year-olds running around the obstacles (other children, adults, and playground equipment), turning sharp corners between the swings, and skipping on one foot as they smoothly move between the tires on the ground. The tricycles, which were approached with apprehension at two, are being zoomed around the yard, constantly slowed down by the teacher on yard duty. Similarly the climbing structures that the toddlers used to walk under or hang from using the bottom bars are now being occupied on the highest point by boys and girls demonstrating their speed in climbing and their confidence in balancing and jumping onto the ground. The preschool child has also developed ball skills, as displayed in the ability to guide the course of a large kick ball or dribble a soccer ball across the field.

The child has also made major strides in the area of *fine motor* development. By age three-and-a-half most children can hold a pencil with a large grasp (fingers and thumb forming a fist around the pencil), draw a face, and write at least one letter of their name. They are beginning to use scissors and often enjoy stringing objects, such as beads or cereal, and painting. By age four they are able to draw a stick figure, copy a shape, draw identifiable objects, and copy numbers and letters. They enjoy playing with small blocks and figures that they can manipulate in and out of cars, toy houses, castles, and planes. They are also able to build elaborate block structures out of blocks of varying shapes and sizes (Linder 1993).

It is also helpful to look at the wide range of *sensory input* that a young child is "typically" exposed to at their preschool setting. If the preschooler is going to have success in any of the motor tasks we just described they need to have a keen sense of where their body is kinesthetically in space. Most children naturally do this each time they stand up in the block area and do not destroy their own or their peers' structures. They can avoid running into them on the tricycle and they are able to find their spot at circle time without stepping on another child. They tolerate a never-ending background of sounds ranging from a child giggling on the swing, a hero yelling at the bad guys, the ringing of the teacher's bell to come inside, a child crying in distress, and musical instruments, to list just a few. They are also exposed to a wide range of smells from their friends' lunches, the school's snacks, the teacher's perfume, their peers' body odors, or a new batch of clay. They will also feel a wide range of tactile sensations as they touch wet sand in the bathroom, dry sand on the playground, clay on the table, crumbs and sticky juice from snack, different types of carpet texture, paper towels, and finger paint. And they can enjoy eating food that is served and tastes differently from what they are familiar with. It is surprising how many variations of graham crackers there are on the market, or how attuned children can be to the taste differences in types of apple juice. Still, the majority of children are able to take these sensory inputs in stride. They may have preferences but they do not have a "melt down" because they feel overloaded or cannot tolerate any changes from ways they are familiar with. One can imagine the problems that can quickly arise in a preschool setting if the child feels overloaded and strikes out at another child or has a melt down, requiring the teacher's undivided attention for reasons that are not immediately apparent to the teacher.

Kopp (1982) proposed that the child's ability to acquire skills in *self-regulation* is related to both biological and social factors that are being impacted from birth. The child is born with its own temperament, sensitivity to external stimuli, and attentiveness to its internal cues. Obviously no infant can survive in isolation. The infant needs a nurturing caregiver that is responsive to his cues, is able to comfort him when distressed, and provides him with a predictable routine so that he is assured that his needs will be met. By the end of the second year the child begins to display some restraint without constant reminding. He knows not to pull the cloth off the table, grab the dog's ears, or pour the water on the floor. By three the child can display more self-regulation across settings, not just in specific, previously experienced situations. He is more adaptive and self-reflective about his behavior. By three years of age the child is expected to adapt to numerous activities in preschool, share with peers, be able to cooperate during play, and apologize if he hurts another child intentionally or accidentally. These are tasks that require the child to be aware of the impact that his behavior has on others, to know what is considered socially acceptable behavior, and to be able to restrain himself when he desires to do something differently.

Table 1.1 Key components of young children's sensory and motor development

- Fine motor development
- Gross motor development
- Muscle tone and motor planning
- Visual-motor planning
- Sensory modulation – hypersensitivity or insensitivity to sound, touch, smell, taste, and/or visual stimuli

---

Communication

The child's *expressive language* takes off like a rocket in the third year of life. The preschool period follows a time when the child's vocabulary has just had a growth spurt of at least 1000 words from the ages of two to three years. This growth continues at a rate of approximately 50 words a month (Davies 1999). Beginning around the age of three, the young child can engage in a simple dialogue with an adult and peers for more than a few turns, using language that is clear and easy to understand. By the age of four, children are speaking in grammatically correct long sentences, they can tell a story using words alone, and they have learned that words are powerful tools that can be used to get attention and determine the direction of symbolic play. The child is able to use prepositions like "behind" and "in front of" correctly, is constantly asking questions beginning with "what" and "how," and is able to talk about his own ideas, feelings, emotions, and attitudes when he feels secure and supported (Linder 1993).

The children's *receptive language* also blossoms during this period. They can sit quietly for long periods of time listening to a story and acquire a wealth of information from conversations with adults and peers, books, videos, and their daily adventures. Beginning at three years of age children can follow three-step commands given in a complete sentence such as, "Put the doll on the chair, pour her a drink, and then put her in bed." By age four they understand and use the prepositions "above," "below," and "at the bottom."

Pragmatic language refers to the child's ability to use new language skills in reciprocal social interactions with peers. Around four years of age children understand that they need to talk differently to their teacher than to a peer or a younger child. They understand the importance of getting another person's attention before talking to them and they are able to use words to get their attention, unlike toddlers who pull on their caregiver's body or clothes to get their attention or grab a desired object from a peer without using words. The three- to four-year-old uses words to request things ("May I?"; "Could you?"; "Please"), and communicate their approval ("That's beautiful"; "This is my favorite") and disapproval ("Stop that"; "That is not nice"; "That is not fair"). If one listens to the conversations on the playground one is sure to hear comments from the "local police officer" and "expert on proper etiquette." This is not to say that these same "playground authorities" are able to follow the advice they are so willing to give out to others when it is they who feel hurt or anxious. What is so striking about the preschool child is how much of his or her language is directed toward social interactions with adults and peers. Around four years of age one can hear preschoolers verbalize out loud their "private speech" which is an ongoing monologue about their thoughts, hopes, and feelings: "I am the doctor, I'm not going to hurt you. I just need to give you seven shots so you can go to Kindergarten. If you hold still and don't cry it will be over very quickly and you can go get a treat. I need to give you the shots." "John" repeats this monologue as he approaches his friend, grasping the thermometer from the pretend doctor's kit with a look of determination that he will administer the shots (Davies 1999). As one can see, the child's developmental paths in communication are very closely linked to the next areas we will review, the child's cognitive development and capacity to play.

Table 1.2 Key components of young children's communication

- The child's expressive language
- The child's receptive language
- The child's pragmatic language
- Observation of the child's speech in social settings with peers in conversations and the level of functional play
- Non-verbal communication
- Level of thinking

Cognitive development

The preschool classroom is filled with little explorers, eager to sort the beads or beans they are using to make a picture by their size, shape, and color. They may spend long periods of time looking at a basket of shells or mixing one of their favorite "delicious" poisonous concoctions from the elements they found on the playground. It is not uncommon to hear the preschool teacher call a group of children "her architects" due to their patience and the time they spend building structures out of blocks. These are tasks that require patience, coordination, planning, imaginative thinking, and flexibility, especially when it involves peers.

Beginning at three years of age, children begin to display discrimination and organization skills. They can sort objects by colors and shapes, match them with pictures, and use them to put together complex puzzles. They are beginning to understand words that represent sequencing such as tall and short, big and small. By four years of age they can understand "more," "less," or "the same" and are beginning to understand questions about what happened before and what is going to happen next. Four-year-olds are eager to show mastery and may prefer to take on challenging tasks given a choice between tasks they feel are "for babies" and those for "big kids." This is not to say that when at home, and not feeling competitive with their peers, they can't still get into pitched struggles with their younger siblings over toys they have not touched for years, or demand to be held when the parents are getting ready to leave the house (Davies 1999; Linder 1993).

The preschool years are when the young child begins to make the transition from what Piaget identified as being *egocentric thinking* to *non-egocentric thinking*, which is not fully accomplished until the end of the fifth year. By three years of age the preschool child is starting to be more flexible. He can tolerate the teacher giving a different name for an object, or accept that a peer may want to use a different color than he does, as long as it does not impose on his own decisions. The preschool child is challenged to move from the egocentric way of thinking each time he is asked to listen at circle time to peers' descriptions of their favorite objects, or share a toy with a friend. Still, the young child's flexibility can evaporate instantaneously when he feels threatened by a peer who wants to play the same role in the house corner or build the bridge a different way in the sand. The young child works on these issues each time he enters into a social interaction with peers.

Another way of understanding this transition from the egocentric to more social way of thinking is what researchers have called the *Theory of Mind*. The theory posits that what makes humans different from all other species is their ability to understand that another person's ideas may be different from their own. Researchers have looked at the developmental process children go through as they move from thinking only about their own thoughts, needs, and desires (egocentricity) to becoming aware that others may have thoughts and needs that are different than theirs (Mitchell 1977). By three years of age most children are starting to identify and interpret other people's feelings in a story or video. They are also beginning to recognize in real life situations that other children may have plans and desires that are different from their own – for example, they may want to play another activity on the playground. That is not to say that they are always empathic, able to respond to their peers' needs first, but rather it is a process that is continually guided by adults at school, on play dates, and in the home. As we will discuss in the next section, one's alarm goes off when, at a very concrete level, the preschool child is oblivious to the thoughts and feelings of others – for example, the child grabs a toy from a peer's hand without asking if he can play with it, or the child jumps onto the back of a peer, oblivious to the clear signals of distress the child is expressing.

As we have alluded to throughout this section, an important part of the preschool child's development is his capacity for symbolic play, the hallmark of the preschool playground. What we sometimes forget is that the child has been working on the skills that lead up to this symbolic play since infancy. We will look at this developmental process more closely in the next section.

> ## Table 1.3 Key components of young children's cognitive development
>
> - Theory of Mind – others may have different thoughts and feelings
> - Verbal and nonverbal functioning, concrete vs. abstract thinking
> - Attention
> - Executive functioning skills

Symbolic representation and play

Pretend play is the stage for the young child's social, emotional, cognitive, and communication development. Most of the research on the development of the child's capacity to engage in pretend play is based on the models of symbolic play described by Piaget in his landmark book *Play, Dreams, and Imitation* (1962) (published in French in 1945 and English, 1962). The book is based on the natural observations of his three children as they moved from exploring their immediate setting with their caregiver to their rich imaginary play world with peers. Piaget's model outlines the cognitive steps that children go through as they move from exploring an object to using it in a sequence of symbolic play. In the first phase (pre-pretense) the child has brief moments when he explores an object but has not assimilated how to use it in his play – for example, he makes a stirring motion with a spoon and then drops it. As young as age one, the child is engaged in the pretend self, pretending how to use these objects independently, tapping the numbers on a cell phone, pulling out the antenna, and then putting it back down. The child then moves from pretending with objects to pretending with others. As young as age 16 months, the child can be observed directing the play towards another person, picking up the pretend cell phone, making a ringing sound, and handing it to the caregiver to answer. The following phase, which Piaget called "substitution," involves the child's capacity to substitute a "meaning-less" object in a creative manner to play a role in pretend play. For example, a block becomes the cell phone that the child uses to call a peer on the other side of the room. At this stage the child does not inform the other adult or child that he is calling him. The play of the three-year-old moves from objects to imaginary objects or beings. One can usually observe on any playground a cup being filled with pretend tea, a swing being transformed into a spaceship, and a stick becoming a weapon to fight the "bad guys."

At about three years of age the child will also begin to animate a toy as he pretends to be feeding a baby doll that is fussing or be the king fighting the ferocious dragon who is shooting flames all over the area. As the play becomes more developed between the ages of three and five, the child has the capacity to integrate more than one act into a sequence or story of acts. The pirates dig for gold in the sand; the berries that they find get sorted into piles of gold or poison and placed into an old plastic cup – the treasure chest, or a bucket for the poison. Lastly, the child's play displays planning as he tells his peers that they need to put all of the gold into their pockets and quickly return to the boat. The peer leads the way, moves the anchor (a log), and announces that they are safe at sea (Gowen 1995).

The themes of the preschool child's symbolic play are often centered around his attempts to display mastery over anxiety-provoking topics such as danger – putting the "bad guys" in jail; pain – going to the doctor; fear – travel, abandonment; as well as mastery over new tasks. Every clubhouse has an authority figure such as the parent, teacher, or police officer waiting to discipline the "bad" child. The preschool playground is filled with authorities on a range of topics such as space, medicine, animals, dinosaurs, and clothing, to list a few. The four- and five-year-olds are the "old timers" of the playground. They know the fastest way to reach the top of a structure, get on a swing, or claim the balls on the playground. It takes only a few moments on the playground to figure out who are the popular superhero figures, and who are the leaders in the class.

Many professionals have noted that the children do not travel this journey alone but rather are aided by the support of parents and teachers who respond to the child's early attempts at play. This may include commenting on the child's actions, adding sound, displaying exaggerated emotions, and providing support for his imagination as the adult tastes the "wonderful" chocolate pudding the child made as the child holds onto the wooden spoon and taps it against the floor, or hands the parent a cup filled with sand. Thus, to understand play one must look at symbolic play as one part of a larger developmental sequence which begins during the infant's early interactions and relationships with his or her primary caregiver (Belsky 1981; Dunn 1985; Fein 1981; Greenspan 1992). The reciprocal circles of communication that the child establishes with his caregivers are the building blocks of the development of mutually satisfying relationships with peers in play (Greenspan

1992). Not surprisingly, if the child has difficulty establishing this type of relationship with a caregiver who is attuned to his cues, he may experience complete failure when it comes to playing with peers who have their own ideas and feelings.

Table 1.4 Key components of young children's play

- Young children engage in symbolic play that has a variety of richly developed themes
- Young children have a wide range of interests
- A concrete object may take on very different meanings and roles in their play
- Young children are able to develop play themes with peers that incorporates others' ideas
- Young children are able to enjoy simple board games with peers, taking turns, tolerating losing

---

Emotional and social development

As with all of the areas that we have previously covered, children this age also mature in the areas of emotional and social development. As we have stressed throughout the chapter, the young child moves from being a toddler absorbed in his own world and needs to being interested in other children and adults. The foundation of such a transition is a secure relationship with one's primary caregivers. Just as we discussed with self-regulation, the infant's caregiver plays a major role in helping the child regulate not only his physical needs but also his emotional needs, at times of delight as well as when in distress. This early relationship is thought to be the foundation of a secure attachment. In simple terms, a secure attachment is one in which the child can feel confident that his or her parent will be there whenever they are needed (Sroufe 1995).

By the end of the second year of life most children are able to maintain a positive internalized image of their primary caregivers even when they are not physically present. This image provides them with the support and sense of confidence in themselves needed to explore the preschool playground, have a play date at a friend's house, or tolerate staying with a new baby-sitter, knowing that their parent will return for them. As Judy Feber (1996) put it:

> The preschool years are the time when the preschool child consolidates
> their concept of age and belonging, to the social category of little girl or
> boy, not baby or grown-up, a time to strike a balance between big and
> little. The young child's ability to recall their history of positive relation-
> ships with their primary caregivers motivates them to develop new rela-
> tionships with their teachers and peers. They can approach new
> challenges confidently and at the same time draw upon adults for help
> and suggestions when needed. (p.39)

The adults play a key role in helping children balance between engaging in
tasks where they can experience mastery, such as superheroes with endless
powers, and feeling reassured that they are still children and that there are
adults whose job it is to take care of them.

By three years of age the average child moves from interacting primarily
with adults to spontaneously engaging other children in play. The parallel
play which is characteristic of the two-year-old's interactions is replaced by
social play with peers that may center around shared interests, rough and
tumble play, as well as long, complicated sequences. The child's pretend play
becomes the stage for elaborate stories which can go on for weeks and change
to incorporate the children's new ideas. What is striking is how most children
this age prefer playing with another child to being alone (Linder 1993).
Sroufe's (1979, 1995) research on the development of human emotions has
demonstrated that most children have the capacity to express a wide range of
emotions by their third year of life. It is so striking to see the wide range of
emotions that most children can express even by the end of their first year.
They are able to express pleasure, delight, wariness, fear, anxiety, distress, rage,
anger, and attachment. By the third year they are able to express a positive
sense of self, pride, love, empathy, anxiety, shame, angry mood, defiance,
intentional hurting, and guilt.

By four years of age the same child who displays a strong sense of pride
and joy in his ability to perform a specific task may quickly become jealous if
he feels threatened by a peer. The intensity of the potential competitiveness in
children this age is evident in any sports class one observes. Even if the coach
makes a point of not keeping score or having a winner and loser there will be
some children trying to determine the winner.

The children are also showing a growing capacity to recognize other
people's expressions of basic emotions such as happy, sad, angry, surprised,
and disgusted based on their actions and facial expressions. Though the
children are also able to understand the causes of emotions in simple
situations it is often easier for them to understand what caused the negative

emotions than the positive ones. The children may also have a superficial understanding that their feelings may change over time but they cannot put their finger on why. What they do know is that a child who is crying may feel better if they get a teacher to help, or that their little brother will be happier if they give him a toy.

Table 1.5 Key components of young children's emotional and social development

- Wide range of affect
- Temperament
- Secure relationship with primary caregiver(s)
- Approach new challenges with confidence, able to turn to adults for support
- Three-year-olds begin cooperative play with peers
- Four-year-olds prefer playing with peers unless absorbed in a project
- Social interactions with peers characterized by talking, smiling, laughing, and playing
- Recognition of nonverbal behaviors

Parent–child relationship

As you can see there has not been a section where the parents have not been identified as playing an important role in fostering all aspects of the child's development, including the foundation for future relationships. We want to stress here the perspective that both the child and parent are active contributors to their primary relationship. A key component of this relationship is the development of positive joint attention between the child and his or her caregiver. These interactions serve as the foundation for the development of mutually satisfying interactions and rewarding relationships.

The task for the parents will be harder if the child's sensory or motor development is inconsistent, his verbal and social cues are hard to read, or his play not welcoming of the parents' input. Similarly the parents are going to be harder to connect with if they do not provide the child with a clear and consistent message that they will always be there to take care of him. The parents must set clear boundaries between themselves and their children, recognize their children's needs as being separate from their own, and accept that their original perception of their child's behaviors may mean something different than what they originally thought. For example, when the child seems hysterical over a small cut, the parent has to recognize that it is not the time to give a lecture on responsibility or to ignore the child's distress but to let the child know that he is safe and O.K. We must remember that the parent–child relationship is not constant but evolving. Just as the child is not stagnant but in a state of constant development, there will be factors constantly influencing the parents' ability to be attuned to their child, such as a change in their paid work or a new baby in the family. What the parents need to be able to do is step back and look at what is working well with their child and recognize when they feel out of synchrony with each other.

Table 1.6 Key components of young children's relationships with their parents

- Both parents and children contribute to the relationship
- Well-adapted relationships are mutually enjoyable and produce minimal conflict

---

Stress and coping

The same child who can leap across the floor to save the day can cling to his parent with all of his might as he approaches a peer's birthday party. It is common to see a child who is able to perform a task with great ease seem "frozen" or confused at other times due to external or internal stresses. Every preschool needs a large box of bandages to cover large scrapes and cuts as well as scratches invisible to the human eye. The young child may have anxieties about the loss of a loved one's approval after spilling paint all over his shirt, forgetting to go to the bathroom, or leaving a trail of sand across the kitchen floor. He may also be concerned about the impact that a bodily injury will have on him. In the preschool age child's imagination a scratch may lead to the loss of a finger, a fall on the penis may lead to its coming off. Most children's anxiety decreases with reassurance and a minor event does not create a major disruption of their daily life events such as eating, sleeping, separation, rela-tionships, or play. The concern arises when a stressful event does create a disruption that does not diminish over time or is generalized to the point that it prevents the child from participating in the activities he used to enjoy.

Given this overview, looking into the world of the young child can seem overwhelming especially if you are a parent wondering if you should be concerned about your child's developmental progress. Nonetheless, we hope that this overview provides a foundation from which we can examine how a young child with Asperger's Syndrome may differ along these developmental dimensions.

CHAPTER 2

The World of the Young Child
with Asperger's Syndrome

The children described in Chapter 1 remind us how rich and playful the world of the young child is. Three- to five-year-olds are embarking on a path of learning to reason, control their impulses, and make friends. They are entering that intricate world of negotiating the complexities of their peer group, a task that continues throughout their lives. In our Preface, we provided a brief overview of what Asperger's Syndrome is, with social and communication issues being core areas of challenge for these children. Given that these areas of development are central to the life of the young child, we can then ask: how does the young child with Asperger's Syndrome manage the tasks of his age? How does he experience and make sense of the social world around him? What does it mean when he talks about friends? What is he feeling when he smiles at times one would expect him to be feeling mad, or when he looks angry when we would expect him to be happy?

In this chapter we explore these questions by walking through the areas of development outlined briefly in Chapter 1, and describing the strengths and challenges that children with Asperger's Syndrome face in each area. It is crucial to remember that every child is unique and that the range of symptoms within each child varies greatly. Therefore, as parents you may read through this chapter and feel that some characteristics describe your child "to a t" while others don't. We hope that even when you read about qualities you think don't fit your child, your understanding of your own children will still increase, because at the root of many of these behaviors (albeit expressed differently) are the challenges in communication and socialization. Throughout this book, you will see that there is a wide continuum with some children struggling with many features of the Syndrome and other children who have much milder presentations.

Let us now look at Max, an energetic four-year-old boy who has a passion for exploring. Through his story, we can see some of the unique challenges and strengths of a young child with Asperger's Syndrome.

Max's story

Max's bookshelves are filled with objects he has found on his explorations: shells, rocks, roots, fossils, and rusted coins. There are rows of model pirate ships. With a deep sense of pride Max can label all of the parts of a ship and tell you about each ship's history. This passion for ships is something Max shares with his father. In fact, they have been spending a lot of time during the weekends working on a ship that they are building in their garage. Max is also very interested in ants and is intrigued by the way each ant knows what it is supposed to do and does it.

His mother, Sarah, enjoys watching the enthusiasm that Max expresses each time he makes a new discovery. Sarah is an artist and has always encouraged Max to explore, collect, and draw pictures of his discoveries, yet she is also aware that he has difficulty getting along with other children who do not want to do things just his way. She knows that his wish to be in charge of what he and others do both in and outside of the classroom is causing a problem for him at school. For this reason she is trying to make an effort to have more friends over for play dates and arrange to meet other children at the park.

A play date at the park

Max loves to go to the park that has a climbing structure that is designed to look like a pirate ship. Before Sarah unlocks the car door at the park she reminds him that he has to share his toys with the other children and come to her if he has a problem rather than hit or grab things from another child. Max nods his head up and down and rolls his eyes as if he has heard this speech a million times. As soon as she opens the door he leaps out of the car and is on the top of the structure before his mother has taken the park supplies out of the car.

From the highest part of the raven's nest, Max looks out onto the park as if he is surveying the ocean and announces the direction of the ship's travel, the temperature, and the forecast for the remainder of the trip. Max does not notice that his friend Steven, who he had arranged to meet at the park, is sitting on the boat. When his friend catches his attention he waves and jumps onto the sand, announcing that he is going to look for lost treasures. His friend is always up for another "Max adventure" so he follows him onto the sand and around the park looking for the spot to begin the next exploration. Steve suggests that he and Max play in the tunnel but Max's mind is elsewhere. Max notices the ends of two poles that construction workers have left under a bench. Max immediately sees the shiny silver jutting out of the seats and decides they are the "parts" he needs to support the sides of the ship. He quickly scurries under the bench and lifts the rods up into the air, almost hitting a toddler in the face. Unaware that the toddler begins to cry because of the near miss with the rods, Max runs with his latest find onto the ship, almost hitting several other children. Max's mother notices the commotion and runs to the structure, telling him to be careful. As he sees her approach, he explains in a very loud authoritative voice that she is interrupting very important work. He must strengthen the side of the ship now, otherwise they will sink! He calls to his friend for assistance hoping that his mother will leave them alone if she sees that he is playing with his friend. Yet she persists until she finds out where he got the rods and makes him give them to her so that she can return them. Max is furious, calling his mother "stupid," saying that she knows nothing about ships, and that she is ruining everything. She tries to offer him something else he can use to work on his ship. He tosses the plastic hammer and nails that she hands him over the side of the ship, crosses his arms across his chest, and begins to cry as he kicks the side of the boat and the sand surrounding him.

Steve knows to leave Max alone when he is like this. He has had the experience of being hit and listened to his mom's advice enough times to know that when Max has a tantrum the best thing to do is to leave him alone until he calms down. Max's mom makes one more attempt to calm him down before removing him physically from the area by reminding him that she has brought one of his favorite snacks and magnifying glasses to the park. In a flash the enraged little boy is joining Steve at the bench for a snack while still looking angry with his mom. Soon his eyes widen and a smile reappears when he sees some ants around the bottom of the picnic table. He quickly grabs his magnifying glass and runs to the table. His mother offers another magnifying glass to Steve who follows Max, yelling for Max to wait for him. Max doesn't acknowledge the call but seems content when Steve joins him under the table. He proceeds to tell Steve all about the ant colony and what each ant is doing. Steve doesn't have much of a chance to join the conversation since Max is so excited to relay everything he knows about ants that he hardly stops talking long enough to give Steve a chance to say something.

At first sight, Max may look like a typical young child playing enthusiastically on the playground. He is busy pursuing his ideas and gets mad when these ideas are thwarted. However, on closer inspection, you can see that Max doesn't initiate any interactions with other children, nor is he very aware of the other children's cues. He enjoys Steve joining him in play but he doesn't incorporate or respond to any of Steve's ideas. If you were to return to observe Max in the park on a different day, you would likely see him still playing the same pirate game or examining ants. Max is an example of a young child with Asperger's Syndrome who has a narrow range of interests and a wealth of knowledge about these interests (ants and ships), poor communication skills with his peers, and difficulty regulating his feelings. He exemplifies how subtle and at times confusing the difficulties for a young child with Asperger's Syndrome may seem. With the understanding that not all of the children with Asperger's Syndrome share the same areas and range of difficulties, let's take a look at the developmental dimensions outlined in Chapter 1 and see how they may differ in a young child with Asperger's Syndrome.

Sensory-motor development

Sensory-motor difficulties in the young child with Asperger's Syndrome may be one of the first signs to parents that something is different about their child. Their child may seem oblivious to certain sounds and hypersensitive to others. He may love to watch his favorite cartoon at a very high volume but cover his ears and complain that the teacher is hurting his ears with her voice. He may only eat foods of a specific shape and texture, be intolerant of having a speck of sand on his foot yet seem insensitive to pain (Dunn 1999; Hoshino *et al.* 1982; Volkmar, Cohen and Paul 1986). Where some children with Asperger's Syndrome may have excellent motor skills while still having sensory regulatory difficulties, others may avoid motor tasks that are difficult for them. For example, if they have difficulty with writing or cutting they may avoid these tasks which may lead to further delays in skill development.

Children with sensory difficulties can easily become overwhelmed in group or crowded situations and develop all sorts of ways to avoid them. Just think about how many visual stimuli exist in a store. Children will go to great lengths to block out excess stimuli by hiding in the corner of the store, covering their ears with their hands, or standing between clothes on a clothes rack. Other children will tantrum and resist leaving their house, preferring the solitude and comfort of the predictable environment their home offers, while still others may throw any object they believe is in their way. These sensory "assaults" can lead a child to feeling very anxious and uncomfortable. Children may have different defensive responses to a stressful situation as seen with our examples. They may withdraw or avoid the stimuli (flight), while others may become outwardly "aggressive" (fight) as a way to try to protect themselves from the sensory "assault."

Other children with sensory regulatory problems may be *defensive towards stimuli presented to them.* For example, if a friend or a sibling should accidentally bump into them they may think that they are being attacked. Yet, when they give a parent or a friend a hello hug, they may squeeze so tightly that the adult is always afraid that someone may get hurt. For Max this was a source of constant conflict. He saw no harm in running into a peer on the playground and slapping him or her on the back, just like the pirates did in the movies, without first saying hello or checking to see if the child was busy with an activity. Of course if a child bumped into him and disrupted his treasure hunt or ant study he would become enraged and with force push the child away. These behaviors can be easily misunderstood because it is confusing to people that children with sensory issues *respond differently to stimuli they initiate versus stimuli they receive.* Children may display adequate motor skills, vestibular (balancing) functions, and body positioning skills but have difficulty when all of these skills need to be *integrated* – for example, learning how to pump their legs on a swing or ride a bike. They often complain of feeling dizzy after activities that challenge them in this area (Gepner *et al.* 1995).

A good understanding of both fine and gross motor development and sensory-motor functioning may also clarify the underlying motivation for certain behavioral problems that can arise when a child is struggling in any of these areas.

Kevin was a boy who complained of a stomach ache every time he was asked to do an art project. He would leave the table and lie down on the classroom couch. His stomach ache "miraculously" went away as soon the children were told that it was time to clean up and get ready to go outside. His teacher began to recognize that the problem arose when he was asked to draw. As soon as they made sure that there was a way that he could participate in the art projects that did not require the same level of fine motor skills his stomach problems disappeared and he began to enjoy the activities. Kevin's difficulty communicating his feelings further complicated the situation. He learned that by saying he was sick he avoided having to talk with the teacher about the difficulty he was having coming up with an idea of what to draw, or about his dissatisfaction with his own drawing skills.

As many of the examples in this section illustrate, sensory-motor problems can lead to behaviors that are challenging or perplexing to a parent. The difficulties with social communication and identifying and expressing feelings only makes it harder to understand these behaviors at any given time. Let us now take a closer look at the communication challenges often experienced by young children with Asperger's Syndrome. We will begin to see how there is quite a bit of overlap in behavioral challenges and how the underlying core issue may be affecting more than one area of a child's development.

Table 2.1 Red flags for motor and sensory functioning in young children with Asperger's Syndrome

- Gross or fine motor delays
- Clumsiness
- Consistent avoidance of motor tasks that may require a specific skill such as balances or handwriting
- Hyperactivity
- Sensitivity to noise, light, smells, taste, touch, or movement

---

Communication

Since communication challenges are described as a core issue for children with Asperger's Syndrome, it is important to understand the various functions of communication and language development and how the functions are not mutually exclusive but are quite interwoven (Linder 1993). A helpful way of understanding a child's language skills is to view them as consisting of three different parts, as outlined in the first chapter. As we explained in Chapter 1, the first part is the child's expressive language that consists of the vocabulary that the child uses in speech, and syntax, the grammatical structure of the sentence. A child with Asperger's Syndrome often excels in this area. Some of these children never have a problem coming up with questions. In fact it seems as if they would be wonderful writers for children's books such as *The Magic School Bus*, due to the endless number of questions and explanations they can come up with pertaining to their area of interest – for example, planets, dinosaurs, architecture, or animal life. A unique characteristic of these children is that some of their language can appear *pedantic or overly formal*. For example, in the case of Max talking about ants, his vocabulary was very adult-like and full of scientific terms he had memorized but there was little intonation in his voice even when you could see that he was excited about his "explorations." Like Max, at times these children can appear to be "very mature" for their age due their use of such formal language, although rarely do they have more than a superficial understanding of the terms they use. Interestingly, though, children often talk in this way when they do not know what else to say or do and/or when they want to redirect an interaction. For example, one child during an evaluation kept saying "Thank you very much, may I please go now?" every time he did not know the answer to a question during the assessment.

The second component of language development we defined is *receptive language skills*. The child with Asperger's Syndrome may have age-appropriate or above average receptive language skills which include the ability to comprehend oral language, such as following simple directions, and identifying pictures after being provided the word. There may be some impairment in his ability to follow directions that have more than one step. Difficulty following directions may be related to the child being internally distracted, having anxiety about a social situation, or one of many other factors. For Max, it seemed impossible to get ready for bed without direct supervision. His mother would ask him to go to his room, get undressed, and put his pajamas on. Max would make it to his room but inevitably he would become absorbed in one of his favorite books or models, soon forgetting why he was sent to his room in the first place. This example (albeit common to all parents!) does illustrate how a parent might be puzzled about whether their child is correctly processing the information heard, particularly if the child consistently seems not to follow through with simple directions. A parent may also get stuck thinking their child is being willfully disrespectful or stubborn instead of recognizing that the child is possibly internally distracted or stuck on his own agenda.

The children can also be puzzling in that despite their rich vocabulary and average receptive language skills *their thinking is very concrete or literal*. When a teacher tells them to take a deep breath they think they need to get down on the floor to be as deep as they can go. They may get in an argument with a peer who is pretending to be a type of bird that they know is extinct. Or they may label the teacher as being "stupid" for suggesting to the class that a cloud could look like a sheep. What a young child with Asperger's Syndrome might do is report in a very annoyed tone of voice that it is impossible for a cloud to be a sheep because a sheep has bones, fur, blood, and a head while clouds are made out of water vapor. If the teacher does not acknowledge that he is correct and understand that he has difficulty in pretending, she might think that he is deliberately trying to disrupt her activity and become the center of attention.

The third part of language, *pragmatic language* (the ability to use words to engage others socially), is the aspect of communication with which children with Asperger's Syndrome have the most difficulty. Children from three years of age can typically engage in a dialogue that lasts for several turns back and forth with both adults and peers; for example, Mom: "Steve, do you want to play ball?" Steve: "I want the red one." Mom: "O.K., you can have the red one but first you have to get your shoes on." Steve: "Here are my shoes." Mom: "Good, sit down and I will help you." This pattern of dialogue is what Stanley Greenspan (1992) labeled "circles of communication"(see Figure 2.1).

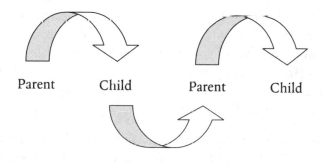

Parent   Child   Parent   Child

Figure 2.1 Circles of communication

Children with Asperger's Syndrome have tremendous difficulty maintaining more than three circles of communication without a great deal of external prompting. Another way that circles of communication are frequently described in the literature on speech and language development is "turn-taking." Turn-taking is critical in maintaining a conversation with another person and is an important social skill to learn not only with regard to communication but also with regard to play. As you will recall, when Max was on the playground he was eager to tell his friend what to do but he didn't respond to Steve's question. Steve was very patient with Max but other children weren't, and many excluded Max from play because he was perceived as "bossy" and as someone who wouldn't share. It is easy to see how these pragmatic language issues interfere with making friends!

Also related to these discourse skills is the ability to move from one topic to another in conversation (Linder 1993). Many young children with Asperger's Syndrome do not read the nonverbal cues in others, nor do they register the comments made by others. They will talk endlessly about something and do not move from their topic to another's easily. For example, you may be asking about how the child's day was when the child responds with a very long-winded account of *Treasure Island* (one of Max's favorite stories). When a child doesn't maintain a topic, what often happens is that he loses his audience. Children don't typically stick around when they are being "talked at." Adults, on the other hand, may spend more time trying to decipher what the child is trying to say. Therefore, it isn't uncommon for these children to be more comfortable seeking adult attention.

As mentioned, these children are having difficulty interpreting or reading nonverbal cues. They keep talking even though the child they are addressing might turn his back to go look at something else or simply break off eye contact and begin fiddling with his hands, two reliably obvious clues of the child's lack of interest. Social communication depends on our ability to read *nonverbal cues*. Having difficulties in this area can lead to many confusions and misinterpretations on the part of the child. The following example of a child, John, during circle time illustrates this:

> John loves circle time. He is always the first to raise his hand ready to participate. Today the teacher asks the class if they know what the next holiday is. John eagerly waves his hand in the air and when called upon proceeds to tell the class about tornadoes. From John's perspective he is doing everything that he should be doing: raising his hand and waiting to be called on. His teacher at first looks a bit puzzled but attempts to redirect John to the question. John continues to talk about tornadoes without acknowledging his teacher's attempts to redirect him. Several other children start to chuckle or frown. Unfortunately, John doesn't pick up on or understand his teacher's facial expressions or the body language of his peers. His teacher tells him it's someone else's turn to talk. John starts muttering "stupid" and he looks visibly tense and mad. John doesn't understand why he can't talk about tornadoes. When

another child starts talking, John starts fidgeting with his carpet square and he isn't paying attention any more.

This example illustrates how both John's difficulty picking up on nonverbal cues (teacher's puzzled look, children's chuckles and frowns) and his pragmatic language difficulties (not maintaining the topic) lead him to getting confused and ultimately distracted from the circle time. Children with Asperger's Syndrome have tremendous difficulty interpreting and reading the nonverbal cues of others and have difficulty giving appropriate nonverbal cues to others. They may be feeling very anxious in a social situation but have a broad smile across their face. This apparent *masked grin* can confuse the people with whom they are interacting. Nothing upsets an adult more than to see a child smile when he is being reprimanded. But if you watch carefully you will see that the broad grin across the child's face is a different expression from the smile he gives when he is feeling happy. Some young children with Asperger's Syndrome will incorporate the exaggerated gestures, facial expressions, and tones of voice of their favorite character from a movie or television show when they don't know how else to respond.

Table 2.2 Red flags for communication in young children with Asperger's Syndrome

- No history of severe speech delays
- Normal expressive and receptive language development, but difficulty communicating with peers
- When engaging others, consistently uses long-winded, one-sided conversations
- Odd use of phrases that may have been learned from a video or book
- Repetitive use of "canned" or "scripted" phrases
- Difficulty engaging in reciprocal conversations
- Poor eye contact
- Misinterpretation of nonverbal cues such as facial expressions or body language

---

It is easy to see how the pragmatic difficulties outlined here lead to social and emotional issues. When a child isn't stopping and naturally assessing a situation by reading the faces, actions, and movement of others, he is likely going to end up doing something he shouldn't. The ability to develop reasoning skills and connect cause and effect is partly based on the ability to read nonverbal cues. It is also connected to the way a child processes information cognitively. Let us now look at the area of cognitive development and see how that ties into how the child perceives the world.

Cognitive development

Children with Asperger's Syndrome typically are bright and show average to above average cognitive abilities on standardized assessments. In the literature on Asperger's Syndrome many references are made to the *Theory of Mind*. As discussed in the first chapter, the theory is based on the presumption that what makes humans different from other animals is their ability to understand the thoughts and feelings of others (Frith, Morton and Leslie 1994; Leslie 1987, 1992). Uta Frith (1991) was the first to observe that children with Asperger's Syndrome are unable to "mind read" and labeled this phenomenon as being "*mindblindness*". Children around four years of age begin to understand that other people may have thoughts and feelings that are different from their own. They can accept that a friend may like vanilla more than chocolate ice cream as long as they are not forced to eat it. In contrast the child with Asperger's Syndrome may refuse to accept that his friend likes something different and, at times, may even tell the child that they are "stupid" to eat vanilla. He cannot conceive that his friend could possibly like something he despises. These issues become the focus of daily battles with family members and friends over topics such as who is the best sports team, the right way to play a game, what is the funniest movie, or the best snack. This behavior pattern often becomes the source of tremendous concern and conflict with parents and teachers, since young children are expected to naturally develop a respect for their peers' differences in taste, style, and activities. What is important to remember here is that research has demonstrated that not all children with Asperger's Syndrome entirely lack this "mindness" (Klin *et al.* 1992) but rather that they may have difficulties to some degree in this area. In other words, a child may show sincere concern over his mother's illness and try to do something to make her feel better, but may still get very upset if his mother suggests that there is another way of playing a particular game.

Children with Asperger's Syndrome are often perceived as having *attention difficulties*. This may be puzzling since they can often spend hours playing one of their favorite computer games or acting out a story with their dolls or dinosaurs. But attention problems are more common for the child who is in a situation where he may need to be more flexible (group activities at school that require turn taking or listening to peers). The same children often can *focus on details that are irrelevant* to the question being asked. For example, at school the teacher may ask the children to look at the calendar and tell what is special about the day. Instead of seeing the picture of a birthday cake the child may notice a different style of printing or a pattern of numbers on the top of the sheet. It is not uncommon to see these children *perseverate*, drawing the same picture several times during the day over an extended period of time. One of the children we worked with was so obsessed with trains that he insisted on having his father draw him a picture of a specific type of train every time he ate. When he was at a table activity every drawing or journal entry was of a train. Another child was so engrossed in numbers that as soon as he was finished with a project or when he lost interest in a discussion he would begin to look for as many numbers as possible in the classroom. To these children their obsessive interests did not feel unusual. Rather, it was the first thing that came to their mind and they could not understand why this should upset anyone since they were not forcing others to share their interest, interrupting the teacher, or teasing another child.

These perseverative interests and the rather concrete way children with Asperger's Syndrome seem to process the world leads to the child having some enormous strengths – such as huge funds of factual information, typically about the more physical aspects of the world (space, how cars/appliances work, dinosaurs, computers, etc.). But it also leads to difficulties in the child's ability to develop reasoning skills which help to navigate social situations. It has been said that emotional thinking, an important skill which typically develops between two-and-a-half and three-and-a-half years, comes from the child being able to make connections between different events/actions and feelings (Greenspan 1992). For example, a child connects his angry feelings to the fact that Mom didn't buy his favorite cereal and says, "I feel angry because you didn't get what I wanted." This ability to connect actions to feelings also helps children predict consequences – for example, if I push John because I am mad then my teacher won't let me go out to recess. These concepts are very difficult for children with Asperger's Syndrome. They don't naturally acquire the ability to connect cause and effect and to interpret their and others' feelings easily. This is why social scripts are commonly recommended for use in coaching and training children what to do when they face situations that require these skills to abstract, predict, and identify feelings. Understanding these "cognitive processing" issues is important to help your child succeed and is very interrelated with the development of communication and play skills.

Table 2.3 Red flags for cognitive development in young children with Asperger's Syndrome

- Inability to interpret others' thoughts and feelings
- Good memory for facts but not for social information such as personal names
- Selective attention to topics of interest to them; can be over focused on one topic
- Difficulties in abstract thinking, jokes, generating novel ideas
- Difficulty organizing thoughts, prioritizing information
- Tendency to take things very literally
- Tendency to focus on irrelevant details

Play

As in the last discussion on cognition, rich symbolic play also requires the ability to develop themes and to connect actions and feelings. A disinterest or inability to engage in *reciprocal imaginary play with their peers* is one characteristic that makes children with Asperger's Syndrome stand out (Attwood 1998; Koplow *et al.* 1996; Leslie 1987). What is confusing is that it may look like they are engaged in very rich thematic play with their peers but if you listen carefully they are often playing next to another child and not with them. They may seem oblivious to the props which are often so compelling to the other children, such as the police hats, animals, or dolls. If they are using the symbolic toys they often are more interested in comparing the *concrete aspects of the objects*, such as organizing the animals by their size or classifications, rather than in acting out a story with another child (Rogers 1998). When they do engage in symbolic play it often is at a much younger developmental level, such as stirring a spoon in a bowl to make a desert or feeding a baby doll (Riquet *et al.* 1981; Sigman and Ungerer 1984; Wing *et al.* 1977). They do not incorporate the roles of the different family members as one typically sees played out in the house corner of the classroom.

Different aspects of the child's development may influence his difficulty in engaging in symbolic play with peers at various times. For example, a child's tendency to avoid playing with others may be related to his poor use of pragmatic speech at one time, difficulty understanding and engaging in the symbolic play at another time, or some combination of both factors (Klin and Shepherd 1994; Losche 1990).

The child's narrow range of interest may also be the source of conflict with peers who do not wish to follow his directions. For example, Josh was a child who was obsessed with cheetahs and their threat of extinction. With a very serious expression he guarded the plastic cheetah that was in the sand area. When he left the area to ride a tricycle another child entered the area and began to use the cheetah to dig a hole. Josh immediately jumped off the tricycle and grabbed the cheetah from the boy in an attempt to "protect" it. He did not use words to ask for the animal back or explain why he did not want the other children to remove the animals from the area. Another child, Craig, was enthralled with the design of buildings. He had memorized a visual image of a floor plan that he repeatedly wanted to make in the block area. Not surprisingly, a battle erupted any time a peer tried to add on to his building or take a block that he thought he would need in the near future. Like Josh, he was not able to explain to his peer his idea, share the materials, or, more importantly, collaborate with him on a shared project that they could develop together.

When these children are engaged in pretend play, it is often *not spontaneous* but rather the *reenactment of a movie story or TV show* they have memorized and become "attached" to. Problems often arise when another child tries to join into the scene and suggest a character or activity that is not in the visual "movie" the child has in his mind. It is not uncommon to see the child with Asperger's Syndrome tell his peers that they are wrong or stupid, and/or physically push other children away if they do not follow his commands.

For some of these children, it may not be that they don't want to play with their friends. It is just much easier for them to reenact a memorized story by themselves rather than to have to explain it to a friend and then incorporate their friend's ideas. And often it is their intense desire to pursue one of their interests (like Max and his ants) that gets first priority. When another child can adapt to this need of the child, the child with Asperger's Syndrome is often content to have a partner to help (such as Steve in the park with Max).

Table 2.4 Red flags for play in young children with Asperger's Syndrome

- Lacks symbolic play not based on scripts (little spontaneous imagination)
- Play involves the concrete reenactment of scripts from videos, TV shows, books
- Obsessive interests in one or two play themes (e.g. "Thomas the Train," space, and dinosaurs)
- The themes may change over time but a limited range of themes still dominant in child's play
- Repetitive use of objects, focus on concrete characteristics (e.g. size and shape)
- Inability to incorporate others' ideas into their play
- The play is at a much younger developmental level than their vocabulary and wealth of information would suggest (i.e. solitary or parallel play, tag vs. pretend play)
- Play lacks spontaneous circles of communication
- Child insists on always being in control of the games

Emotional and social development

Young children with Asperger's Syndrome do not seem to have the range of feelings one would expect. Most children by three years of age express a wide range of affect and can identify most types of emotions, having talked about feeling happy, sad, tired, frustrated, shy, scared, and proud. (As early as 24 months old most children know the feelings "happy" and "mad.") It is striking how many of the young children with Asperger's Syndrome either aren't able to define how they feel or describe everything in terms that are very black and white. When they do use feelings in their conversation it often is in a scripted phrase that they have been taught by their parents, such as "You are making me feel very frustrated" or "I am very angry with you." When you listen to the other children on the playground they sound very different and usually do not need to label their feelings for others to know how they feel. Rather, they show it in nonverbal mannerisms like walking off, stomping their foot, saying the other person's name in a very angry tone, and/or pushing away an object.

Socially, children as young as two years of age are beginning to form friendships, understand differences between themselves and others, and understand social rules. There are numerous factors that may influence the child's capacity to develop friendships. Most of the children with Asperger's Syndrome are securely attached to their primary caregivers. The problems arise in the second stage of social development when the child moves away from the caregiver and begins to build upon his earlier experiences to develop new relationships with other important adults in his life, such as his teacher, and then peers (Koplow 1996).

What seems to occur in the children with Asperger's Syndrome is that when they go off to explore the world during their second year of life they do not refer back to the caregiver for guidance or cues but rather keep moving on. They appear not to have internalized the social heuristic that tells them to check in and make sure they are on track. One can easily imagine the alarms that go off in a preschool setting when a child wanders off the grounds or seems to be on another planet when a teacher calls him back into the classroom.

Given these differences in the way the young child with Asperger's Syndrome is making sense of the social heuristics, how then is he feeling internally? The answer to this question of course varies depending on the child; however, many of these children do end up experiencing varying degrees of anxiety. They are bright and are often highly tuned into what feels difficult to them. As we have described throughout this chapter, many things can feel challenging – the fact that peers and adults aren't always behaving in predictable ways, the fact that the world can be an assault on the sensory system, and the fact that people communicate in subtle or abstract ways that they cannot understand. These challenges can lead to the young child feeling very anxious and nervous. Anxiety is expressed in different ways but it is common to see children who are feeling this way become more rigid or at times oppositional. They may express the anxiety by becoming hyperactive, aggressive, or withdrawn. We have seen some children get more fixated on their particular interest when experiencing stress, and have been impressed by their ability to be more flexible with interests when the stress is reduced.

Table 2.5 Red flags for emotional and social development in young children with Asperger's Syndrome

- Poor eye contact
- Restricted range of affect – may seem flat
- Avoidance of other children, or inability to sustain brief interactions with another child
- Failure to initiate any friendships with peers
- Narrow interests and repetitive behaviors, preventing child from engaging socially with peers
- Separation difficulties across settings and/or extreme fearfulness and/or avoidance of situations
- Interaction patterns with peers can be aggressive, controlling, intrusive, or passive
- Lack of empathy, very egocentric, and unaware of others' feelings
- Tendency to interact better with adults who follow the child's cues, modify demands, organize play, and adapt to child's interests
- May show adequate social abilities in structured developmental testing and structured play, but have poor social abilities in unstructured play
- Can become increasingly anxious, and disorganized in play, communication, activity level, and thought as the social demands increase, or the expectations or routines are disrupted

Emotional and social difficulties can often be masked by behavioral problems. If a parent or teacher doesn't understand that a child may be having difficulty understanding the social world and the complex set of rules many of us take for granted, the child can be mislabeled as aggressive or hyperactive. Therefore, as with other areas of development, it is very important to try to understand these emotional and social issues in order to help the child develop more adaptive behavioral responses, as well as help him make connections between his feelings and actions.

The parent–child relationship

Inherent in much of the development outlined above is the child's ability to relate to and interact with others. Young children with Asperger's Syndrome generally appear and act differently depending on the people they are with and the context in which they find themselves. It is striking how well adapted most parents of children with Asperger's Syndrome are to their child. They very frequently experience mutually enjoyable interactions with their child. They may share a love for similar interests such as science, trains, and nature or activities such as swimming and art. They are often incredibly attuned to their child, reading their child's cues and constantly decoding their messages.

Interestingly, parents may not be aware of how much their lives have shifted to accommodate their child. For example, they may have stopped going shopping with their child or taking their child to church. They have learned to incorporate into their activities the extra amount of time that it takes their child to make a transition. This adaptation may result in a good fit between parent and child temperamentally, but tension can rise if the child has a behavior that the parent attempts to change before he or she has fully delved into the complexities of Asperger's Syndrome and developed a better understanding of what the behavior represents for the child. For example, parents may be able to tolerate a lot of difficult behavior but become very upset when their child does not say "please" and "thank you." Other parents may be anxious over their child's difficulties with toilet training because it means that he will not be able to go to nursery school. They may worry about how aggressive their son is towards his peers on the playground and fear that if they are not strict the community will ostracize both their child and them. Some parents worry every time the phone rings that it is their child's school telling them that their son is in trouble again.

Relational difficulties can lead to a lack of support for the child in many different arenas. Many of us enjoy the gratification of a small smile or a pat on the back when we have accomplished something or made an overture towards someone. If a child is different in this area and lacks or has impaired relational abilities, he can often be frustratingly difficult to reach. Teachers, caregivers, and parents alike may feel ineffective, overwhelmed, or even angered by this type of child, leading to further social isolation.

Table 2.6 Red flags for the parent–child relationship in young children with Asperger's Syndrome

- The parent may seem overprotective or anxious about the child's safety and/or frustration level
- There is very little mutual pleasure between the parent and child when they are playing together
- The parent appears to become easily frustrated with the child

---

The child's environment

We all have different tolerance levels for things such as noise, chaos, solitude, crowds, and so on. As we discussed in the section on sensory-motor issues, children with AS are particularly sensitive to their environments. The sensitivity is to both the physical environment and the emotional climate of a given situation. Some environmental factors are more predictable than others. *Noisy, crowded, chaotic* scenes can be overwhelming to some children with Asperger's Syndrome. Situations where the rules are *ambiguous* or *constantly changing* (e.g. during recess, birthday parties) can be confusing and anxiety provoking because of the child's rigidity and need for structure. Highly charged *emotional* situations are also disorganizing for children with Asperger's Syndrome. They can't accurately read and discern the feelings of others and are easily frightened by the strong emotions directed towards them.

Some parents feel that their child does better in an unstructured setting where he can do as he pleases. This may be true as long as the environment isn't chaotic and physically overwhelming. However, are the child's social needs being served by that situation? It may be that the child retreats and can occupy himself easily by doing tasks of his choice but he isn't interacting with, or being challenged to engage, other children. There is a place for this type of setting in a child's life. Many children, after a full day of school with all its various demands, welcome unstructured down time (watch TV, play with favorite toy). Like all children, children with Asperger's Syndrome often need time to recoup or to just be part of a group without the pressures to engage. However, in general, a structured, predictable environment tends to decrease anxiety and foster increased social interaction and communication for children with Asperger's Syndrome. It is also important to *avoid rigid and inflexible environments.* These types of environments may initially appeal to a parent because they profess "structure." However, the contrary is true. A rigid environment can evoke strong control feelings and increase the chances for a child with Asperger's Syndrome to become quite oppositional and/or anxious. We will take a closer look at how these issues pertain to selecting a school for your child in Chapter 11.

Stress and coping

We have referenced different ways a child copes with some of the developmental challenges throughout this chapter. For both children and adults some coping strategies are more adaptive than others. A typical coping pattern that we see in young children with Asperger's Syndrome is *avoidance* of situations that are either socially demanding or not well-structured and have poorly defined rules such as playground activities. Some children may complain of extreme boredom and fatigue, and become very *rigid* leading to *oppositionality* when challenged to do things differently (e.g. play a ball game a different way), or engage in an activity they do not feel comfortable with (e.g. go for a bike ride). They may respond to such a request by rejecting the offer or giving an excuse. As their anxiety rises so does their hypersensitivity to their external environment, leading to their complaints that the space is too noisy, too hot, or too crowded. And in some cases, the children are so overloaded that their behavior degenerates into a tantrum.

Not surprisingly, children with Asperger's Syndrome are often described as being very *controlling*. They need to do things a certain way and aren't able to adapt others' ideas. For these children, controlling others is their way of saying, "This is the only way I know how to do things, thus it is the right way."

Other children respond to being challenged with *aggression*, which is often an act to protect themselves from the onslaught of stimulation and confusion. At times, it is a very effective short-term way of scaring away a child who is frustrating or scaring him, but in the long term it always leads to his getting in trouble and possibly being ostracized. "Steve" hit a child in his class every time that child sang a jingle from a TV commercial. He did not know anything about the song but he assumed that if his friend was looking at him and smiling then the song must be an insult directed at him, causing him to strike out at his peer. This was a coping pattern that led to numerous discipline issues at school.

Some young children with Asperger's Syndrome cope with uncertainty in social situations by adopting a powerful character from a favorite video or book and imitating the way that the character (such as Tyrannosaurus Rex) interacts with others. Part of these characters' appeal is that their behaviors are quite clear and direct (T-Rex attacks everyone), which is attractive to a child who has difficulty picking up on subtle social cues. Often the children's parents feel tremendous pressure from their child's school to eliminate certain of their child's maladaptive behaviors, such as lunging at a peer (without first understanding why the child takes on these roles), and provide their child with more adaptive alternative behaviors.

Children will cope differently depending on their temperament, support, and the severity of developmental challenges. It is important to recognize what the behavior means before trying to change the behavior. With this understanding, parents, teachers, care providers, and clinicians will be better equipped to help the young child find more adaptive ways of dealing with his stress.

A developmental approach for conceptualizing young children's strengths and challenges

The approach described throughout this chapter attempts to integrate the relevant aspects of a child's life. We hope that by the time you have finished reading this chapter two points will stay with you. The first is that children with Asperger's Syndrome are bright, creative, and enjoy sharing their interests with other people. The second point is that Asperger's Syndrome is a developmental disorder in which the overriding characteristics showed by all of these children is difficulty in developing and maintaining social relationships, reciprocal communication with their peers, and spontaneous imaginary play (National Research Council 2001). In the following chapter we will apply this developmental approach to the diagnosis of young children.

CHAPTER 3

The Diagnosis

Any parent who notices that his child seems a little different than the child's peers or siblings wonders if his concerns are valid or if he is making too much out of nothing, not respecting the child's differences. It takes a great deal of courage to go to a professional for help, especially when your child is young and may seem to be "on target" in so many ways. Often it isn't until a preschool or kindergarten teacher begins discussing concerns that the parents are forced to try to confront their child's issues. Many parents have an underlying fear that a "label" will be more harmful than helpful to their child. Understandably, some parents worry that a diagnosis will stigmatize their child and lead to others having lower expectations for their child. We hope that this chapter will take away some of the fears that are often associated with taking a child to a mental health professional for an evaluation. In our opinion the goal of a good assessment is to provide you with insight into your child and guidance for helping him in the areas where he is experiencing difficulty. We will provide a guideline for an assessment that is based on the same developmental approach to the child that we have used in the first and second chapters. As you can see in Figure 3.1 the model examines not only the child's strengths and weaknesses but also the stresses and resources in his family and community.

We also hope that this chapter will take away some of the mystery behind the diagnosis of Asperger's Syndrome by exploring how the information gained during the assessment is used to determine which diagnosis best fits the child. Once again we want to stress that a diagnosis can have many different objectives. First and foremost a diagnosis has the potential to foster parents' understanding of their child, providing a base from which to look for both educational and support resources. Of course, care must be taken so that this information is not presented in a way that affects their ability to see their child's strengths. Second, it provides a term that has a shared meaning

53

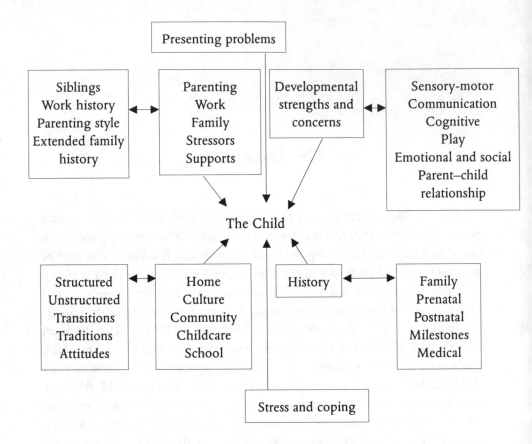

Figure 3.1 A developmental approach for understanding the young child

between professionals which then in turn can help inform clinical and educational decisions. Third, the diagnosis is often the one factor that helps children qualify for inclusion into a program that is funded by their school system and/or health insurance. As children grow and begin to ask questions, having a diagnosis can also help them make sense of why they experience some things differently than their peers. It is our goal that by the end of this chapter you will be able to see the benefits of having an assessment and recognize that how and when one chooses to use the diagnostic label is a separate issue. The first question frequently asked is, to whom do you go for an assessment?

Who should complete the comprehensive assessment?

It is easy for parents to become confused about who to turn to for help. There is a wide range of mental health professionals who may have experience assessing young children for developmental and behavioral problems. This group includes social workers (MSW), marriage, family and child counselors (MFCC), psychologists (PhD), psychiatrists (MD), and developmental pediatricians (MD). Speech and language pathologists and occupational therapists can also conduct developmental screenings to determine if a developmental evaluation may be helpful. Yet to give the diagnosis of a Pervasive Developmental Disorder, including Asperger's Syndrome, the clinician must be a licensed psychiatrist or psychologist. Since not all professionals are trained to assess young children, it is important to ask if they have experience working with young children with Pervasive Developmental Disorders (PDD) and Asperger's Syndrome (AS).

In cases where the behaviors and development are confusing, an interdisciplinary assessment which involves the collaboration of a team of professionals can be most useful. The team may include a psychiatrist, psychologist, speech and language pathologist, and occupational therapist.

Some families may initially have had an assessment by a speech and language pathologist or occupational therapist (OT), since these children's initial presenting difficulties are often within these areas. Speech and language pathologists are qualified to assess and treat communication disorders. They treat developmental and physical conditions that interfere with communication. For children with Asperger's Syndrome this typically entails both the ways in which they use and understand words and the gestures that they use to communicate.

Occupational therapists assist an individual to participate in their daily "occupations." They assess the many factors that contribute to the ability of a child with Asperger's Syndrome to participate in daily activities, such as fine and gross motor skills and sensory integration issues.

Table 3.1 Key elements to consider when selecting a professional for an evaluation

- Experience with young children
- A developmental perspective
- Experience with Autistic Spectrum Disorders/Pervasive Developmental Disorders and specifically Asperger's Syndrome
- Observation of the child in different settings interacting with adults and peers
- Ability to collaborate with others involved in the child's care
- Sensitivity to parents' needs, fears, and challenges

The components of a good assessment

As we stated above, a good assessment requires a professional or an interdisciplinary team of professionals who have expertise in working with young children on the autistic spectrum and in particular young children with Asperger's Syndrome. The assessment needs to be child centered, which means that it must be sensitive to the developmental issues of the child. It evaluates his strengths and weaknesses along the multiple dimensions of functioning outlined in the first two chapters in order to develop a working understanding of the whole child. An evaluation ideally should include observations of the child for more than one session in both structured (standardized testing) and unstructured settings (a play session with both his/her caregivers and the examiner). An assessment should also include standardized evaluations of the child's communication skills and intellectual functioning to better understand the child's areas of strength and difficulty.

Given that communication and social difficulties are central to the condition, it is also important that the professional see the child interacting with other children outside the context of his home. If this is not possible, then this information may be obtained second hand – for example, by telephone interviews with previous or current teachers.

Psychological testing is also helpful for getting a complete picture of the child's development. Not only do you obtain information on language, motor, and cognitive functioning, but also a good examiner can assess the child's attention, relational, and coping skills. Standardized questionnaires completed by parents and/or teachers about the child's behavior and development can also be very helpful, but they should not be the only source of information about the child. Depending on the child's presenting problems and the structure of the clinical setting, an assessment may also include a speech and language evaluation and an occupational therapy evaluation. When a group of professionals works together to understand the child it is often referred to as an "interdisciplinary diagnostic evaluation."

Table 3.2 Key aspects of a developmental assessment

- Family history/cultural factors
- Medical history
- The child's coping patterns, behavioral problems, and adaptation
- A development evaluation which looks at the child's:
  - Sensory regulation and motor skills
  - Communication
  - Cognition
  - Play
  - Emotional and social development
- The quality of the child's relationship with his/her primary caregivers
- The child's environment (home and preschool/daycare)

The evaluation process

The first step of an evaluation typically will be an appointment for the parents with a mental health professional, commonly called an intake meeting. Parents often feel very anxious about what will be found and whether a diagnostic label will hinder rather than help their child. As mentioned, many parents may fear they are making too much out of nothing. They may also receive very mixed feedback regarding their child's behavior. Their pediatrician may say everything is fine while the teacher is quite concerned. Usually, if you are seeing a clinician who has experience assessing young children with Asperger's Syndrome, he or she will assure you that these feelings and mixed messages are common, and that you should feel free to ask any questions that arise throughout the evaluation process.

The first meeting will typically include gathering information about the child's early developmental history, medical history, family history, behavioral problems, current developmental functioning, including the quality of the child's play, the child's social-emotional relationships, the child's school experiences, and current stresses. We will now look at each of these areas in greater detail in relationship to how they may be addressed in an assessment.

The family history

It is very common for parents to wonder if their child's difficulties are due to something they did, or if the problems are inherited from one side of the family (Bristol 1987). Therefore, during an assessment, a thorough family history is important to both identify key events in the child's and family's life and to identify potential *hereditary factors.* These issues may impact how the parent copes with, understands, and accepts the problems. Since siblings of children with Autistic Spectrum Disorders are more at risk for having Autistic Spectrum or related disorders, both parents and professionals need to be attentive to their siblings' development as well (National Research Council 2001). Many parents may feel a high degree of guilt if there is a close relative with autism or perhaps a very socially isolated and eccentric relative that reminds them of their child. However, *parents are not to blame for this disorder.* Being sensitive to the feelings and anxieties that surface for the parent during the initial history taking is very important.

It is also very important to be attuned to how their culture may influence what a parent or professional perceives as being a child's strengths or difficulties. *Cultural sensitivity* and the understanding of the norms within the family's culture also prevent misinterpretation of certain aspects of the family history, style, and behaviors. For example, it is not uncommon to see that some families with a child who has Asperger's Syndrome demonstrate great pride in, and have very high expectations for, their child's academic achievement. The emphasis in these families may be more on education than on the child's capacity to play, which may lead them to overlook their child's social difficulties with peers. Other families may have different cultural norms regarding autonomy and separation from the family. One family may view favorably their child wanting to stay home and not wanting to spend time with children outside the family, or they may admire characteristics of leadership in a child and think very positively about the child who acts like the class director. It is important to be able to explore these cultural attitudes without assuming that they are causing your child's difficulties.

Sensitive history taking should include a discussion of *learning difficulties* (e.g. dyslexia or attention difficulties) and academic strengths on both the maternal and paternal sides. The examiner will also ask about the social trends within both the immediate and extended family (e.g. do members of the family prefer to spend holidays alone or as a group?). It will also be important to get a thorough history of *mental illness* (e.g. depression, anxiety, and obsessive-compulsive disorder) that was diagnosed or suspected in family members, as well as other medical problems.

A thorough history will also include all life events that have impacted the child since birth – for example, history of childcare, birth of siblings, moves, or any specific traumas. It is helpful to also explore *parenting styles*. Most parents are motivated to have their child succeed but major differences in how this goal is achieved are common. In discussing these differences, tensions that exist between partners can surface. Although parents are seeking an assessment for their child, it is important to explore these parental tensions in order to help parents gain the support they often so badly need from one another.

Discussing parenting styles also frequently leads to identifying the gifts and natural talents of the parents. Many parents have intuitively learned how to support and tune into their child's needs without having concretely verbalized and identified what it is that they do so well. For example, parents have described how they will frequently go to the park equipped with doubles of certain toys that are of interest to their child (without these they know that their child will likely play by himself and avoid any social contact). When other children approach them to see the toy, the parent takes an active role engaging the kids until their child can begin to participate. These are examples of how many of these parents maintain an active role in building connections between their child and other children.

It is common that an intake interview can raise questions for parents about what they were like as children. Some parents may begin identifying with their child's difficulties and recognize their own discomfort in social situations. This recognition can create a whole new set of issues for the parent and for the parent's partner. *Normalizing the flood of feelings* that can occur is important and providing support is essential in order to help parents embark on this new journey with their child and family. In Chapter 5 we will take a closer look at the thoughts and feelings that many parents experience after learning about their child's diagnosis and the journey they take from seeking professional help to becoming advocates for their child.

Medical history

Like the family history, a thorough review of the child's medical history should be conducted. Included in this review is the *child's prenatal and birth history, developmental milestones*, illnesses, allergies, or other medical issues that may impact the child's functioning. It is also very important to explore the family's *relationship with the pediatrician* and to advocate for informing and including the pediatrician, where appropriate, in the assessment process. Some families feel very supported by their doctor while others have had difficulty getting help. It isn't uncommon for a parent to hear that the child will "outgrow" a behavior or that the parent should "wait and see how things develop." Some parents feel angry that their pediatrician did not identify the "red flags" for this type of problem. These parents may harbor angry thoughts and fears that they lost important time to help their child. However, it is important to remember that these children *have* made many developmental gains and the difficulties can initially be much subtler and therefore harder to recognize when the social demands on the youngster are few.

Behavioral problems

When families seek help, they are often asked to identify the presenting or current problem(s) and list other areas of concern. In the process of identifying problem behaviors, *patterns of behavior* are being explored and efforts to understand what underlies the behaviors are made. Additional help from structured testing, observations, and detailed history taking enables clinicians and parents to evaluate the child's behavior in different settings and under different circumstances. The clinician will want to understand what the child experiences as stressful. For one child it may be not drawing a perfect picture, for another child it may be not winning every game, and for still another it may be separating from his parents at drop-off time.

Coping behaviors can be best understood as how the child reacts and responds when under stress and when supported by his environment. Some children cope by displaying *externalizing behaviors* such as aggressiveness, hyperactivity, and/or oppositionality. Other children may respond with more *internalizing behaviors* such as avoidance, shutting down, and tuning out others, or obsessing about things. And of course, there are children who present with a mix of both externalizing and internalizing behaviors.

How one defines a behavior problem is also influenced by the relationship the individual has with the child, and their understanding of the child's behavior. The same behavior that may be viewed as a strength by one parent, such as the child's ability to stay focused on an area of special interest, may be seen as a problem by a teacher who is trying to get the child engaged in a group activity or shifted to a new task. Exploring these patterns of behavior will help set the stage for understanding their root causes and influences and will lead to developing interventions that support healthier ways of developing.

The developmental assessment

By now you are familiar with the developmental areas you would expect clinicians to look at when they are evaluating your child in both informal observations and standardized tests. As a reminder, the areas include motor and sensory development, communication, cognitive thinking, play, social and emotional development, the parent–child relationship, and the young child's adaptation to his home and school environment. Now let's look at what actually happens when your child meets face to face with a clinician for an assessment. Let's assume that your child is having an interdisciplinary evaluation that includes a mental health professional/psychologist, a speech and language pathologist, and an occupational therapist.

The *psychologist* may conduct a play observation as well as cognitive testing. Many parents question the need for intelligence testing, especially when their child seems so bright. However, much can be learned from this assessment. Typically, a *cognitive assessment* will include IQ testing but also evaluates the child's executive functioning skills, attention, and organizational skills. Children with Asperger's Syndrome typically show average to above average cognitive abilities on standardized assessments. The standardized assessments capture the child's strengths in rote recall of information, definition of words (vocabulary), factual knowledge such as the number of days in a week, and tasks that have visual cues such as arithmetic and block design. Typically, the score given on IQ tests will reflect overall performance on verbal and nonverbal functioning. Given at an early age, the most helpful aspect of the IQ test is its ability to reflect the child's current level of functioning in the above areas and identify areas of significant delay, rather than predict future performance level.

Children with Asperger's Syndrome may show strengths in one area and weakness in another. This is often described as having an uneven scattering of results. The challenge here lies in understanding why there is a discrepancy. A child's unusual ability may be more related to their areas of special interest as in the case of numbers, rather than reflecting an understanding of arithmetic concepts. As children increase in age their cognitive test scores may reflect their academic achievement and school success but their adaptive behavior may be a better predictor of their level of daily functioning.

Part of the psychological assessment will also be looking at *executive functioning skills*. As we have discussed in the previous chapters, executive functioning refers to the child's ability to organize his thoughts, prioritize information, carry out complex multi-step problem solving tasks, and be flexible in his thinking (National Research Council 2001). It is important to remember that these are skills that are just beginning to develop in young children. Therefore, a clinician will make observations regarding these skills but a full evaluation cannot be conducted until the child is of school age.

The psychological testing can also help us understand whether or not a child has *attention difficulties*. What is often so confusing about children with Asperger's Syndrome is that they can spend hours playing one of their favorite computer games or arranging furniture in a dollhouse but not seem able to sit still during circle time or a meal for longer than five minutes. Standardized testing will evaluate the differences in the children's thinking and attention when they are given verbal cues, visual cues, manipulative objects, concrete ideas, and abstract ideas. It is interesting that the same children who appear to have attention problems can focus intently on details that are irrelevant to the question being asked. For example, at school the teacher may ask the children to look at the calendar and tell what is special about the day. Instead of talking about today's field trip to the bakery the child may give a very long-winded description of the new carnivorous plants his parents purchased over the weekend.

The psychological testing can also provide insight into which behaviors may challenge a child's success in the classroom as well as strategies that may foster the child's adaptation. For example, was it hard to keep the child's attention on questions that did not have any visual cues? Was the child's ability to stay focused on a task increased when the clinician provided visual cues? Did the child appear much more attentive when he was provided with a sticker each time that he completed a set of questions?

The clinician will also be observing the child's social-emotional development throughout the evaluation. Assessing social-emotional development will include looking at the range of feelings that the child expresses as well as examining behavior. It is important to assess how comfortable or anxious a child is in both structured and unstructured settings. For example, does the child look like he is having fun when engaged in free play or does he seem angry for no apparent reason? Is the child chewing his shirtsleeve during the entire session? The clinician will have to decide whether the chewing is related to anxiety or sensory issues. The clinician will also note how quickly a child can move from a positive to a negative mood and vice versa. Some children with Asperger's Syndrome seem to wake up in an angry mood and stay that way for the entire day for no apparent reason, while others may quickly move from being happy to mad and happy again, leaving their parents on "pins and needles" constantly.

Up until this point most of the assessment has been focused primarily on the child, but as we have stressed throughout this book a good evaluation must also look at the child's social development within the context of his family and school. The psychologist or mental health specialist will typically gather this information but all members of the diagnostic team can contribute to the assessment of social-emotional functioning since they see the child in different contexts. It is very helpful to have a sense of what a typical day is like for the child and his family. How does the child adapt to the daily routines? Understanding what the family does at meal time and how they handle getting ready for school, bath time, and bedtime can provide very helpful insight into how much effort the parents have to put into these events and how smoothly they are working with the child. It is also helpful to have a play session that looks at how the child interacts with each parent as well as the entire family. A *structured play session* may include little glimpses of the child's day by asking the parent to engage with the child in free play, a structured play activity such as building something out of blocks, a teaching task such as putting a puzzle together, a snack, and cleanup time. It can be very helpful to see what the parent and child enjoy doing together, who is the leader of the activity, how the parent sets limits, and how the child responds. The play session provides an opportunity to look at how easily a child gets upset, the types of things that upset him, and what helps him cope with this stress both with a clinician and with his parents.

A good assessment will also include a school observation. The school observation gives the clinician a chance to see what the school experience is like for the child. Again, the clinician is looking at the child along all of the developmental dimensions. Some common questions to be asked are: how does he handle the transitions both to and from the playground? What are his relationships like with his teachers? Does he spend most of his time in one activity or does he play with a wide range of materials? Does he engage in mutually satisfying play with his peers or is he mostly playing next to them or by himself? What is his communication style with peers? How accurately does he read his classmates' cues? What typically triggers the child's upset feelings and how does he cope with these feelings?

As mentioned earlier, the two other professionals who are frequently involved in the assessment of young children with Asperger's Syndrome are speech and language pathologists and occupational therapists.

A *speech and language pathologist* draws from a range of methods to find out as much as possible about the different aspects of the child's communication. This includes the use of standardized tests, developmental scales, parent questionnaires, and observation of the child's interactions and behaviors in different situations. In a speech and language evaluation the language component includes: receptive language – what the child understands; expressive language – what the child says or gestures; and the pragmatics of language – how the child is able to use language to communicate. The speech component of the assessment looks at the motor skills involved in vocalization and articulation of sounds in words. Another component of the speech assessment is auditory processing – making sense of what the child is hearing. This includes the child's ability to follow oral directions that include more than two steps, and staying attentive to conversation when there are sounds that are competing. Some children may also find certain sounds overwhelmingly negative, such as the sound of chalk on the chalkboard or a humidifier. It is possible to make a speech and language diagnosis solely from test scores, but a good assessment also takes into account the way in which the scores were obtained and all of the observations that were made during the assessment process.

Table 3.3 Areas to be assessed in a speech and language evaluation

- Receptive language
- Expressive language
- Pragmatic language
- Articulation and voice quality
- Play

The speech and language pathologist then needs to integrate all of the diagnostic testing results and decide whether or not a diagnosis of speech and language disorder should be made. DSM-IV provides several possible diagnoses. The first two are Expressive Language Disorder and Mixed Expressive–Receptive Language Disorder. Neither of these is given if a language delay is part of a general cognitive delay. Others are Phonological Disorder, which means problems with articulation; Stuttering; and Communication Disorder–Not Otherwise Specified. The diagnosis of Semantic–Pragmatic Disorder has been used in England for some years and is now being used in the United States school system, but it is not in DSM-IV. A speech and language clinician may diagnose and treat speech and language disorders without using a DSM classification, but for insurance purposes (in the U.S.) the DSM classification can be important.

An *occupational therapist* (OT) can also be an important member of the diagnostic team. As you may recall, Asperger originally described these children as having delayed motor skills as well as being physically clumsy. An OT assessment may be recommended following the screening conducted by the mental health professional and at times it is the first step in the diagnostic process because of the parents' concerns about their child's motor delays, sensory differences, or responses.

As with other disciplines, information may be obtained from the parents using questionnaires, standardized testing (if available and appropriate) of sensory and motor abilities, and observation in specific activities. The therapist can choose from a great variety of tests. Observing the child in less structured activities may provide a different picture than that seen during structured testing and may add to understanding the child. A single skill or behavioral description can have a variety of reasons behind it. Therefore, interpretation of results involves not looking at one behavior alone but at how the pattern fits together in a specific profile. "The key to assessment is to focus on *how* the child processes sensory information and manages environmental challenges and not to focus solely on the specific skills or milestones the child displays" (Williamson, Anzalone and Hanft 2000 p.155). The areas addressed in the occupational therapy evaluation of sensory integration can be found in Table 3.4.

Table 3.4 Areas addressed in the occupational therapy evaluation of sensory integration

- Tactile Input – perception of touch
  - tactile defensiveness – defensive response to ordinary experiences
  - tactile discrimination – interpretation of input
- Proprioceptive Input – perception of input from muscles and joints
- Vestibular Input – perception of input about movement and gravity
  - influence of vestibular-proprioceptive input on motor skills
- Input from Other Sensory Systems – visual, auditory, olfactory
- Praxis – the ability to develop the idea, plan, and execute a novel task
- Sensory Regulatory Abilities – the ability to respond in an organized way and self-calm following a sensory experience

---

The evaluation of the various sensory systems and their impact on the motor, social-emotional, and behavioral responses has indicated that many children with Asperger's Syndrome have inefficiencies in sensory and motor functioning which impact daily functioning. If present in a specific case, these findings may then be incorporated into the team's diagnostic formulation and recommendations.

Diagnostic issues

The next question you should be asking is how we integrate all of this information to formulate a diagnosis. A good clinician or assessment team will take all the information gathered and begin to look at patterns of behavior and development. The challenge always is to integrate what has been learned about the family, the child's medical history, and cultural factors with all the information obtained from the developmental assessment. For example, how might a child's difficulty in social interactions and communication be influenced by the fact he is new to the country or comes from a home where they speak a different language? After all this is accomplished, the team or clinician will determine which, if any, diagnosis best fits your child.

When an assessment is complete parents may or may not receive a definitive diagnosis. Particularly when children are young (under five), clinicians may err in the direction of caution. Some clinicians may discuss delays and difficulties without ever using a label and others may provide a list of possibilities and defer diagnosis until interventions have been attempted.

Currently Asperger's Syndrome is diagnosed primarily in children between the ages of five and nine, yet there is a growing consensus among professionals that Autistic Spectrum Disorders can be identified as early as two years of age (National Research Council 2001). Since children with Asperger's Syndrome show no significant delays in the areas of expressive language or cognitive development they are typically not being identified prior to three years of age, when children are expected to display skills in social interactions, communication, and symbolic play with peers. It is important to remember that Asperger's Syndrome is a relatively new diagnosis. It was first included in the DSM-IV (Diagnostic and Statistical Manual of the American Psychiatric Association, Fourth Edition) in 1994 and ICD-10 (International Classification of Diseases, World Health Organization, Tenth Revision) in 1993. Because it is one of the newer diagnoses, clinicians are still working to fully understand the disorder and to separate it from the other diagnoses. Before looking at how clinicians rule-in or rule-out the diagnosis of Asperger's Syndrome, we will review several of the screening tools currently available.

If you were to conduct a search on this topic over the Internet you would find a growing number of tools designed to screen children for Asperger's Syndrome, to provide research data on specific aspects of Asperger's Syndrome, and even act as a set of diagnostic criteria. One of the most widely talked about screening tools is the Australian Scale for Asperger's Syndrome, developed by Attwood and Garnett (Attwood 1998). It is a rating scale designed to help parents and teachers determine if a school age child *may* be at risk for Asperger's Syndrome. The scale is to be used as a screening tool, not a diagnostic tool. And like so many of these tools, the examples are more attuned to issues relevant to school age rather than young children.

Clinicians who work with young children are very excited by a recent screening tool called ADOS which stands for Autistic Disorder Observation Scale (2001). What's exciting about this scale is that it provides the clinician with a set of play-based activities to use in rating the child on a set of behaviors that cover the primary components of an Autistic Spectrum Disorder: communication, reciprocal social interaction, play, stereotyped behaviors, and restricted interests. One of the strengths of ADOS is that it is based on criteria shared by both DSM-IV and ICD-10. The current edition of the scale has a cutoff number for autism and autism spectrum but not Asperger's Syndrome. However, we believe that it still provides clinicians with a very descriptive and standardized way of observing how the child responds along the key diagnostic dimensions.

Let's now take a look at the criteria used by medical and mental health based institutions to diagnose Asperger's Syndrome. DSM-IV and ICD-10, even though they are worded differently, are relatively close to what Asperger originally intended. They differ primarily in how the material is presented. ICD-10 presents a more detailed clinical description of the children's early development, how they vary in terms of social interactions, interests, and motor development, and how they differ from children with autism. In contrast, DSM-IV cites the clinical criteria but directs the reader to look into the larger handbook for more detailed descriptions of them and the range of severity.

It is helpful to know that ICD-10 was intended to have two separate versions. The first was a more descriptive version to be used by clinicians, and the second was a more detailed version of diagnostic criteria to be used by researchers (see Appendix I). In contrast, DSM-IV was to be used in both clinical and research work with a more detailed description in the adjoining handbook. Thus ICD-10 has been found to provide a more detailed description of how the child may look along the same dimensions covered by DSM-IV. Both consider autism as part of the diagnostic spectrum, but ICD-10's research criteria explicitly addresses that Asperger's Syndrome shares many of the same criteria as autism, while DSM-IV simply says that other Pervasive Developmental Disorders must be ruled out.

Putting these differences aside, both ICD-10 and DSM-IV use criteria from early development to differentiate Asperger's Syndrome from autism; if there is a history of significant delays in language or cognition then the child cannot meet the criteria for Asperger's Syndrome. Still, ICD-10 gives a more detailed description of areas in which there may be delay. They both cite social and communicative difficulties along with restricted interests as the key diagnostic areas. And neither addresses the issues that may arise when a child's early language delay is due to a medical problem such as a hearing impairment or cleft palate (Klin, Volkmar and Sparrow 2000). Thus the debate over which set of diagnostic criteria is better will certainly continue. The diagnostic criteria for both DSM-IV and ICD-10 can be found in Appendix I.

One of the most frequently asked questions by both parents and professionals using both diagnostic criteria is: what is the difference between the diagnoses of Asperger's Syndrome and High Functioning Autism? Based on the ICD-10 or DSM-IV criteria, if the child has a history of early language delay (i.e. single words not used by two years, communicative phrases not used by age three years) or if they meet the criteria for another specific Pervasive Developmental Disorder, they cannot receive the diagnosis of Asperger's Syndrome, even if a delay is not apparent at the time of the evaluation. As many of these children approach school age there may no longer be a significant difference between the two groups, but the child's early history is considered a key issue in the diagnosis. Thus it is not surprising that there is an ongoing discussion in the professional community regarding the value of differentiating Asperger's Syndrome from the larger body of Autistic Spectrum Disorders (High Functioning Autism, PDD-NOS). At times it may seem that the distinctions are arbitrary, relating mostly to the number of symptoms reported and the severity of the handicaps. This question will continue to be examined by researchers as they fine-tune the diagnostic classifications and test their validity and reliability (Klin and Volkmar 1996; Klin et al. 2000; National Research Council 2001).

Another area of debate is the view that social intent is an area that may better differentiate the two rather than the child's early language history. The research on this topic has identified children with Asperger's Syndrome as being more motivated to have social contact with peers than are children with autism.

The diagnostic process becomes even more complicated as different communities use different criteria to determine a child's eligibility for special services. For example, in the United States the school district has its own criteria of autistic-like behavior based on a summary of the determinants for autism to evaluate whether or not a child qualifies for special education services. Still other criteria have been designed for research purposes and may be viewed as being more descriptive and less pathological, but they have not gone through the same extensive research to determine their validity and reliability as diagnostic criteria.

These are all valid points, making it even more important to remember that the diagnostic classification is only a small part of the more important diagnostic process of understanding the whole child (Klin et al. 2000). What we feel is most important is that we do not lose sight of the characteristics that they share, and what makes Asperger's Syndrome unique, namely the impairments in the areas of social interactions, communication, and imaginary play combined with restricted interests and habits, and no significant cognitive delays. We cannot stress enough the importance of not losing sight of the goals of the evaluation. For the remainder of the chapter we will be referring to the DSM-IV criteria. For a more complete look at other popular criteria you can refer to Appendix I. Let's now go back to your child and assume that he has received the Asperger's Syndrome diagnosis using the DSM-IV criteria.

The DSM-IV criteria can at times be confusing or ambiguous for parents of young children. They may seem to be too focused on the child's limitations without any room to incorporate the child's strengths and account for the wide range of functioning seen within this population. Both parents and clinicians know that children with the same diagnosis can look very different from one another, some with significant problems and others only mildly affected. Most of all, both parents and clinicians rightfully wonder what these criteria may mean for the young child in his everyday functioning. Table 3.5 redefines each diagnostic term in a way in which a parent may view their child.

Are there significant variations between children with this diagnosis?

The short answer to this question is absolutely yes, and this can lead to confusion in making the diagnosis, especially if the clinician has seen only a limited number of young children. As stated before, there is a range of behaviors with which the children present, which is influenced by factors such as the child's temperament, his fit with the environment, and the severity of his developmental difficulties. The diagnostic criteria may also present differently in some children. For example, many of these children, instead of having a special area of interest, may have obsessive preference for a specific type of activity such as water play or computer games. Some children may be clumsy while others are quite athletic. Often the behavioral problems are minimal when there is a very good fit between the child and his care-giving environment. But underlying issues with communication, imaginary play, and social interactions with peers must be present in order to meet the criteria for Asperger's Syndrome.

What are the other diagnostic categories often considered when evaluating a young child who has communication, relational, and behavioral problems?

Here are some of the diagnoses that parents may encounter in the process of having their child evaluated:

Table 3.5 DSM-IV criteria for Asperger's Syndrome adapted for young children

A. *Qualitative impairment in social interaction, as manifested by at least two of the following:*

   1. poor eye contact; the child doesn't naturally and consistently respond when you smile or frown at him; hard-to-read facial expressions; doesn't pick up on social cues of others

   2. hasn't made friends on his own from preschool or daycare; has difficulty engaging in give-and-take with peers his age; difficulty expanding play beyond his own interests

   3. doesn't spontaneously seek out peers to share enjoyment in his creations and projects or to demonstrate interests

   4. just as happy playing by himself or next to a peer; seems indifferent to another child's interests and/or feelings

B. *Restricted, repetitive, and stereotyped patterns of behavior, interests, and activities, as manifested by at least one of the following:*

   1. child is overly focused on a daily basis on one or two special interests or activities (e.g. dinosaurs/space/computer games/replaying a video by rote)

   2. repetitive rituals around things like eating, travel, bedtime, and bath. Child demands that one follows rituals

   3. finger flicking, spinning, hand flapping

   4. can get absorbed in an aspect of his special interest or object but not able to integrate it into the larger context (e.g. may have an interest in brand names of cars but no interest in making up a story about the people who drive these cars)

C. *These difficulties impact ability to make friends, manage daily transitions in family life or school life, and in general impact the ability to adjust to routines typical of preschool age children.*

D. *There is no clinically significant general delay in language – child used phrases to communicate by the age of three.*

E. *There is no clinically significant delay in cognitive development (child's IQ is average or above) and child can feed self, dress self with help, but may still have difficulty with potty training. Child is not totally absorbed in his own world.*

F. *If child meets criteria for autism, mental retardation, schizophrenia, or PDD, child can't have Asperger's Syndrome. Child can be given other diagnosis such as ADHD, anxiety, or depression concurrently.*

- Pervasive Developmental Disorders – these include Autism, PDD–Not Otherwise Specified (NOS), Asperger's Syndrome

- Anxiety Disorders

- Attention Deficit/Hyperactivity Disorders

- Communication Disorders – these include Expressive Language Disorder, Mixed Expressive–Receptive Language Disorder, and Communication Disorder–Not Otherwise Specified (NOS)

- Semantic-Pragmatic Disorder

- Nonverbal Learning Disorder – NLD (a type of learning disorder that is not a DSM-IV diagnostic category)

- Motor Skills Disorder – Developmental Coordination Disorder

- Dysfunction in Sensory Integration or Sensory Integration Disorder (not a DSM-IV diagnostic category)

This list can be overwhelming and confusing for both the parents and clinicians. Many of these diagnoses rely on seemingly similar behaviors and characteristics. The defining issue is determining which features are most prevalent and consistent across settings. Again, we want to stress that the diagnostic evaluation is *a process that can evolve over time.* The clinician may feel that the child has the capacity for beginning imaginary play and wonder if the child's anxiety is preventing him from engaging in the rich symbolic play that is more age-appropriate. The clinician may choose to see the child over a longer period of time to see if the child's communication and imaginary play skills increase once he is more comfortable with the clinician in the clinical setting. Before making a formal diagnosis, a clinician may also want to have the opportunity to observe the child in a school setting with peers, especially if the child seems to be very verbal with adults, since the clinician knows that that is very different from communicating and interacting with peers. Diagnostic questions also arise when the child comes from a home where English is the second language and the child's primary caregiver does not speak English. In this case, the clinician may want to enroll the child in a speech and language early intervention program to see if his capacity to communicate and play with peers increases as he expands his English language skills. However, it is important to remember how easy it is for most young children to engage in reciprocal interactions and joint play even with children who do not share the same primary language. Similarly, one would expect to observe age-appropriate communication and symbolic play when the children are engaged in play with their parents.

Another factor that is considered is whether or not the diagnoses are mutually exclusive. For example, a child cannot receive the DSM-IV diagnosis of Communication Disorders (a more limited diagnosis) if he meets the criteria for a Pervasive Developmental Disorder such as Asperger's Syndrome (a more all-encompassing diagnosis).

Because anxiety in young children is often manifested by withdrawal and controlling behavior, *General Anxiety Disorder* (GAD), and more specifically *Social Phobia*, is often considered, especially if the child's difficulties were not noticed prior to school. Children with GAD have a sense of anxiety and worry that is much greater than is more typically seen as a response to daily living. They can seem to be worried for no apparent reason and their anxiety may be displayed in physical symptoms such as difficulty falling asleep, muscle or limb twitching, headaches, nausea, poor eating, sweating, and irritability. During times of stress, such as going to a birthday party or having a new baby-sitter, these symptoms are often increased. Thus it is easy to see how young children with Asperger's Syndrome may initially be given this diagnosis, since they often appear anxious when they are asked to do things that they do not feel 100 percent confident about. These tasks may appear to the outsider as perfectly natural or intuitive, like joining in at circle time, sitting at the lunch table with peers, or playing on the playground. Yet, unlike in children with an anxiety disorder, the anxiety of children with Asperger's Syndrome often decreases once they feel comfortable in the activity, although their difficulties in reciprocal communication, social interactions, and interactive social play do not improve.

Other types of anxiety disorders often considered are *social phobia* or general phobias. In the case of social phobia young children develop intense fears of being left alone by their parents at school or childcare setting. The child's inability to separate from their caregiver and make the transition into the classroom lasts much longer than the period of time expected. The child's response is very intense, often causing him to panic, hyperventilate, vomit, wet his pants, and isolate himself from his peers. If the child had his way he would stay at home with familiar family members and adults. It is so striking that when in familiar settings, such as their home or a family member's home, the children with social phobia may seem very typical in their interactions with family members and peers. It is important to remember that the children with Asperger's Syndrome have difficulty in their communication, interactions, and play with peers *across all settings*: in the school, the community, and in the home.

Children with Asperger's Syndrome may appear to be much more relaxed and outgoing at home than at school but that is because they are generally engaged in routines that are very familiar and include their areas of special interest. They may seem to be much more communicative and social at home, but closer observation often reveals that they are engaged in parallel play, directing their sibling or parent on what they should be playing and how, or following an older sibling's directions. Frequently not until these children are assessed do the parents or caregivers realize how much they have structured their lives to adjust to their child's needs.

Obsessive-Compulsive Disorder (OCD) is another diagnosis often considered with these children. A child with OCD has repeated and unwanted thoughts (obsessions) and/or behaviors (compulsions) that interfere with their daily lives and seem impossible to stop. One common compulsive behavior in young children is refusing to throw away objects of special interest such as drawings, regardless of the object's condition or the availability of storage space. One child we knew had not thrown out a picture for the past two years. The mother was always trying to find a new way to demonstrate to her daughter why it would be nice to rotate the pictures that were covering every nook and cranny of their kitchen and den walls! Another common compulsion for young children is washing and drying their hands to the point that the skin becomes irritated and bleeds. Obsessive thoughts are not as common in young children but they have been reported. One such obsession is the fear that a poisonous spider will bite the child. The challenge in differentiating OCD from AS is separating the child's area of special interest from an obsession. One of the things we consider when differentiating OCD from AS is how easily the child can let go of their area of interest when they are engaged in another activity they enjoy. Children with Asperger's Syndrome tend to be able to shift ideas more easily when they are presented with an option that they find attractive. For example, when a young child with Asperger's Syndrome is being shown an exciting puppet show he can stop talking about trains and become engaged in the show. In contrast, the child with OCD will continue to be looking for all of the numbers he can find in the room, not noticing that there is a puppet inviting him to participate in the activity. When the children are doing an art activity, the child who has a special interest in trains may draw trains until he is given some visual examples of other things he might draw. The child with OCD will continue to draw numbers or trains even after he is given other ideas and stickers to include in his picture. The other factor that one must always consider when making the diagnostic differentiation is the child's capacity for social interactions, communication, and play. With young children it is often only the parent who is aware of the OCD-type behaviors, while at school they seem to be very well adapted and social with peers. It is for this reason that OCD is typically not diagnosed before school age, when the child's OCD interferes with his ability to do his schoolwork.

Attention Deficit/Hyperactivity Disorder (ADHD/ADD) is another diagnosis that is frequently considered. ADHD is a neurobiological disorder that is characterized by the individual's inability to sustain attention, control impulsivity, or a combination of the two. The challenge is understanding what is reasonable to expect from young children along these dimensions. For example, it is reasonable to expect a four-year-old to sit in opening circle for 15 minutes but it is not reasonable to expect a young child to stay engaged in a self-directed workbook activity for 30 minutes. There is a growing body of standardized assessments that looks at the preschool age child's attention and impulse regulation skills. Many children with Asperger's Syndrome also become overly active and avoidant in social situations where they are confused and anxious. This isn't necessarily a manifestation of ADHD but of anxiety due to the difficulties the child has in understanding social rules and nuances. Still other children with Asperger's Syndrome may be very impulsive, overly active, and display a short attention span whether or not significant stress is present. Once again, the key difference between the two diagnoses is the qualitative differences between the child's behavior and development. The young child with ADHD/ADD should not be showing significant delays or atypical behavior in his symbolic play, social interactions, or communication with peers. These children may not be maintaining eye contact with the clinician while they examine all of the toys in the playroom but they can maintain a reciprocal conversation while they survey the room. Their play may be more simplistic and concrete than that of their peers, for example playing a favorite video game or game of tag, but the child is able to come up with original ideas for symbolic play and incorporate others' ideas into the play. In fact, young children with ADHD often are very popular kids on the playground because of their endless supply of energy and ideas. The problems typically arise during the school years when their impulsivity and/or inattention becomes disruptive in the classroom. As with all of the diagnoses we have discussed, the child may be given Asperger's Syndrome as the primary diagnosis and ADHD as a secondary diagnosis, inferring that in addition to AS they have attention difficulties that should be addressed in their intervention plans.

Another diagnosis that is often considered is *Nonverbal Learning Disability* (NLD). NLD is a type of learning disability and not a psychiatric diagnostic category. The term NLD was initially used by Myklebust (1975) to describe a group of children who had a learning profile that was characterized by difficulties in visual-spatial-organizational, tactile-perceptual, psychomotor, nonverbal problem-solving, concept formation skills, and nonverbal communication skills on standardized cognitive assessments. How this translates to the children's everyday life is that they may have a large vocabulary, excellent rote memory, but they use the words quite literally, and so adults often assume that they understand more than they actually do. They typically are very attentive to details but lose sight of the larger picture; thus they may seem to be easily distracted and have a hard time completing tasks. The children with NLD may also be early readers but as the material becomes more complicated in the later elementary school years they will show difficulty in reading comprehension. Not surprisingly, both the parents and teachers are confused over how a child who was thought to be at the top of the class in reading is not able to answer the open-ended questions about what the class is reading. These children also show difficulty in math, especially as the material becomes more complicated and requires computation of math problems, abstract thinking, and word problems. It is also quite common for these children to have difficulty in the areas of fine and gross motor development. Lastly, these children experience a great deal of stress in social situations because of their tendency to interpret what everyone says quite literally and their difficulty in reading their peers' nonverbal cues. If a child calls them a pig they may get in an argument over the fact rather than being able to walk away or laugh. By now you should be noticing how similar children with NLD sound to school age children with AS.

The research on NLD took place parallel to the research on children with Pervasive Developmental Disorders (Asperger's Syndrome), with very little interaction between the two. More recently, the experts in these fields have begun to examine the strong similarities between children with an NLD profile and Asperger's Syndrome. Though every child with an NLD learning profile does not necessarily meet the diagnostic criteria for Asperger's Syndrome, a large percentage of them do. As Rourke and Tsatsanis (2000) put it, "There is strong evidence to suggest those individuals with AS present with virtually all the characteristics of NLD"(p.248). Now you may ask, what does this mean regarding your child's assessment? If this pattern is seen on cognitive tests and the child has difficulties in social communication and relationships with peers, the clinician will need to determine if the child meets the DSM-IV criteria for a Pervasive Developmental Disorder, as well as a Nonverbal Learning Disability. As the child's learning needs are better defined over time, it may be very helpful for parents to request more formal neuropsychological testing when the child is in elementary school.

Semantic-Pragmatic Language Disorder (SPLD) is used to describe children who, despite having adequate speech and vocabulary, are delayed in the area of pragmatic or communicative language (Bishop 1989, 1998). As with NLD, this learning disorder has a lot in common with Asperger's Syndrome and may overlap with children who have a milder case of AS. Both sets of children have difficulty in conversational skills – for example, beginning, maintaining, and shifting topics, maintaining a coherent message, and making sure that they have another person's attention before they begin speaking out loud. Research has demonstrated that even though the children with SPLD may have a lot in common with children with AS they do not necessarily have difficulties in social relationships with peers, symbolic play, or have restricted areas of interest. Still, it may be helpful for these children to be routinely screened for Asperger's Syndrome, since a speech and language pathologist is not able to give that diagnosis and thus may not consider it as an alternative explanation for the child's difficulties. Many parents ask if a child who is diagnosed with AS could benefit from the interventions designed for children with pragmatic language disorder. The answer to that question should be an obvious yes, as long as the speech and language pathologist has a working understanding of the other factors which may impinge upon the child's ability to use the communication skills they learn in therapy.

Dysfunction in Sensory Integration (DSI) *or Sensory Integration Disorder* (SID) is another diagnostic category that may be used by occupational and physical therapists to identify a child's inability to effectively and efficiently process sensory stimuli. As with the diagnosis of Semantic-Pragmatic Language Disorder, a child may have DSI and not have Asperger's Syndrome, and DSI may not explain all of the difficulties a child with Asperger's Syndrome is experiencing. Children with Asperger's Syndrome may have sensory and/or motor difficulties that may influence the child's ability to navigate his interactions with other people and external stimuli.

As you can see there is quite a bit of overlap among these diagnostic categories and Asperger's Syndrome. This fact illustrates the need for a thorough evaluation. It also helps explain why these children may receive multiple diagnoses, with Asperger's Syndrome being their primary diagnosis, since it is a developmental disorder that impacts all aspects of the children's lives. The other diagnoses, when used as secondary diagnoses, may provide insight into specific aspects of the child's behaviors, such as their OCD habit of washing their hands, and offer insight into interventions more attuned to address this behavior, such as a specific type of medication or occupational therapy intervention. It also may explain why sometimes it takes several clinicians to understand fully a child's diagnosis. What we cannot stress enough is the importance of not losing sight of the goals of an evaluation. An evaluation is of little help if the clinicians are not able to use the information to develop with the family a plan for intervention and ongoing monitoring of the child's social, emotional, developmental, and behavioral goals (Linder 1993; National Research Council 2001; Sparrow 1997).

Who do you tell about the diagnosis and when?

This question may pose the most difficult challenge parents face after receiving their child's diagnosis. As with every issue we have presented, there is no one set answer that fits every family, and the issue will arise every time you enroll your child into a new program or school. A lot depends on how the parents feel about the diagnosis and if they feel it will help others understand their child. Generally speaking, we feel that when the parents believe that the diagnosis is a vehicle for understanding their child and advocating for the services he might benefit from, they will feel more comfortable sharing the information with the other adults in their child's life. Clearly this is a hard process that will vary for individual parents. Some parents and clinicians may decide that it would be more helpful for the child if they give a detailed description of the child's strengths and challenges, and the helpful behavioral strategies they use, without labeling the child with a diagnosis. This decision is often based on past experiences of the child being rejected from a program after the staff learned about the child's diagnosis. Of course, it is impossible to know whether or not the school administrators would have rejected the child, regardless of what terms the consultant used, as long as they felt that their concerns about the child's behavior were justified. Other parents may decide that their child needs services that he cannot qualify for without a diagnosis, and feel that justifies informing the school. Another possible scenario is that the parents decide to tell those individuals who have the most direct contact with their child – the caregiver and grandparents, for example. They may not feel a need to tell the child's teacher if he only goes to school two mornings a week and the school has not expressed any concerns about their child. Certainly one of the most frustrating experiences for parents who gather up the courage to share the diagnosis or other detailed information with a family member, the child's pediatrician, a teacher, or friend is to be told that they are exaggerating, that their child has too many strengths to have a developmental disorder, and that the labeling will harm him. The most helpful advice we can give for this extremely frustrating situation is that you must realize that these adults may be at the same place that you were when someone first suggested that you take your child for an evaluation, or when you initially suspected that something was different about him. You naturally want them to be at the same point that you are in understanding your child's strengths and challenges, but they will need time as you did to absorb the information and integrate it into their image of your child.

When should you tell your child that he has Asperger's Syndrome?

The answer to the question of when to tell your child is very similar. As with adults, you will not be able to discuss the diagnosis with your child until you feel comfortable enough using the term yourself. You may initially choose to talk with your child about things that he finds frustrating and strategies that may help him. For example, if he finds soccer frustrating because it is hard to know what the players are supposed to do, then help him choose a sport that is easier to understand, such as swimming. Another example may be talking with him about why he always ends up mad when a friend comes over, and working together to develop strategies that might make his next play date go more smoothly. Initially, the child may think nothing of going to see a speech and language pathologist or occupational therapist, or attending a therapeutic playgroup, since these are mostly enjoyable experiences. Yet as the child becomes more aware that his neighbors or friends from school do not have similar activities, he may begin to ask why he has to go for therapy while his friends do not. If he has overheard one of your conversations about him, or read the word "Asperger's" on the cover of a book, he may want to know what it means. We find it most helpful to initially give children brief responses to the specific questions they raise. We suggest that you keep the answers brief and simple since we are always surprised by how little the children actually want to know. It may be sufficient to tell them that "Asperger's" is a diagnosis named after a pediatrician from Vienna who worked with children like them, and enjoyed getting to know them and helping them. Most young children will not ask for anything else. If your child wants to know more, keep the answer connected to his question and avoid overly complex issues such as the newest findings from neuroscience research. For example, if he asks what the children were like you might explain how Dr. Asperger noticed that they were like him: that is, smart, active children who sometimes had trouble getting along with others who wanted to do things differently, yet liked having friends. Rest assured that the topic will come up again, often at the most unexpected times such as during a bath or a car ride home from the park. By the time the child reaches first grade we feel that it is helpful for him to be familiar with the term, realizing that a basic understanding of what Asperger's Syndrome means to him and his daily experiences will evolve gradually.

It is around seven, when children begin to really notice how they look and act compared to others in terms of their height, weight, hair style, learning strengths, athletic skills, and special interests, that they may begin to notice that a child with Asperger's Syndrome is different. They may wonder why a child wants to talk about one specific topic all the time, that their friend seems to be quoting things out of context, or that their friend knows a lot about some things and not much about others. You should remember that this process of noticing how they are similar or different from their peers is not static but involves different attributes and different levels of understanding over time. Thus it is a natural time to explore with your child how he understands Asperger's Syndrome and his perceptions of his peers. This may also be a time when the child chooses to share something about Asperger's Syndrome with his classmates. We can say with confidence that the other children typically do not hold onto the label but, like most adults, forget about it and respond to how the child interacts with them, the interests they share, and the ways they differ.

The following chapter will take a closer look at three different young children with Asperger's Syndrome. Though they display very different strengths and behaviors, and ways of adapting to their home and school settings, they share the same challenges that are unique to children with Asperger's Syndrome.

CHAPTER 4

The Many Faces of Young Children
with Asperger's Syndrome

How does a young child with Asperger's Syndrome act? How does he communicate? Relate with others? What kinds of things does he enjoy doing? To fully answer these questions, one must understand that Asperger's Syndrome, like other conditions, can present quite differently from one child to the next, depending on the child's temperament, strengths, experiences, and environmental supports and stresses. This chapter will illustrate the diversity of young children with Asperger's Syndrome based on their presenting problems. The three cases we present will show the importance of respecting the child's uniqueness and understanding his areas of strength as well as his weaknesses in order to form a thorough understanding of the child and develop interventions attuned to his needs. With time it is likely that the diagnosis will be more finely differentiated to encompass the diverse group of children who have significant difficulties in the areas of communication, symbolic play, and social relationships with peers.

In describing the three cases for this chapter, we found it helpful to differentiate the children according to their presenting problems. Many of the children sent for assessments are referred for behaviors we typically describe as externalized behaviors: the child is acting out or is overtly expressing symptoms. Other children are referred for behaviors more commonly considered internalized behaviors: the child is shut down or withdrawn. And some children present with a mixture of both externalized and internalized behaviors. To illustrate the diversity of the presenting issues we will describe one child who could be considered representative of each of these groups. We will describe the child's early development, the behaviors that caused the parents or caregivers to be concerned, what was learned from the evaluation process, the recommendations the family received, and the paths of intervention they chose to follow. It is striking that at times these children can look like they are right "on track," while at other times they appear dramatically different, particularly when one pays close attention to the quality of their communication, social interactions, and play with peers. Table 4.1 outlines some of the behaviors which are characteristic of the three groups.

Table 4.1 Behaviors which often precipitate a professional referral

Externalizing Behaviors

- Impulsive
- Poor attention span (for others' demands)
- Disorganized
- Loud
- Aggressive
- Insensitive to others

Internalizing Behaviors

- Withdrawn
- Shy
- Distractible in groups
- Intense focus on own interests
- Rigid – perfectionist
- Obsessive
- Hesitant to enter new groups/activities

Combined Behaviors

- Combination of the other two
- May vary depending on the day, time, setting, activity, other children, etc.
- Behavior seems unpredictable

Steven – the active and impulsive (externalizing) child

Steven was a tall, handsome four-and-a-half-year-old blond-haired boy who viewed the world as a race in which he was determined to be first in everything, be it his position in line, answering a question, getting a drink, or selecting a toy. His parents always thought he was very active but they had no real concerns about his behavior until he was four years old and was not meeting the social expectations that they had for him both at home and at school. Steven was the first child for Mike and Debbie, and neither of them had family or friends with children the same age to compare him with. Steven's mother was a business consultant and had been working full time up until Steven's birth. She returned to work when he was four months old and maintained her work schedule until she became pregnant with her daughter, at which time she reduced her paid job hours to part time. Steven's father was an engineer and had always been one to seek out very demanding jobs. It was not uncommon for him to work in the evenings after dinner and during the weekends.

Debbie's pregnancy was planned and had no complications. Steven was born three weeks early, weighing 8 pounds and 11 ounces, and received a good bill of health. She remembers Steven as being an easy baby. He ate well, slept well, and seemed to be very calm as an infant. After three months of breast-feeding, Debbie switched to bottle-feeding so that she could return to work. They had hired an older nanny who had a very special relationship with Steven. He seemed to thrive with her calm, predictable, and nurturing caregiving style. Steven reached all of his early developmental milestones on time. The family looked forward to having a second child, and Steven's little sister was born when he was two years old. He loved showing her toys or helping with her bath and feedings. This, of course, changed as she became more independent and unwilling to follow Steven's direction, but this was not until her second year of life.

Debbie finds it difficult to recall any red flags that may have indicated to them early on that Steven's development was taking an atypical course. She can recall wondering if his speech was delayed, because he was not a big talker prior to the age of two. Still, he was able to use a combination of words, whining, or hitting to get his desires known. Yet these concerns were erased following a two-week visit with her sister's family. His expressive language seemed to "take off" after spending two weeks in non-stop interactions with his older cousins. When Steven was just over two they enrolled him in a preschool setting that was play based and he seemed to make the adjustment well. It was clear that he had a very hard time standing in line or waiting his turn but this could be expected for all two year olds, especially those that were active like Steven. The family went on a three-month sabbatical and reenrolled him in the same school when they returned, but this time he clearly was having a very hard time adjusting. The teachers' expectations were higher and they were concerned that he was having difficulty in maintaining eye contact, participating in the group activities, and controlling his aggressive behavior towards peers who had an object he desired. Debbie felt that Steven needed a school that was more attuned to his individual needs rather than trying to get him to conform to the school's agenda. They placed him in a smaller preschool that seemed to be more flexible and able to support Steven's need to work at his own pace.

Debbie recalls starting to feel perplexed about Steven when he was about four years of age. It didn't make sense to her that his younger sister was better able to handle the bedtime transition than he could. She also did not understand why he was having such a difficult time with toilet training. He was doing well during the day but seemed oblivious to his cues and unmotivated when it came to nighttime control. Lastly, she wondered why he was having such a hard time getting along with the other kids at school. It seemed as if he wanted to play with the other kids but he did not know how to enter into or initiate play, so instead he would spend an entire recess riding a tricycle in circles or playing in the water area. Debbie consulted her pediatrician for advice and can remember being told that he was doing fine, and that she was making too much out of nothing. His position was that boys simply develop more slowly and that she needed to be more patient with him. Still, she could not figure out why things went much more smoothly at home than at preschool. Steven seemed to love playing outside at home and could spend hours exploring with a bunch of sticks or rocks he found in the back yard. In contrast, his father was becoming increasingly frustrated with Steven's social behavior at home. He did not think it was asking too much to expect a four-year-old to be able to sit at the dinner table, participate in a conversation, and be more polite when interacting with others. He wanted him to be a better role model for his younger sister.

Debbie sought advice from a parent guidance counselor regarding Steven's potty training and difficulty adjusting to his preschool. After several sessions the counselor felt that he would benefit from a social skills group to help him learn how to get along with his peers. The first step in joining this particular group was a mental health evaluation to make sure that the group would be a good fit for him. Steven's parents were comfortable with an evaluation. They were clearly starting to have different opinions about Steven's problems and what he needed. His father wondered if he was hyperactive since there was a history of ADHD in his family. He had heard his brother talk about his nephews who were diagnosed with ADHD and he felt that Debbie needed to be firmer in setting limits. In contrast, Debbie felt that he just needed more attention and she decided to take leave from her paid job so that they could get a better grip on Steven's needs. They were both eager to learn anything that might make his experiences both at home and in preschool more pleasurable for everyone involved.

The preschool observation

The first step of the evaluation was to observe Steven in his preschool setting. Steven's teachers expressed concerns over his inability to read other children's cues and his tendency to hit other children as a way of getting their attention or obtaining a desired object. They also wondered why he had such a hard time during transitions to circle time or table activities. In fact, the school was so worried that another child might get hurt that they insisted on his mother being with him as a condition of his continued attendance. The school appreciated his energy and enthusiasm but they felt that they could not give him the undivided attention he needed. At the time of the observation Steven attended his preschool three mornings a week with his mother.

When the clinician arrived, the class was ending circle time while Steven was working with his mother with the blocks at a table. As soon as the teacher announced that it was time to go outside, Steven was the first child out the door and onto the playground. He ran straight to the water table and reached across the table to get the blue boat he wanted. He seemed delighted to push his boat across the water but appeared not to notice the other children at the table unless they were standing in his way or attempting to get a boat he claimed as his. At one point he was splashing so hard with his boat that the water splashed the other children standing around the table and one little girl started to cry. Steven smiled and continued to play with his boat. When his mother stepped in to make sure that the little girl was O.K. and explain to Steven what he had done, he merely nodded and then looked for something else to do. He quickly ran over to the playhouse where some girls were playing and pulled the purple sheet off the top of the house and ran with it across the sand. When the girls reported the "theft" to the teacher, Steven smiled and ran with the sheet like he was a tornado until the teacher caught him. Steven could not explain his actions or apologize to the girls but was able to follow the teacher's directions that he needed to return the sheet if he was going to stay on the playground.

His teacher then brought the hose out into the sand area in an attempt to engage Steven in an activity that he enjoyed and could tolerate playing with other children. She obviously knew him very well since he immediately expressed delight in being able to hold the hose while other children washed objects in the water or built a path in the sand for the water to flow. However, Steven did not engage in any reciprocal conversations with his teachers or his peers. He spent the remainder of the extended outdoor time oscillating between playing with the boats in the water table or holding the hose in the sand. Conflicts arose any time a peer attempted to take over his role of holding the hose. He guarded the hose as if he was the commander in charge of the water play.

The clinic evaluation

After the preschool observation the clinician decided that she needed a better understanding of how Steven perceived and interacted with the world around him. For example, was his breadth of "fact knowledge" (e.g. about transportation) matched in depth by his understanding of the social cues he is presented with on a daily basis? The clinician wanted to know if Steven splashed other children because he was angry with them or if he was simply unaware of the impact that his actions had on others. She was curious to see if his smile was an expression of pleasure in seeing the other children upset, or an artificial grin that masked his anxiety about not being sure what to do. To answer these questions she gathered information from many different sources, including questionnaires which asked the parents to rate his behavior as it related to different developmental tasks and problem behaviors. She also conducted standardized tests to assess his cognitive development on both verbal and nonverbal tasks and used assessments that provided insight into how Steven read social cues and understood relationships.

From the start the clinician was struck by how attuned both Steven's mother and father were to his strengths and difficulties. On the Child Developmental Inventory (Ireton 1992) both parents identified him as having more than a two-year delay in the area of social skills while being on target in the areas of fine and gross motor development. The parents were also given the Child Behavior Checklist (Achenbach 1991) which asks the parents to check off those behavioral problems that they feel describe their child. What was interesting here was that neither parent's ratings were in the clinical range. The one area where they cited the most difficulty was attention problems, which included behaviors like having difficulty sitting still, nervous behavior, and immature behavior.

The next phase of the evaluation included standardized assessments of his cognitive, social, and emotional functioning. The assessment also included both structured and unstructured play sessions with his parents and the clinician. Steven performed best on those tasks that had a clear beginning and end, and greeted most new challenges with the phrases "I can't do this" or "I want to go now!" Next he was administered a standardized cognitive test which is designed to tap skills that a child his age should be able to perform. On the Wechsler Pre-Primary Scale of Intelligence–Revised (WPPSI-R), he performed in the average range on the Verbal IQ, Nonverbal IQ, and Full Scale IQ. Steven performed exceptionally well on those tasks that provided visual guidelines, such as following a path in a maze or putting a set of pictures together to tell a story. He had a much harder time when he had to listen to a story and complete an arithmetic problem or put pieces of a puzzle together to make a horse. Once he became frustrated or distracted with an object he could not return to the task without a great deal of external support.

When he was asked to draw a picture of a tree, a house, a person, or a family – a task that most four-year-olds find enjoyable, not overwhelming – he repeatedly got stuck on the details. For example, when he drew the tree he insisted that he needed more time or else nobody would be able to notice all of the tiny apples and flowers on the tree, which in truth looked like just tiny scribbles. He was so overwhelmed by the task of drawing a tree that he refused to even try to draw a house or a person but rather scrunched up the paper and tossed it on the ground.

The clinician also administered the Children's Apperception Test, which consists of a series of black and white drawings of animals in stressful human social situations, such as a child misbehaving at an adult party or having your father look over your work. Steven's responses were of two different types. The first was a very concrete description of the animals – for example, the animal is in bed, and the kangaroo is on a bike, "The End." These stories lacked any reference to the themes or feelings they were trying to replicate such as the mother on the bike looking like she was in a hurry with her child trailing behind her, or a bear sitting up all alone in his bed feeling lonely or scared. The second type of responses centered on the theme of separation. Either the child was upset and ran away or the child was afraid and felt alone. In Steven's stories none of the children were able to come up with a solution to the problems, such as calling for a parent (who in the picture is sleeping in the bed next to them) for help, or apologizing for what they did wrong. Steven's confusion over the pictures was very similar to the look of confusion he expressed on the playground when a child expressed distress towards Steven's actions or an adult asked for an explanation of his negative behavior.

The play sessions

The evaluation also included two play sessions so that the clinician could observe the quality of Steven's communication and interactions with his parents, and his capacity to engage in age-appropriate play. Steven was very excited about going to the playroom, and challenged the clinician to a race to see who could be first to the room. His enthusiasm was quickly replaced by expressions of frustration that the room did not meet all of his expectations. It was smaller than he thought it would be, it did not have the "right" kind of blocks, and there were not enough chairs at the table. Once distressed, he was unable to calm himself down or find another activity to engage in without his mother's assistance. He used the same phrases during the play sessions as he did during the testing when he was not sure what to do ("What's this?"; "I need to go now"; "I don't want to"). Steven made very little eye contact with his mother when exploring the materials or engaging in a joint project with her. When he did reply, his comments were often not related to his actions. For example, he might comment about a spaceship while building a road. It was also noticed that he tended to respond to his mother with an echolalic replication of the last word or phrase she used.

Steven was able to function at a higher level when his mother expanded, or "scaffolded," his play by frequently reminding him of an area of interest, suggesting ways he might go about doing it and then expanding upon his ideas. For example, when they were presented with a box of blocks and directed to make something together he seemed confused. Debbie suggested that they make a road. (One of Steven's special interests was construction work.) Steven cheered up and quickly became the director, only to be frustrated when his mother was unable to follow *all* of his instructions. When she ran out of a certain type of block she started to use a different one that was a little bit higher and a different color. Steven could not tolerate this; the block had to be the exact height, width, and color of the other blocks. For Debbie, the slightest sense of compromise was a major victory. She appeared to be on "pins and needles" hoping to prevent a major meltdown. When the clinician entered the playroom she attempted to incorporate human figures into

Steven's play with the various vehicles. Steven acted very rigidly and was unable to expand his play of moving the cars around the road.

Steven displayed the beginning stages of symbolic play as he fed the doll baby a bottle or led the toy elephant on a walk. However, he was not able to engage in a series that included more than one object or theme into his play, nor was he able to incorporate others' ideas into the play.

Steven's profile

Steven's rich vocabulary and wealth of information about transportation vehicles and construction work stood in sharp contrast to his inability to engage in reciprocal and mutually satisfying interactions with his parents, peers, or the examiner. The quality of his social interactions was more representative of a two-year-old than a bright four-and-a-half-year-old. Steven could use toys to act out very simplistic symbolic play, such as feeding a baby doll, but he spent most of his free playtime creating structures of which he had a pre-formed visual image, such as an elaborate road. This pattern often resulted in aggressive behavior and meltdowns when Steven could not get the objects to work the way he planned, or his parents or peers had different ideas about how the materials could be used. He seemed oblivious to the fact that another child might be using the object he took, or did not like getting splashed by the water he was pushing in his play.

Steven also had a very difficult time modulating his emotions. He typically greeted any new situation with an expression of negativity that could quickly change into pleasure and delight once he felt comfortable doing what was asked of him. At one moment he would be eager to participate in an activity, yet the next moment he might be kicking and crying in distress over not being able to get the materials to work the way he thought they should. His quick changes in emotional states put everyone who worked with him on edge, hoping that he would not become distressed. When this did happen he would need a caregiver to sit with him and gradually find another solution. At other times his rigidity could not be overcome and he had to leave the setting kicking and crying.

Steven was most responsive to his parents and teachers when they asked questions about his areas of special interests. It was striking how attentive he could be when engaged in play on these topics, such as playing in the water area at school. During the evaluation he spent over 30 minutes building a road with his mother's support, stopping only because they ran out of blocks. He was also very attentive to tasks that tapped the same visual-motor strengths during the structured testing, such as puzzles and mazes. A child with primarily attention difficulties may be able to stay more attentive in certain situations, such as watching TV, but they may still have difficulty staying seated even during activities they can excel in. The key difference is that children with attention deficit disorders as their primary problem would not show such extreme difficulty engaging in reciprocal social interactions with their peers or demonstrate play that was as severely delayed as Steven's. Steven's qualitative impairment in communication and social interactions, restricted areas of interest, difficulty in giving and reading others' social cues, along with his average IQ, were all suggestive of Asperger's Syndrome.

Recommendations

Steven's family was given several recommendations, including getting an aide for him in the classroom with the goal of facilitating his social awareness, shared attention, and reciprocal communication with peers. It was very difficult for Steven's mother to have the combined role of mother and classroom aide on a regular basis. As a mother her primary attention was on facilitating Steven's positive interactions with peers; as an aide she needed to do that but she would also need to set limits and protect the other children while explaining Steven's behaviors to fellow teachers, parents, and peers. Debbie also wanted to have some individual time with her daughter since Steven demanded so much of her attention when he was at home.

The family was also encouraged to have a series of family sessions to help them understand Steven and develop strategies for engaging him as well as providing consistent limit setting. The parents were also encouraged to enroll in our group program, which provided them with a chance to learn more about Asperger's Syndrome from professionals and fellow parents. The program also gave them the chance to observe Steven interacting with peers and professionals and learn about different strategies targeted at his communication, interactions, and play with peers. Since Steven was in a regular preschool the clinician was not concerned that he would not have the opportunity to learn from neurotypical developing children. What was clear was that he was not going to pick up their social cues without intervention. The group setting would also allow the clinician to see if he might benefit from an occupational therapy or speech and language evaluation. The parents were also given the names of community resources. Steven's family followed up on all of these recommendations. You will hear more about his progress throughout the book.

Ben – the shy and withdrawn (internalizing) child

Ben was a very cute little five-year-old boy who looked like Charlie Brown with his large round face, big brown eyes, and a look of confusion as he observed the social world around him. His parents' initial concerns centered on Ben's gross and fine motor skills. He seemed to achieve all of his gross motor skills a little bit later than the child development books suggested, and did them in a different order. For example, he started to walk at 16 months before he crawled at 21 months! A neighborhood friend noticed the difficulty Ben was having at four years of age kicking a ball, skipping down the sidewalk, or riding a tricycle. She shared with his parents how she had taken her own child to an occupational therapist for help in these areas and suggested that they might want to get a consultation for some ideas on how to help Ben's motor development. When he was assessed by an occupational therapist he was found to be two years delayed on both gross and fine motor tasks. After one year of occupational therapy he had made great gains and was almost up to age level, but continued to demonstrate other behaviors which concerned the therapist, such as his intense interest in calendars and letters, poor pragmatic speech, and lack of interaction with peers during a school observation. The occupational therapist recommended that they see a clinical psychologist.

Ben was the first child of Sarah and John. He was the product of a planned pregnancy that went very smoothly. Both parents were employed full time as engineers. Ben was born one-and-a-half weeks late at an alternative birth center. Beginning at birth, his parents had a sense that Ben was going to be a child who did things at his own pace. Breast-feeding had a slow start because of Ben's tilted jaw but things went well after Sarah received some guidance from a lactation specialist. Ben was breast fed for the first 19 months and began solids when he was five months old because he was such a big eater. The combination of Ben's personality and difficulty regulating his eating and sleeping made him an irritable baby. Sarah recalls that this improved a great deal around six months of age when he started sleeping through the night for about ten hours a night. Sarah returned to work when Ben was six months of age and the family hired a nanny who played an active role in the family.

Just like Steven, Ben's early development seemed to be on target to his parents, the nanny, and their pediatrician. He began to smile around one month, babbled around six months, showed stranger-anxiety around eight months, and spoke in words other than "mama" and "dada" around 14 months. As mentioned earlier, the area with which they were most concerned was his motor development. They thought that since he was so large it would take him longer than other children. When Ben was 13 months old he had a brain MRI just to make sure that his large head size was not representative of a neurological problem. The scan was fine and Ben's family and pediatrician just felt that Ben was not going to do anything until he felt ready to. When Ben was two years old his parents had a second child, a girl, of whom Ben seemed to be very fond.

Ben attended a Montessori preschool from three-and-a-half to five years of age. From the teachers' reports he was a "dream child" – he was quiet, easy to get along with, and seemed to enjoy school. It is important to note here that this Montessori school paid a great deal of attention to the child's capacity to self-regulate, follow the classroom rules regarding how to play with different materials, and participate in snack time and cleanup. They gave much less attention to the child's capacity for social communication or symbolic play with peers. Ben was the type of child who thrived on having all of the rules spelled out. If they were not spelled out he would attempt to do so himself.

Ben's nanny expressed concern about his lack of interest in other children and his "grown up" speech. When he was around four years of age she began to notice that he spent most of the time on the playground talking with her or playing by himself. The parents did not see this as much as the nanny because when they took him to the park or played with him at home he seemed to love to engage in pretend play with them. What they did not realize at first was that his play was repetitive and that he could not accommodate any new ideas into his play. For example, the main focus of his play with his mother was playing store where he was the storeowner adding up the bill, his interest being more on the numbers than the different themes she and his sister acted out in their play. She was aware of his intense interest in calendars and the alphabet but she attributed that to having parents who spent a lot of time on the computer and encouraged him to explore ways that he might enjoy the computer as well. Sarah did not find it difficult to talk with him; in fact, it seemed that she could not get him to stop talking. Still, she wondered if his resistance to trying anything new was getting in the way of his making new friends. She did notice how shy he was when they went to a friend's house or a classmate's birthday party but she wondered if that was because such events did not happen too frequently.

John was beginning to wonder if Ben's limited range of interests was normal for kids his age. He found it hard to get him involved in activities that did not center around water play, pretend cooking, or the calendar. He also could not understand why such a smart kid seemed to get so confused anytime he was given directions to follow, such as "Take off your jacket, put it in your room, and wash your hands for dinner." Still, John's way of dealing with this was to go out of his way to expand Ben's range of interests. For example, he transformed Ben's bedroom to look like his new favorite movie, *The Wizard of Oz*. Ben seemed to love all the details, props, and costumes and he would engage in elaborate recreations of segments of the film with his father and sister, without ever thinking of or incorporating others' spontaneous or original ideas. For Ben, the focus was on setting the stage, a task that usually left no time for play. The parents were also surprised by the fact that he was not toilet trained until he was four-and-a-half, since he seemed to be so concerned with being clean.

When Ben was five, John had moved out of the home and the parents were in the process of filing for a divorce. Both parents wondered if his difficulties in relationships and falling asleep in his father's home could be related to the stress associated with their separation. The arrangement was for Ben and his sister to spend two nights a week and one weekend night at their father's house. What was helpful was that the nanny made the transition with them. At both homes Ben often ended up moving into his sister's room during the night. By the time Ben's parents sought a mental health consultation they had heard his occupational therapist gently raise concerns regarding his rigidity and lack of communication and relationships with peers.

The play sessions

Both Sarah and John met with the clinician and decided that it might work best for Ben if he met her before she did a school observation since he was so shy with strangers. The clinician arranged two play sessions: one with Ben, his mother, and sister; and one with his father and nanny. During his first session with his father and nanny Ben spent most of the time examining the toys and then putting them back into their original locations. He looked like he was in a fine china store, anxious that he might break an item or put it down the wrong way. The majority of his communications were centered on asking questions about where the items belonged. The only time that he engaged in any form of symbolic play was when he followed his father's lead to set up a road like the one in *The Wizard of Oz*. He then began to search for doll figures to represent the different characters from the play. He used very detailed sentences to describe what he was looking for or to inquire about an object he was interested in but he did not engage the clinician in any form of play.

Ben's interactions with his mother and sister took on a slightly different form, but the lack of spontaneous symbolic play and reciprocal communication was the same. Ben's attention was caught by a Lotto game that he decided to play with his mother, sister, and the clinician. Yet Ben's idea of how to play the game was unique. He wanted it to be like solitaire where he could see if all the cards matched his board. The concept of taking turns was very difficult for him. Ben seemed most comfortable when he could set up a strategy for solving a problem such as lining up all of the letters from an alphabet puzzle on the table before placing them back in the puzzle. The challenge that symbolic play posed to Ben was most evident when his mother attempted to engage him in the doll play she was doing with his little sister. In a very controlling, anxious, but "polite" manner he asked his mother to stop playing and leave him alone. After much persistence and sensitivity to Ben's need for modeling as well as support to enter the play at his own pace, his mother succeeded in engaging Ben briefly in the play. With a sigh of relief Ben found a piece of paper and a marker to write down "important" numbers: the date and time the clinician planned to observe him at the school.

The school observation

Ben noticed the clinician's arrival right away and greeted her by running into a cupboard so he could not be seen. His interactions at school were very reminiscent of his play sessions. He was drawn back to join the activity that the children were engaged in, making their own puzzles using numbers and colors. He wanted very much to play the game and constantly asked a teacher or his sister, who attended the same school, to play with him. Over an hour he was observed talking to another child only once and this was at an art activity where he repeatedly asked for more materials, as modeled by his teacher. Ben's teacher commented that this was typical for Ben, that he seemed most happy when he was following his own agenda. The school personnel were also aware of how stressful it seemed for him to participate in social activities with other children, so they did not try to force it. They thought that he was ready for kindergarten based on his knowledge of letters and numbers, but they recognized that they could not complete many of their assessments due to his unwillingness to participate. With all of this difficulty it was striking to the clinician that his teachers never recommended an evaluation. It seemed that in this setting, externalizing behavior problems were taken much more seriously than a child's difficulties interacting with or communicating with peers.

The evaluation

As with Steven, following the preschool observations and play sessions the clinician believed that it would be helpful to get a sense of the areas in which Ben had strengths as well as difficulties. It was hard to tell if Ben avoided activities because he could not understand what was going on, or because he felt he could not do them perfectly. On the Wechsler Pre-Primary Scale of Intelligence–Revised (WPPSI-R) he performed in the average range in the Verbal IQ, Performance IQ, and Full Scale IQ. Even though they were all in the same range, his Verbal IQ was significantly higher than his Performance IQ. This is not surprising when one considers his delays in fine motor and visual motor tasks. Ben's strength was in his vocabulary and fund of information. The challenge for Ben was that both visual and social cues were much more difficult for him to understand.

Ben's profile

Ben was a child who seemed most comfortable playing by himself or sharing his ideas with an adult. His rich vocabulary, interest in details about a favorite movie, and photographic memory of calendar dates seemed to provide the armor that he hid behind on the social field. The activities that drew his attention had a clear set of rules and visual cues that he understood, such as a puzzle that required him to focus only on the activity rather than manage the attention and input of his peers. Unlike Steven, who expressed his frustration outwardly, Ben tried desperately to stay in control, and the adults who cared for him appreciated his drive to do things the "right" way. They supported his polite behavior even as they were aware of the stress he experienced any time he was encouraged to participate in reciprocal interactions with peers. They realized that he could talk endlessly to an adult about *The Wizard of Oz* or about dates and numbers, with no awareness of the social world surrounding him and making no attempts to engage another child in reciprocal communication or play. These differences became remarkably clearer to them when they were asked to contrast his capacity for symbolic play and conversations with those of his three-year-old sister. His difficulties were indicative of Asperger's Syndrome. The clinician gave him a provisional diagnosis since he had not had any intervention to address the quality of his communication skills, social interactions, or play.

Recommendations

Ben's parents were given several recommendations. The first was dyadic therapy targeted at helping them understand Ben and finding ways to expand his capacity for social interactions and play. The clinician was also concerned about his high level of anxiety and wanted to monitor it to see if it decreased when he became more competent in knowing how to play, or if it continued to be such a burden that medication should be considered. She also recommended a therapeutic playgroup that could be a source of support and education for both parents as well as a supportive setting in which Ben could work on his social communication and play skills with peers. It was understood that Ben's parents, teachers, and therapist could all find ways to foster his use of pragmatic language and help teach him how to play, but the real test for Ben would be to develop his capacity to engage in mutually satisfying interactions and play with his peers.

The clinician also addressed the issue of school placement since Ben was to enter kindergarten in the fall. It was recommended that since he was so ready for school academically he should not participate in a Young Fives program that would give him another year to work on social skills before entering kindergarten. His parents were advised to inform the district's department of special education about Ben's needs and request additional support in the classroom, in particular intervention targeted at his pragmatic language and social interactions during unstructured times like the playground. It was also recommended that he be monitored for nonverbal learning difficulties as the complexity of the tasks at school increased. A speech evaluation was also recommended because of his difficulty in the articulation of specific letters. Ben's family, like Steven's, was relieved to have a clearer understanding of Ben. The diagnosis, however, was especially hard for John, who saw his son as having too many strengths to have a neurodevelopmental problem. Still, both parents agreed that a therapeutic group would help them better understand their son and learn what they could do to help him. They also agreed on informing the school to see what they could do to help make his transition to kindergarten a smooth one.

Mark – the sensitive and impulsive (combined internalizing and externalizing) child

Mark's parents, Linda and Robert, had always felt that something was "off kilter" with Mark since birth, as he seemed extra fussy, impulsive, and highly sensitive to any changes. In addition to Linda's training in special education, both parents had a great deal of experience with young children from their large extended families who they saw on a regular basis. Robert was an engineer who always wanted to have a large family. Their plan was for Linda to finish her graduate program in special education before they had children, so this unplanned pregnancy took them by surprise, yet they were soon very excited about becoming parents.

Linda had a difficult pregnancy, requiring bed rest and IVs due to her dehydration. During the delivery, forceps were used but by the time they took Mark's second Apgar everything looked fine. As an infant he was colicky, and highly sensitive to sounds and new settings. His parents had a very hard time developing a regular pattern of eating and sleeping for him. They felt that they were always trying to find ways to make his and their lives more relaxed. Looking back it seemed to them that he never was a cuddly child, and he was easily overstimulated in situations that most children enjoyed, such as a family gathering, the toy store, or on the playground.

All of Mark's early motor milestones seemed to be on target. He crawled by six months and walked by ten months. His speech development was a little slower. He spoke his first words at one year but continued to use only a few words up until his second year, and began to put three words together when he was about three years old. At around three-and-a-half his language dramatically improved and he began to speak in very elaborate sentences with a rich vocabulary and clear articulation, but his pragmatic language remained delayed and somewhat atypical.

As a toddler, Mark required constant supervision during social gatherings due to his tendency to be too rough with other children or go into an off-limits area in search of a hiding place. Robert and Linda felt like they were always on their toes since his favorite thing to do with other children was to give them a large bear hug. The problem with this was that he never asked if the other child wanted a hug but just hugged them very tightly anyway, ignoring the other child's yelling at him to stop or crying for an adult to help. When Mark was two he was diagnosed with having food allergies. Medication and a change in diet decreased his irritability but he still seemed to be incredibly challenging to his parents and to any other adult who cared for him.

As a toddler, Mark seemed to be the most content when he was playing in a quiet, familiar setting by himself with an adult in close proximity to help him when he became frustrated with a task. Even when Linda tried to keep a pretty routine schedule and not overwhelm Mark with activities, peers, or too much sensory stimuli, he still continued to become increasingly active, irritable, and frenetic as the evening approached. Linda enrolled him in a parent–child playgroup for two-year-olds, hoping that he would benefit from an opportunity to practice playing with other children in a small setting with a great deal of adult supervision. Soon, both Linda and the school felt that the toddler class was too hard for Mark. The other children were avoiding him because of his bear hugs and they could not find other ways to engage him in the activities. Linda decided to reduce her time working at the university so that she could provide more opportunities for Mark to learn to behave with other children in one-on-one play dates.

When Mark was three, Linda enrolled him in a cooperative nursery school, placing him in the two-year-old class because of the higher adult:child ratio and more flexible schedule. Even in this situation, Mark typically required the full attention of one parent since he could easily become overstimulated by the group activities, requiring an adult to redirect him to a quiet area and help him calm down. Mark's teachers were also concerned about his poor conversational skills and the difficulties he was having in fine and gross motor activities, resulting in his avoiding many of the table activities. When Mark was three-and-a-half they took him to a child psychiatrist who recommended Ritalin for his "hyperactive behavior." The psychiatrist did not do a school observation or play session with Mark, or request a cognitive assessment. Neither Linda nor Robert felt comfortable with giving medication to a child so young, so they did not go back to that clinician.

At this time the parents began an evaluation with a child psychologist. The clinician was able to conduct a parent interview and school observation but the remainder of the evaluation was put on hold because Linda was pregnant with her second child; experiencing difficulties similar to her first, she was ordered to bed rest. After an extremely stressful pregnancy Linda gave birth to a healthy little girl. The parents were delighted when she seemed to be a much easier baby than Mark had been. However, with a new baby to care for they could not give Mark the undivided attention he had been receiving, and they noticed that he was having an increasingly difficult time coping both at home and at school. The family decided to remove him from preschool and focus on understanding what was making their son so unhappy, aggressive, and temperamental. Due to the concerns about his motor and language development it was recommended that he have an occupational therapy and speech and language evaluation.

The occupational therapist found his fine and gross motor skills to be significantly delayed. She also thought that he had a sensory-regulatory disorder, based on his hypersensitivity to sound and defensiveness to tactile stimulation. However, this was not sufficient to explain the severity of his behavioral problems both at home and at school.

The parents reconnected with the clinician and brainstormed about all of the stresses which may have contributed to Mark's difficulties: the birth of his sister, the death of a grandparent, and witnessing their dog being killed by a car. He seemed to be oscillating between being a very quiet and withdrawn little boy who was most content when playing on the computer or watching videos, and being a very active and impulsive child in social settings, who often became aggressive towards children who he thought got in his way. When they placed limits on his computer/video activities he would roam around the home, or engage in repetitive motor activities, such as jumping on the bed or kicking sand out of the sandbox. When he was excited he would flap his hands and run in circles like a tornado he saw on a TV documentary. Both parents felt that it was impossible to engage him in play, that he'd much rather tell them information about dinosaurs or endangered animals. The parents also thought that he was getting even more resistant to following any of the daily demands they made of him, such as getting dressed, brushing his teeth, or getting ready to leave the house. The grandmother who was taking care of him also told them that it was becoming too difficult for her to handle him with his sister. He was becoming a tall, strong little boy who threw fierce tantrums when demands were made of him to share with his sister or make a transition, such as leaving his play activity to get ready for lunch. They all noted that it was much easier to take care of him alone, when they found him to be delightful because he always had a great deal he wanted to tell them about or show them. Both Robert and Linda were frightened by the idea of Mark's inability to adapt to any kindergarten with his "aggressive" behavior, so they decided to give him an extra year in a small pre-kindergarten program where he would be the oldest child. Both parents had a family history of developmental and psychiatric problems and they worried endlessly about Mark's future.

The preschool observation

The psychologist who initially referred the family to an occupational therapist observed Mark on the last day of his parent-participation preschool. Consequently they did not follow their regular routine; there were fewer structured activities and more parents' participation. Still, most of the children seemed excited about the entire end-of-the-year special activities. In contrast, Mark spent most of the one-hour observation riding a tricycle down an inclined path and crashing into a grassy fence. He was not the only child engaged in this activity, and at times he would copy some of the silly gestures or sounds that his peers made but he did not engage in any reciprocal communication with them. The majority of his play was solitary or parallel with the other children. The same pattern occurred at the water table. The children were looking for toy fish that were hidden at the bottom of the water table and making up an elaborate story about their fishing adventures. Mark approached the water table and began to look for the fish but he seemed to be unaware of the conversations and symbolic play that were going on around him. After a few minutes he walked away and went into the classroom where he sat down and had a snack by himself. Another mother encouraged him and another child to look at rocks with a magnifying glass. He seemed most content, focused, and relaxed when engaged in these quieter parallel activities which required very little social interaction and allowed him to demonstrate his large store of scientific facts.

The play sessions

Mark was seen with his mother for several sessions both prior to and after the intellectual testing. During the first sessions Mark's level of play was dramatically delayed. He was unable to sustain any sequences of interactions centered on a symbolic play theme. His favorite activity was to arrange the army men in a line. He would graciously accept any other men the clinician had to offer but he didn't respond to any attempt that was made to engage them in social interactions. He seemed to enjoy watching a story being played out by the clinician but made no attempt to expand it. In the second part of the evaluation he began to use the dinosaurs to act out an aggressive interaction based on his favorite videotape. In his last sessions he repeated the theme of objects getting into crashes with cars, people, and dinosaurs. Even with adult support and guidance Mark would become easily overwhelmed and the play would quickly degenerate into the objects being tossed over and over again into a large pile until an adult placed limits and redirected his play. With support and modeling, Mark was able to repeat the script of rescuing an injured man or dinosaur, and checking to see if they needed help, but he could not elaborate at all on what the clinician had modeled.

Over the evaluation period Mark's mother became a very active partici-pant in his play, providing support without being too intrusive. With the clini-cian's guidance she became more accepting of his aggressive play, labeling his feelings as well as providing ways for coping when he became frustrated. Linda was able to share with the clinician her fear that if they allowed Mark to act so aggressively in his play he would think it O.K. to act that way towards his baby sister or peers. This concern was very realistic, and thus the clinician introduced the idea of creating a safe place in Mark's room (under his desk) where he could go and hit a pillow or kick a soft pad when he felt frustrated, or if he felt the need to be alone. The clinician's hypothesis was that Mark struck out when he was feeling overstimulated or upset. Not surprisingly, Mark visited this space frequently, considering how challenging it was for him to play with his peers and siblings. Over the three month evaluation period, Mark could not sustain any theme in his play for longer than five minutes without a great deal of adult support and guidance.

The psychological evaluation

Due to the difficulty Mark had in sustaining any reciprocal social interactions, the clinician decided to reduce the length of his visits and extend them over a period of time. She wanted to get a sense of Mark's optimal development since she had already seen him when he was "shut down." She was curious to see at what level Mark could engage in symbolic play when he had structure and support. She also wanted to know if Mark's statements about feeling sad, or his lectures about vicious dinosaurs, were representative of his own issues or if they were memorized scripts that he said when he did not know what else to say or do.

The parents were asked to fill out the Behavior Assessment System for Children (BASC) and the Conners' Parent Rating Scale to better understand his behavior and how it related to other children his age. On the BASC both parents viewed Mark as having significant attention problems, and poor adaptability, while Linda rated him as being in the significant range for hyper-activity. On the Conners' both parents rated him in the significant range for learning problems and in the "at risk" range for conduct problems and anxiety. Put together, these scores from the parent behavioral rating scales were consistent in suggesting that, compared to other four-year-old boys, Mark had a great deal of difficulty focusing his attention, was often restless and impulsive, and had adapted poorly to the world around him. He was also more anxious and had difficulty interacting with other children. What these scales could not tell us was why he was having so much difficulty staying attentive – was it that he did not process what others were asking of him, was he distracted by internal ideas, or was he easily distracted by external stimuli? The next step was to conduct a standardized assessment of his cognitive development to see if it would answer some of these questions.

The clinician administered the intellectual testing over four sessions because of the difficulty Mark had staying focused on the tests. He seemed in constant motion as he moved back and forth in his chair trying to get comfortable. He was easily distracted by every sight or sound, or by his own thoughts, so much so that one could see him frequently trying to bring himself back to the test after the clinician's prompting. Mark also seemed to be distracted by his own anxiety over his test performance. While he wanted to be cooperative and please the clinician he also tried to avoid any task which he felt he would not do well. He would respond to support up to a point and then become very silly and totally inattentive when he reached his limit.

Mark gave very lengthy responses to the verbal questions, using very good vocabulary, but he had difficulty organizing his ideas. He also did a very poor job explaining his responses, seeming more like a younger child who expects everyone to know exactly what he is trying to say. Mark needed a lot of structure, visual cues, and support to stay focused on a question. At times he would get stuck on an idea and keep coming back to it throughout the evaluation. He also displayed difficulties with fine motor tasks when he was asked to hold a pencil or turn a page.

On the Wechsler Pre-Primary Scale of Intelligence–Revised (WPPSI-R) Mark performed well within the average range on the Verbal IQ, Nonverbal IQ, and Full Scale IQ. He performed at age level on almost all of the verbal tests. He displayed strength on the subtest that assesses word knowledge and somewhat below average on the scale that measures verbal conceptual thinking. He had difficulty identifying what two objects had in common, often choosing the color and ignoring the shape.

Mark displayed more variability on the visual-motor tasks. Despite all of the movement that was going on during the verbal subtests he approached these tasks in a very organized and non-impulsive manner. He had more difficulty on visual-motor tasks that did not have clear visual cues about how things fit together.

Mark's profile

Mark had a long history of hypersensitivity to sensory stimuli, such as noise and light touch, while craving strong tactile stimuli, such as banging his head into walls and very tight bear hugs. He had a history of being irritable and having sleep difficulties since birth, though these problems decreased some-what after he received treatment for food allergies. He seemed to be most content when playing by himself in a familiar setting with adults who were active observers of his shows. His elaborate scripted stories stood in sharp contrast to the tremendous difficulty he had staying engaged in a simple reciprocal social interaction with peers in a one-on-one or small group setting like preschool or his church class. Although he was of average intelligence, with no large discrepancy between verbal or nonverbal skills, the social demands of preschool had always been a struggle for him, even when it was a very small program with a large number of adult participants. Mark's rigidity over things such as being first in line or insisting that his play be the exact reenactment of a specific video was a constant source of conflict between him and his peers. He did best in very short play dates with very active adult super-vision. He seemed unattuned to the suggestions that his peers made for symbolic play ideas or was so focused on winning a game that it took priority over having friends.

Mark's average intellectual development, poor social skills, poor use of social language, delayed play both alone and with peers, fine and gross motor difficulties, hypersensitivity to tactile and auditory stimuli, tendency to flap his hands when excited, walking or riding his tricycle in circles when not engaged in an activity, and overriding specialized interests (e.g. dinosaurs) were all suggestive of Asperger's Syndrome. Yet the clinician was not comfort-able giving that diagnosis since she wondered if his problems could be attributed to his difficulties with sensory and affective regulation. She speculated that his irritability, sadness, and, at times, oppositional stance could be the reaction to his regulatory and developmental difficulties. For these reasons the clinician gave him a diagnosis of Disorders of Childhood–Not Otherwise Specified (NOS), an Adjustment Disorder with Mixed Distur-bances of Emotions and Conduct, and cited Asperger's Syndrome and ADHD as diagnoses to rule out following intervention. The goal of the intervention was to foster his capacity to communicate and engage in social interactions with peers.

The family was given treatment recommendations that were very similar to the interventions recommended for Steven. The psychologist recom-

mended that they take Mark to see a child psychiatrist to determine if he could
be helped by medication. She felt that medication was worth looking into
because of the severity of his symptoms (particularly his anxiety and poor
attention) and his inability to function in a small group setting. It was also recommended that he participate in a therapeutic group program that could
address his difficulties in communicating and playing with peers. The
therapist also felt that he could benefit from individual therapy but that if they
had to prioritize the intervention due to financial constraints they should
choose the group program. The family was also advised to continue in occupational therapy to address his fine and gross motor and sensory-regulatory
difficulties. The parents were advised to notify the school so that an individualized education plan (IEP) could be set up. This would enable them to
educate the school and the teacher about Mark and determine which type of
interventions would be available for him in the school. The therapist felt that
he might qualify for speech and language therapy targeted at his pragmatic
language delays, a behavioral consultant to help him adapt to the classroom
and playground, a shortened morning in the beginning to help with his
transition to school, and an aide if the teachers felt that it was needed. The
evaluation process began when he was three-and-a-half years old but the
diagnosis of Asperger's Syndrome was not formalized until he was five years
old. Over time it became clearer to all of the clinicians involved that he was a
very complicated child. He was a very bright young boy who had the primary
diagnosis of Asperger's Syndrome, at times appearing depressed and at other
times hyperactive-impulsive, combined with sensory-regulatory problems
and, later, learning difficulties. At several points in the chapters ahead we will
explore aspects of Mark's development, and the impact that his diagnosis had
on his family, which are illustrated in the poignant words of his mother in the
final chapter of this book.

CHAPTER 5

The Parents' Journey

This chapter will provide a guide to the journey that parents travel after learning that their child has Asperger's Syndrome. It is important to remember that the direction, pace, and meaning of this journey will vary from parent to parent depending on their personal histories, their role in the child's daily life, their perception of the child's strengths and difficulties, and their experiences with other young children. It is not uncommon for mothers and fathers to see their child very differently and feel as if they are on different paths, meeting each other only intermittently along the way. The diagnosis of Asperger's Syndrome is a lifelong journey, causing parents to reexamine the diagnosis each time their child passes through a new developmental phase, masters new skills, or is confronted with new challenges. We have learned that while the path is not uniform many parents experience, at different stages, a sense of denial, rage and anger, bargaining, depression, advocacy, and acceptance. The chapter will look at each of these phases and how they may differ between parents.

Many parents have passed through the phase of *denial* long before they take their child to a professional for an evaluation. Often these are the parents who believed very early on that something was out of sync in their child even when others told them they were making too much out of nothing, that all they needed to do was relax, set better limits, or find a new childcare arrangement. For these parents the diagnosis can be a great relief since it confirms their observations that their child is different and that they are not "crazy or neurotic" for being so worried. This does not mean that they do not experience feelings of anger or sadness but rather that they are able to move more quickly after the assessment to becoming their child's advocate. For these parents the feelings of *bargaining* may be present when they choose to take time off from work or get a loan so that they can enroll their child in an extensive intervention program, hoping that he will be on track by the time he gets to kindergarten. The feelings of *depression* may occur when their child experiences difficulties at school, even after all the efforts they have made to make his school experiences a positive one. What adds another layer of complexity to this issue is when one parent, typically the mother, is at a different stage of acceptance than the partner, who often does not see the child in a social setting. For this reason it is helpful for all parents to be attuned to where each is in their understanding and assessment of their child, and how that impacts their relationship as both parents and a couple.

A parent's history

To understand more fully the journey parents undertake when learning their child has Asperger's Syndrome, one must remember that parents are individuals with their own personal histories and experiences. These histories will influence how parents cope and how they make meaning of having a child with Asperger's Syndrome. For example, a parent who had a sibling with special needs may be well aware of the pressures that this places on a family. They may also have a heightened awareness of how important it is to be an advocate for their child, even before they fully understand their own child's needs. They may also wonder if their genetic make-up is the reason for their child's difficulties.

For parents with a history of physical or mental health problems, the news that their child has a developmental problem can feel especially overwhelming. Parents with a history of depression or anxiety may feel extremely vulnerable and insecure about their ability to bear the increased responsibilities. They may be at risk for worsening of their own symptoms and need professional help in addition to the support of friends and relatives. The anxiety that all parents feel about being the cause of their child's problems can be magnified in parents who have learning or social difficulties themselves. Regardless of how many times they have been told that the cause of Asperger's Syndrome is unknown, these parents may feel that *they* are the cause since they can so easily relate to their child's problems. The identification can serve to either immobilize a parent or be a catalyst for understanding the child's needs.

On the other side of the continuum are parents who feel that the characteristics that professionals identify as being problematic for their child are the same qualities that they view as being strengths in themselves and others. These individuals may believe that their photographic memory, selective attention span, and wealth of factual information on a specific topic all contributed to their "success," both academically and professionally. These parents may find the journey extremely difficult since they are being asked not only to understand their child but also to reexamine their own sense of self.

Not surprisingly, the same issues are relevant to the couple. Having a child with special needs places unexpected stress on all couples. Those with a history of high conflict, poor communication, and little mutual support are going to be more vulnerable at these times than those who have a mutually satisfying relationship. For many parents, the journey of understanding their own child sheds light on the rewards and stresses they have been experiencing as a couple. It is very common for a parent to discover that the strategies they use to help them stay connected with their child and make their days run more smoothly may also help them stay connected with their partner. Other parents may need professional help to rediscover what attracted them to each other and how they can complement each other's strengths and difficulties. Thus special attention must be given to how the parents as a couple support each other's ways of coping or place additional stress on their relationship.

The following case vignette is used to illustrate how a *parent's history* can influence how parents come to understand their child, accept the diagnosis, and seek intervention. In this case, it was the grandmother, Carol's mother, who was the first to question her grandson's development. Carol has an older brother who is autistic and her mother was the first to notice some similarities between her brother and Lance, a connection that Carol initially rejected. However, over time Carol began to look for answers to explain her son's difficulties. Carol vividly tells the journey she traveled, from struggling with coming to terms with her child's needs to becoming the best possible advocate for her child.

Carol's story

Lance's first years were marked by high-pitched screaming and full-blown tantrums. By the time he was one year old people would notice his unusual tantrums in public, and stare horrified. Lance's screams would sound like someone was hurting him, but would be about something as minor as a diaper change. It soon got to the point where taking him out became embarrassing.

By the time he was two, I retreated more and more to the house until I became almost afraid to go out. I was afraid to go to the park because Lance might throw one of his screaming fits, and other mothers were afraid for their own children, or curious if I was hurting Lance to make him cry like that. Even our Sunday church service became a problem because other well-meaning parents were certain if we only parented our child correctly, he would act normally. He was just spoiled, we heard many times.

The first help I sought was a hearing test. At two, we checked Lance's hearing and it was fine. At two-and-a-half, I took Lance to see a clinician, where she initiated testing.

Not ready to hear the results, I convinced myself we were fine and didn't even wait to hear the results after all the testing. Then at four, we started Lance in a preschool three mornings a week. Getting him to go was like pulling teeth. He would barricade himself within the van door and I would have to pull him out. Usually, I succeeded only two days a week, the other day it simply wasn't worth the fight to me. Once at school, the teachers were of little help. They saw Lance as a behavior problem, and a Mama's boy. But once he was established in the classroom, he would do fine, until circle time. Then he was lost and would wander about the room aimlessly, again securing his title as a problem child.

I forged ahead. Looking back I wish I had that year back. I wish I stood as my child's advocate instead of forcing him into this social time that didn't have enough structure for him. While Lance was in this preschool, I took him back to the previous clinician. Unwilling to have my child labeled, I wanted private counseling, and so all testing would be confidential.

Lance started kindergarten at the local public school about this same time. Lance was incredibly smart; he was reading whole readers by the first six months of school. But when I'd test him myself, he had no idea what certain letters were. I figured out that Lance was listening to the other kids read the books, and moving his fingers along like they did at a reader's pace, and completely faking all learning. By the time he finished school he didn't know his basic alphabet sounds.

His kindergarten teacher loved Lance and was mortified she hadn't noticed Lance's ruse, but he was very good at it, and she had twenty other children. She loved Lance unconditionally, and that was all he needed to have the drive to succeed. He saw that when he did well, people loved him and treated him better and so he really wanted to please. That was the first time I really saw that in him – although it had been there all along. It was just me waking up to it. Lance's teacher gave me lots of phonics to work through over the summer, and encouraged me to work on rhyming with him.

I had Lance signed up for kindergarten again at a Christian school that uses a very visual curriculum. This curriculum had flash cards, and associated letter sounds with a picture. Lance knew his sounds almost immediately.

During this same time, Lance was attending a therapeutic group called the Friends' Group. Once a week, he would go and learn how to function with other children, and to address kids by name. After two years, I think he outgrew it because he knew how to function on his own in public. We still have issues at birthday parties, and entering into play, but we are working on them.

I told his new teacher all about the diagnosis, how Lance would get confused and would need a little prodding if he started to retreat. His teacher saw very few problems with him, and said he was one of the better kids in the class, both educationally and emotionally. This school was very structured, and that has worked wonders for Lance. He knows that on Friday at ten, writing will be worked on, or Chapel will happen earlier that morning. The hardest days for Lance are the field trips and the parties, because he doesn't know what to expect, or what will be expected of him. But with only sixteen children in a class, and only one class per grade, there are very few changes for Lance and he is thriving.

A note about fathers

Most of the examples used throughout this chapter show the mother playing the more active role in the parenting of a child with Asperger's Syndrome. This is not to imply that the fathers are not just as affected by their child's struggles and accomplishments or do not experience the same range of thoughts and feelings, as do the mothers. Rather, fathers often express these things differently than mothers. Every father's experience is unique. Nonetheless, there are some patterns of coping which seem more common than others. We attempt to portray those now, but recognize that many may not relate to all of the following.

It is almost impossible for both parents to maintain full-time paid jobs and care for their child's special needs, unless they have both an exceptional childcare provider and flexible work schedules. When the father's job permits him to take time off he is often most involved in the early stages of the diagnosis and intervention. Fathers may seek out second opinions if they are in denial, express anger towards the clinician, do extensive research on the topic, and participate in the early phases of intervention as they struggle with the diagnosis. Depending on the father's own history and comfort with expressing grief, he may cope with any feelings of depression by becoming more involved in his paid work, withdrawing from the child, or, in the best case scenario, becoming very attuned to his own, his spouse's, and their child's feelings.

By the second stage the father and mother are either in agreement about the child's diagnosis and have decided how they want to divide the parenting responsibilities or they may be on quite different paths. The father may take on a passive role, supporting the mother's decision to leave her paid job and financially supporting the intervention, while being ambivalent or even frankly disagreeing with the diagnosis. Some of these fathers identify so strongly with the child that what some people see as problems they see as strengths. Still others believe that the child's difficulties stem from the couple's parenting and childcare decisions, and that if they had a more tradi- tional household with more authoritarian parenting their child would be fine. In these situations it can take years of phone calls from the school before the father can accept the diagnosis. If the child does not present with behavior problems in the home setting, the father may never reach this level of acceptance. Sometimes it requires a clinician to develop a therapeutic relation- ship with the father and work through his fears and feelings of pride before he can let down his protective shield and work through the emotional upheaval of having a child with special needs. This process may also occur at the work place if he meets another father who has traveled a similar journey, in a parents' support group, or in the worst case it may never occur. What is clear from our experience is how much easier it is for the family when the parents feel supported by their partners in their attempts to understand and help their child.

The following vignette is from a father whose strong identity with his son makes him a loyal friend and a strong advocate. As the father explains, the strong identity he feels towards his child can at times represent the confusion they both feel towards the social demands they experience outside of the home.

> Since I became a father, all of my emotional highs and lows have been connected to my children. All their successes, achievements, and triumphs, all their injuries, sicknesses, and failures resonate with me. I wonder if I over-identify with them or if I just feel for them very deeply. When our son Mike was little, I felt closer to him than I ever have to anyone else in the world. I still feel close to him. He and I seemed to be on the same wavelength on many things. What he did made sense to me in a way that I could not explain at that time. I felt a profound kinship with the way he acted and played. When he got his first toy animals he began organizing

them. He started with the elephants, lining them up, changing their order or direction and lining them up again. What else are elephants for?

From a very early age he began drawing his favorite cartoon character, Woody Woodpecker. I searched all over the area where we live for woodpecker books and videos. He soon began doing all things "woodpeckerish." Drawing seemed to be his main métier. He would draw very happily for two to three hours each day. When he was two we tried sending Mike to the same preschool his older brother loved; however, he had an extremely difficult time of it, understanding what they were doing and why he should do what they wanted him to do. We withdrew him from the class in less than a month when the teachers informed us that they could not cope with him. After two years in a loving, in-home family day care he returned to the same preschool. He seemed better able to settle into the routine. His sensory hypersensitivity was becoming less acute, and he could tolerate more sensory input. He wore sunglasses on the playground and found activities like digging a secret burrow with his peers that absorbed his full attention.

My first awareness that something was not right was when the preschool had an art show and there was nothing from my "artistic" son being displayed. A sinking sensation hit me as I realized there was a serious problem. When I went to his teachers for some insight the most they could say was that Mike did not cooperate doing the art projects. The explanation struck me as being very strange, given his love for drawing. When we asked Mike he knew exactly why he did not have any drawings in the show. In his preschool everything was on a 45 minute schedule. He was often not aware of the announcements so that meant he would get started late and have to stop before he was finished. His way of coping with this problem was not to start at all.

When it came to the end of the year evaluation, the teachers told us in no uncertain terms that Mike was not ready for kindergarten because he was not cooperating, not getting with the program, and that would be necessary in kindergarten. We (I) did not have any idea what might be different about Mike, not a clue. Both of us had attended an Ivy League school where we met and fell in love, so we had plenty over-achieving conditioning in our upbringing, especially mine. The thought that my son should "fail," not graduate, was very traumatic for me. As we grappled with this unexpected experience we realized that the most important concern was not our egos, but Mike's well-being. We realized that he has always had his own rhythm, and that he never responds well to having the rhythm disrupted.

I have always been aware that there are often some points I miss from other people, although I did not know any explanation until the invention of Asperger's. We were quite relieved when Michael finished that preschool, but all three of us looked forward to kindergarten with increasing apprehension. This is a feeling we were reminded of when we recently sent our son off to Junior High School.

With the awareness that a parent's coping is likely to be influenced by his or her own personal history, we will now explore the different stages described earlier in more detail, using the voices of parents to bring them to life.

Denial

For most parents the news that their young child has Asperger's Syndrome, or characteristics of AS, is shocking and they are overwhelmed with disbelief. Exceptions to this are the parents who have another child or relative with an Autistic Spectrum Disorder and see similarities between them, or the parent who has been insisting that something is different with their child since he was a toddler. For these parents the diagnosis, as frightening as it is, confirms that their parental intuition was on target.

The question for many parents, though, is: how can a child who is so bright, curious, and connected with his parents have any similarities with a child who has Asperger's Syndrome? The first part of the answer is often connected to how involved the parents were in the diagnostic process. Were they able to observe with a clinician, or hear descriptions of, their child giving answers that were unrelated to the questions being asked during the structured testing? Did they see the child attempt to end the session by politely saying that he did not want to play and if that did not work attempt to flee the evaluation room? Did they observe how much the child enjoyed leading the clinician around the playroom in contrast to the difficulty he had following a parent's or clinician's attempts to engage him in an activity that was not centered around his agenda? Without these experiences it is understandable that the parents would be in a state of *disbelief* since the child they know is so different from the child the professionals describe.

For parents who have not experienced any difficulty playing with their child, the idea of their child having difficulty engaging in reciprocal play with others seems unbelievable. They and other adults in their child's life may enjoy following the child's lead, becoming actors in the play he is directing or assistants for the museum he has set up in the family room for trains and dinosaurs. They may think that their child enjoys playing more with them than with peers because the peers cannot understand his complex ideas, or are not interested in knowing things to the same level of detail as their child does. What these parents typically have not seen are the tantrums their child throws when a peer suggests that they do something differently, or his pattern of going off and playing by himself if a peer is not interested in his ideas.

Still other parents do not understand what type of play is typical for a child of their child's age. They may not remember playing with other children when they were young, and don't have the opportunity to see how their child plays when they pick him up at the end of the day at his childcare setting or school. They may have spent a lot of time exploring outside by themselves as a child, collecting things, drawing, or just being alone. Furthermore, they may not remember anyone's parents ever being actively engaged in play. Thus, if a parent works with computers he or she may think that it's a great idea to get the child comfortable with playing on the computer as early as possible. If the parents enjoy movies they may be proud of their child's ability to memorize the scripts, and if they love science then they may encourage their child's desire to put things together in a very exact matter or count everything they see. They typically do not ask what their child enjoys doing with other children that does not include following their own child's interests.

Another important issue in this process is what triggered the evaluation in the first place. If it was because the child was having trouble following the teachers' directions then they may have thought of a hearing problem. If the child was oppositional at home and at school then they may have anticipated receiving some parenting guidance. If it seemed that their child could not sit still for more than a few seconds unless he was doing an activity he selected, then they may have anticipated a diagnosis of ADHD and referral for medication. The diagnosis of Asperger's Syndrome, though, often comes as a surprise. After hearing this diagnosis they may search the Web, libraries, and their favorite bookstore for information, hoping that the descriptions they read will not fit their child and finding that they have a hard time retaining much of this information. It is very common for parents to return for a conference with an impressive number of articles on the topic, and questions regarding their child's diagnosis. They will struggle with understanding how their child could have an Autistic Spectrum Disorder since he is so very different from the stereotype they hold of what a child with autism looks like. This feeling of uncertainty may never go away but only recede into the background as they take on the next task of seeking intervention for their child. One can be sure that each interview the parents have with a new clinician includes the question of whether the diagnosis is correct. The following vignette is from the mother of a four-and-a-half-year-old boy who received a provisional diagnosis of Asperger's Syndrome and Oppositional Disorder.

> When we were told that Sam might have Asperger's Syndrome I could not believe it. We had very little difficulty with him at home, and I thought his problems at school arose from the fact that he did not have much experience with children his age. He has an older brother but he is ten years older. We had talked with him several times about not hitting other children, grabbing things from them, or calling them names and he seemed to understand it just fine. Every time I saw him at school he was usually playing by himself, smiling, not bothering anybody. I did notice that he was starting to talk about the other kids not being nice to him, but I told him that he had to be nicer if he wanted friends. He seemed content to work on his drawings of home interiors and planes. He is a perfectionist and can spend hours working on a drawing, which is a good skill for his academic work.
>
> We came from the Philippines where nobody ever talks about developmental or mental health problems. There is a huge taboo, and everybody keeps those things a secret. I have no idea if there were other people in the family with similar problems.
>
> My husband is from the United States, and he thinks Sam is fine, he thinks that we just need to be a little bit stricter with him. I thought that if we get him into a different school and a baby-sitter so he does not have to spend the entire day in day care he will do much better. He really is a nice child. I would never have guessed that he would be thriving two years later in a special communication class.

Frustration and anger

The next phase is characterized by feelings of frustration and anger. Parents of a child with impulsive or aggressive behaviors may feel angry with the child for not listening to them and for behaving poorly at school or in public places. It can seem that no matter how hard they try to make the situation work for the child (e.g. spending more time with him or offering him a reward for good behavior) their child ends up with a tantrum. They may feel angry with their child's teachers for not being more sensitive to their child's needs, even if they have not shared the diagnosis with them. They may feel like they are continually on "pins and needles," afraid that every time the phone rings it is the school calling to tell them that their child has been expelled for hitting another child. They may also feel angry and confused by the mixed messages they are receiving from their pediatrician, family members, and teachers, who may insist that their child is fine and just needs a little bit more discipline, time to mature, and opportunities to learn how to play with other children.

The situation is even more confusing for parents of children who are more withdrawn and reserved, since these children may not be seen as having any problems at school or social gatherings. In fact they may be a favorite of the parents' friends or adult relatives since they love to talk to adults about their favorite topics. Sometimes the adults never see how isolated the child is from peers and may think that the parents are over-anxious, attributing pathology to every quirk the child has. The parents are understandably angry at themselves for thinking that either they are making too much out of something minor or they have a parenting style that is causing their child's problems. This is especially true if it is the parents' first child. Even if they feel that the diagnosis is correct they may feel guilty that they did not intervene sooner, missing some "critical" time to intervene, despite being told this does not apply to Asperger's Syndrome.

This is the time when parents sometimes search for factors that they can blame for causing the child's problems, hoping that finding a cause will lead them to a cure: for example, removing the nanny who did not speak English to improve their child's ability to communicate with peers; withdrawing the child from the daycare center that did not spend enough time teaching the children social skills, and finding a baby-sitter more attuned to his needs; eliminating from the family's diet foods thought to be associated with hyper-active or autistic behavior; reducing the father's tendency to engage in rough play with the kids, since it gets the child in trouble when he tries to duplicate it at school; eliminating the child's habit of watching aggressive cartoons on the television or playing violent computer games. They may also comb through their child's medical history, wondering if they may have caused the AS by having their child vaccinated, putting their child on different medications for his ear infections, bottle feeding, or following a specific type of diet. They may read testimonials from parents who are convinced that their child's devel-opment halted after one of these events and they will have to balance feelings of fear and guilt against the reality that none of these factors has yet been found to be a cause of Asperger's Syndrome.

Some parents may feel overwhelmed by feelings of guilt, anger, and rage, not only if they were never told about a family member with a similar presentation, but also with the realization that it cannot help them understand how to better treat their child. They are suddenly aware of article after article in the popular press about potential cures for autism and are shocked and angry to see how preliminary these studies actually are.

At another level this process may challenge an already stressed relationship if one of the parents, in our experience typically the mother, begins to wonder if the diagnosis fits their spouse. It is quite common that parents who may not be ready to accept the diagnosis for their child find that it sheds light on their partner and on their relationship. The process may also place additional stress on the couple if the parents see the child differently. One can anticipate this if the behaviors that are being used to diagnose the child are the same characteristics that a parent takes pride in: for example, working independently, focused attention, perfectionism, strong memory, a desire for control, and natural leadership qualities. This parent typically spends most of their time with the child only in one-on-one situations, engaged in a limited range of routine activities or play with the child. Because of their usually demanding career they may not have the opportunity to observe their child during a play date or at school during unstructured time. The challenge of parenting a child with AS is increased tenfold if the other parent feels that their partner is criticizing him or her. The following vignette highlights the conflict that Steven, who is the impulsive child described in Chapter 4, aroused between his parents until they developed a shared understanding of both his strengths and challenges.

Steven's mother was surprised by the reports of his aggressive behavior at preschool but quickly understood their seriousness after the school insisted that if her son was going to stay she would have to be his aide and help him during times of transition and interactions with peers. She had not observed these difficulties at home since he did not have regular play dates and seemed very content to play in the back yard with his sister.

Steven's father was convinced that the difficulties stemmed from his wife's permissive parenting style, and what was needed was firmer limit setting and consequences for Steven's behavior. He worked very long hours and typically only interacted with Steven on the weekends, when they did a special activity together. He had no problems with Steven as long as they did one of his favorite activities like wrestling, going hiking, or watching a nature movie. When he did see problems was at the dinner table, when Steven would not sit still. If anything he felt that Steven might by hyperactive, but as far as he could see his communication and play skills were just fine.

In this family the journey to understand Steven was very different for each parent. Steven's mother quit her part-time consultation job and began to help out in the preschool until they could find an aide. She also began to set up and facilitate play dates for Steven on a regular basis and enrolled him in a therapeutic playgroup. Very early on in the process she realized that her husband, who she thought had a lot in common with Steven, would not accept the diagnosis, yet he also did not forbid her seeking professional guidance. She felt frustrated towards him for making her feel responsible for Steven's difficulties rather than supporting her for the intense effort she was making to help him. She was mad that nobody had noticed her son's difficulties earlier, so that he could have received intervention sooner; and she was fed up with all of the adults who thought nothing of giving her inappropriate advice on the playground, at a store, or at their church. Over time she realized that, as a couple, they had a lot of shared interests, values, and goals, but the day-to-day parenting of their child was a role she was going to have to carry out alone. This task was made easier as she sought out the support of professionals, parents of children with similar needs, and a very supportive nanny.

Bargaining

The next phase is called the *bargaining phase*. Here the parents may agree to enroll their child into many of the recommended interventions while at the same time not fully accepting the diagnosis. In fact, many of the first interventions they choose, such as speech and language therapy and occupational therapy, may never mention the diagnosis of Asperger's Syndrome. The professionals who address areas such as pragmatic language, fine and gross motor, and sensory motor integration can seem less threatening than a mental health professional who may have made the initial diagnosis. The children are dropped off, they seem to enjoy their sessions, and the therapists may talk about the child's individual goals and suggest strategies that may help them both at home and in the school setting without ever mentioning a specific diagnosis.

Parents may also explore alternative diets and nutritional supplements which have been associated with allergy and asthma problems, found at a higher rate in children with Autistic Spectrum Disorders. Again, this can be a solitary journey. Most pediatricians discourage these interventions since they have not been substantiated in controlled medical research, which is very hard to conduct in a child population. Still, nutritional or allergy specialists may be consulted, since many families have heard that food allergies can exasperate AS symptoms.

The more difficult step for many parents is consultation and intervention with a mental health specialist who uses terms like PDD or AS. One can argue that getting the child the services he needs is what counts, not the diagnosis, since one does not need a diagnosis for therapy. The diagnosis is typically needed only for insurance coverage or to qualify for services provided by the local school district's or special education programs (see Chapter 11). The situation is a lot trickier in a therapeutic group program that is tailored for children with AS. It is not uncommon for parents in this phase to enroll their child in a group or even participate in a parent program, hoping that even if their child has some of the characteristics of AS he does not have enough to warrant the diagnosis. For these parents it can be very frightening to hear another parent describe how they felt the same way when their older child was first diagnosed or when a teacher began to point out similar problems in their younger child. The bargaining parent may insist that their situation is unique. They know their child better than anyone else and may believe that their child is making so much progress in such a short period of time that he will no longer meet the diagnostic criteria by the next school year. They may feel that their child has delayed rather than atypical development.

In many cases the clinician who diagnosed their child is the only person with whom the parents have discussed the "taboo" term of Asperger's Syndrome, and they want to keep it that way. They may be afraid that if other people are aware of the diagnosis they will treat their child differently and not encourage their children to be friends. They may fear that teachers will have lower expectations of their child, providing only a mediocre education or, even worse, placing a mark on his school records that will prevent him from being accepted into competitive programs. It can feel hard to trust that their child's school experiences and play dates might go better if other parents or teachers knew something about their child. Often, only time and experience can convince a parent that the other parents' or a teacher's insight can actually be used to support and advocate for the child – not prohibit the child in ways they may fear.

In this phase of *bargaining* we often see parents divide into two different groups. The first group is starting to understand that there is a wide range of children who meet the criteria for Asperger's Syndrome, and their child is one of them. They see that there is a wide range of interventions, some of which might help their child and some which may not be necessary or even beneficial. The parents realize that they will have to make the best educated decisions that they can, understanding that what works for one child or one family may not work for them, and that an intervention skipped now can always be tried later.

The second group, which is often smaller, is made up of parents who still disagree with the diagnosis. Sometimes the progress their child has made is proof to them that the diagnosis must be wrong. For still others, they view the progress the child is making as being due to maturation rather than intervention. Yet some of these families may underestimate how much effort they are putting into making sure their child gets the interventions recommended as well as not recognizing the changes they have made to accommodate their child. The next vignette illustrates a family's struggle with doing everything possible for their child, yet still bargaining with the diagnosis.

> Jonathan was a very quiet and serious four-year-old boy who was referred for an evaluation because of the difficulties that he was having keeping up with all of the transitions in his day. Both parents were very bright, well-educated professionals who delighted in their son's wealth of information, concentration skills, and adult-like behavior. The mother was able to see that he also had difficulty engaging in reciprocal play with peers and had a restricted range of interests. The mother immediately sought out professional help and set up an intensive intervention program that included dyadic play therapy, occupational therapy, a special diet, participation in a therapeutic group program, music lessons because he loved the piano, and participation in a sports program. In contrast, Jonathan's father did not accept any aspect of the diagnosis. He saw his son as being very much like himself: bright, very focused, and disliking social gatherings. He marveled at his abilities in chess and music, but actually spent very little time with him during the week because of his own very busy schedule.
>
> The parents initially decided not to tell the school about the diagnosis with the hope that if the intervention worked they would never need to know. However, the teachers were very concerned. The parents were called in for a conference regarding Jonathan's aggressive behavior on the playground: he was acting like a dinosaur. At that point they shared information with the school and had a consultant come in for the teachers. The teachers felt misled and wished that they had known this information from the beginning. The staff decided that their program was not the best place for Jonathan, which was devastating for his parents. With hindsight they agreed, but that did not make the process any less painful, especially since the mother had made such an effort to connect with the other parents and

develop a social network for her son. The situation was even more complicated since they had enrolled his younger sister at the same preschool.
Jonathan's parents chose not to share the diagnostic information with their
friends and not let the next administration know before he was accepted.
Once he was accepted they informed the administrators and his teacher, but
felt strongly about not letting the other families know. He has thrived at his
new elementary school which is much smaller, more structured, has very
limited free time on the playground, and rewards his academic strengths.
What the school does not address is his lack of interest in making or
sustaining friendships with his classmates. His mother feels this loss very
strongly every time she watches him at a party, or during a free time at
school when all of the boys except Jonathan start up a ball game.

Depression

The parents' feelings of depression can come at many different times
throughout the child's life and are most frequently associated with feelings of
helplessness at not being able to make the child's problems go away. As
described in the previous section, parents may be quick to see their child's
special needs, get him enrolled in a more appropriate class, and begin intervention. They may see his behavior dramatically improve. Yet with their
child's progress comes the hope that the diagnosis no longer holds and the
subsequent painful awareness that it still does.

Nothing is more upsetting than to watch a child who is doing so beauti-
fully in school completely melt down during an activity that was planned as a
special treat for him, such as a trip to the zoo or a birthday party. Many parents
describe how depressing it was to watch their child "fail" in an activity that
they felt he was ready for, such as going to Sunday school or participating in
group sports, and then be told that he cannot stay unless a parent is with him.
At these times the parents feel helpless. They wonder if others were right
when they said that all their child needed was stricter parenting. They
question the worth of all of the interventions they have tried if their child is
not going to be able to generalize any of these skills to different settings. They
are overwhelmed with the fear that their child's needs are not going to go
away and they wonder if they have the energy and stamina it takes to care for
their child as he gets older, stronger, and enters arenas where parent participation is not welcomed. At these times the parents' minds often become flooded
with feelings of anxiety and depression.

The parents may rethink earlier plans they had to terminate treatment after one year because of its interference with their paid job and/or their family commitments. They may worry about the cost, both financially and emotionally, that the child is having on his siblings and on the couple's relationship. Most of all they may feel overwhelmed if they are the only ones looking after their child's care, integrating all of the professionals' recommendations and explaining them to every new adult the child works with. These feelings of depression and helplessness are a normal response and often a reminder that the parent needs to find sources of support, either from fellow parents, clergy, support groups, and/or clinicians. Recognizing that these feelings exist, make sense, and are expected is sometimes not enough to maintain the stamina that is needed to help their child. Some parents, even when they have a helpful social network, are afraid of overburdening others with their chronic issues. At these times it is very helpful to seek professional support from an individual you do not have to worry about overburdening, since helping you is their job. A poignant story at the end of the book reflects the wide range of feelings parents of children with Asperger's Syndrome often experience.

Advocacy

At this point the parents often realize that their child works better with adults who are attuned to his strengths and needs and in settings which do not have excessive visual, auditory, or sensory stimuli. Parents often find that when they have reached a place where they are comfortable being a strong advocate for their child, they may come up against others (teachers, family members) who think they are making too much of things. They often sound just like the parents did when they were in the denial phase, reassuring the parents that their child looks just like a lot of the other children in their class. This can be challenging since they, in their own right, are often just coming to terms with sharing their child's diagnosis with others. Parents understandably can become extremely frustrated with the teacher for suggesting that they are pathologizing their child's behavior or encouraging them to rethink the diagnosis.

If a teacher has had experience with a student with Asperger's Syndrome, he or she may want to make the class work for the child but indicate that extra help is required to provide for the child's needs. One aspect of the parents' role as advocates is to do what it takes to help their child get the services they feel he needs. In the case where the teacher is helpful, together the parent and teacher can advocate for the child. But it is not uncommon for parents to find out that what they feel is best for their child may not be provided by their school. Therefore, parents benefit from developing a collaborative relationship with the child's school to maximize the possibility of implementing strategies and interventions to support their child's needs. (These issues are explored further in Chapter 11.)

Even though the parent's role of advocate is clearest in relationship to the child's educational plan, it does not end there. Advocacy is required in every setting in which the child participates in social relationships with peers – for example, sports teams, religious school, youth groups, performing arts groups, and camp programs, to list a few. Each new activity presents the dilemma of whether or not to tell the adult in charge about their child's special needs, and whether they should share any information about their child, including the thorny issue of a formal diagnosis, with the other parents or children. Strategies to get their child's attention or change the topic of a discussion are things that can be discussed more casually. Understandably, this is an issue which takes on different meanings depending on the developmental stage of the child and the parents' level of comfort with the diagnosis.

A father of a child who was diagnosed when he was four years old writes the following story.

Doug's observations

One of the best pieces of advice received during our four-year journey with Adam and Asperger's Syndrome was, "Welcome to your new full-time career as Adam's advocates." Whenever we deal with public school teachers, special education professionals, care providers, other parents, and his peers, I'm reminded that we alone are responsible for educating those involved in Adam's life as to the nature of his condition and methods for dealing with his challenges. Helping him be successful at home, in school, and at play obviously requires much more vigilance than children without Asperger's Syndrome. With Adam, early intervention has meant a Herculean amount of effort and involvement in every aspect of his life from the age of three-and-a-half but the reward has been longer and longer periods of calm and constructive play, age-appropriate behavior, and steadily improving self-management on his part. There are definitely setbacks, the most severe of which are when he strikes another child or a teacher, but these incidents are decreasing in frequency and severity as he learns to manage his impulses and seek help from others. We can go weeks with no incidents, then two or three in one day. He's beginning to show remorse and understanding of the consequences of his actions (typically after the fact), but every day I still hold my breath as I pick him up from after school care, waiting to find out if he had a "good day" or not.

As the advocate, the issue of whom, what, and when to tell about Asperger's Syndrome is central. In advocating for their child, parents are also faced with the question of what and when they should tell their own child about the diagnosis. Many parents choose to wait and follow the children's cues on this topic, while others give their children a brief explanation of the challenges they confront, and still others choose to use the label of Asperger's Syndrome with children as young as kindergarteners. One mother's strategy was to set a book about Asperger's Syndrome out on the table so that the child could see it. As anticipated, it led to a series of questions from her son, the nanny, and extended family. It is reassuring to know that most children are very skilled at obtaining just as much information as they can handle. Once again, what seems to be key to this process is the parents' level of comfort with the diagnosis. If the parents believe that the diagnosis is wrong, confusing, disabling, or transitional they will choose not to disclose it to others, including their child.

Acceptance

The *acceptance* that one's child has Asperger's Syndrome or traits of Asperger's Syndrome is a stage which parents frequently transition in and out of depending on how well their child is currently functioning at home, in school, and in their social activities. Most parents' acceptance of the diagnosis does not occur until they experience and understand that it is not synonymous with delayed development but rather atypical development. In practical terms that means accepting that the same child who may excel in music, have extensive knowledge about one specific interest, or read at four levels above their grade will need help learning how to listen and respond to another person's thoughts and feelings. Some parents will insist that their child simply has a different way of learning and that their job is to find the academic and living situations in which their child can excel. These parents associate a diagnostic label with closing the door on opportunities for their child. They may be more comfortable describing their child as having a different learning style, such as a nonverbal learning difficulty, rather than accepting the diagnostic label of Pervasive Developmental Disorder or Asperger's Syndrome.

It can honestly be said that most parents, after months or years of deciding whether to share the diagnosis with family members, schools, and friends, have found that this action does not have the negative impact they thought it would have. If anything, they find themselves defending a diagnosis that they initially doubted. They are shocked that after sharing the information with the school, copying articles for their child's new teachers, and hiring a clinician to consult, the teachers still forget the difficulties that the child may be having if they see him doing well academically. When teachers do identify problems it is usually related to the child's difficulty keeping up with the academic demands of the classroom or "bossy personality" and not in the areas of social communication with the teacher or peers.

Unfortunately, when some parents inform family members or peers they are often told that the diagnosis is more of a hindrance than a help. Others may give the parents example after example of how the child reminds them of a parent, friend, or other relative who is a very successful professional. They may not acknowledge, remember, or address the difficulty that the person has had in social situations at school, work, and community. For many parents the acceptance of their child's diagnosis occurs very indirectly, often through educating others about ways that have been found to foster their child's development and ways that accentuate their child's difficulties. Some teachers and parents dismiss the information, ignoring the insights that have been offered, while others are very appreciative of learning about ways in which they can facilitate the child's success.

It is in these experiences, where sharing the diagnosis fosters their child's growth, that parents develop the confidence to use the diagnosis of Asperger's Syndrome to help build paths for success for the child. The challenge is so strong because these issues are often replayed each time the child approaches a new situation. For example, educating the child's preschool staff may have fostered the staff's roles as your child's advocates and friends. But the issue recurs with any new schools you are considering, from kindergarten to high school, or the new sports team your child is trying out for. At each stage is the hope that, since the child has made so much progress, the new programs do not need to know. This decision may be followed by tremendous feelings of disappointment and sadness if the child's attempts to connect with others are misunderstood by their teachers or peers, leading to social isolation or even punitive responses.

Parents understandably will ask about the long-term effect of sharing the diagnosis of Asperger's Syndrome with others. The diagnosis is too new to answer that definitively. One can guess that if the child presents with primarily internalizing problems, they may come across professionals who discount the diagnosis, friends who may never need to know, and sensitive teachers who will appreciate knowing so that they can foster the child's success in all aspects of his education. These children may seek counseling to help them develop more adaptive ways to cope with the anxiety they experience in relationship to the social and performance aspects of school, perhaps including medication. For the child who displays externalizing behaviors, the diagnosis will play an important role in helping others understand his impulsive and, at times, disruptive behavior.

Regardless of what diagnostic labels the parents use, the challenge will remain to find the best ways to help facilitate the child's ability to communicate with his peers, develop positive relationships, and experience success in the choices he makes in school, play, and work. We expect that parents will choose to use a diagnostic label when they feel it will help rather than hinder their ability to attain these goals. We recognize that many parents may hesitate to use the label for fear that their child will be labeled and prejudged, leading to lower expectations by teachers or programs not willing to work with their child. In our experience, these fears rarely transpire but it is important for parents to discuss them in order to gain acceptance.

The following vignette was chosen to illustrate yet another mother's journey to becoming an advocate for her child.

Sarah's story

After eleven years being a parent to a child with Asperger's, I have so many stories in mind. My difficulty is telling about one or two snapshots from the whole dusty album.

I will start on an ordinary but hardly typical day last week. My son had an appointment for allergy testing. He has suffered for years from skin rashes and nasal congestion. But he has such a profound aversion to needles and injections, even if he could tolerate testing, I thought to myself, how would he ever be able to go for the regular series of desensitization shots? This was one of many instances when one parent responsibility, for his health, conflicted with my ongoing parent assignment, to manage his Asperger's Syndrome.

How had I arrived at the point where this trip to the doctor's office was even possible? The answer encapsulates the whole journey. First I learned to love him. This sounds odd to me even today. But my son was not an easily comforted baby. If he was too stimulated by light or by noise he couldn't accept the nursing or rocking that might calm another baby. I began to feel unequal to being his mother. Maybe we weren't a good fit.

Parenthood was turning into the ultimate Catch-22, total responsibility for the child with zero control over him. I felt this acutely at the wedding of my husband's sister held when my son was eighteen months old. By then I knew the little guy hated lights and buttons. I knew I could not make him like them.

So when we were told to be dressed in full regalia two hours before the ceremony for the family photo shoot, I had a powerful foreboding. But my experiences and intuitions did not have much weight against the prevailing social pressures. On went the dress shirt, off went the flash bulbs. My son howled, I fled the scene and missed most of marriage festivities. The looks followed me out, as on a crowded airplane, could she get him to be quiet! I was frustrated, embarrassed, and angry with everyone, my wild son, my extended family, and the guests I never would meet.

I also felt the stirring of a new resolve to trust my own instincts. Clearly, I had an extraordinary, sensitive child. We were feeling our way towards closeness with each other. We both enjoyed quiet afternoons when I could read while he carefully lined up his dinosaur figures in some precise taxonomy only he saw.

Hearing the diagnosis of Asperger's Syndrome was both alarming and confirming at once. No parent wants to hear the word autism associated in any way with his or her child. Yet the diagnosis let me focus on what I needed to help my son and get myself off the hook. He wasn't a bad boy and I wasn't a bad mother. Also I realized that the discovery of an Asperger child meant I belonged to an Asperger family. My son's therapist would identify my husband as having Asperger's Syndrome: newly aware, my husband and I found that our older son has nonverbal learning disabilities as well.

So last week my youngest son and I roll into the allergy clinic. I left plenty of time that morning for my son to finish his morning rituals without hurry, time in bed with the dog, the usual cartoons, the Pop Tarts, and Prozac. He left prepared and informed about what was going to happen. I had given him answers to his questions, short answers when he could not process a lot of information, and long answers when he wanted to fill in all the details of the picture.

I felt almost smug. My predictions came true for my son; the skin scratch tests hurt no more than the thorns do when we pick blueberries, though the subsequent itching and stinging started to overload his sensory tolerance. Still, he was able to do his funny show-biz routines while I fanned him. We were coping together. He trusted me, I felt proud of him.

Then the doctor started talking false negatives. It seems that for every scratch test negative, an injection of a stronger concentration needs to be given. Real shots, seven of them in a row. We hit the most dreaded contingency: the new thing. I did not know about the shots beforehand. I could immediately feel the waves of confusion and worry come over my son as he asked, "Will it hurt?" And the doctor gave false hope, "Not much."

In walks the nurse with a tray of syringes like a Grade B horror movie. Still, my son tried to cooperate with the program, sat on my lap, held still. But then the nurse said "I won't lie to you, this is going to hurt a lot," and swiftly, cunningly, gave the first shot. All of a sudden, my son and I were hurtled back to the very beginning, him howling and flailing, me trying to restrain him but knowing he needed to be left alone.

"If it was my kid he would have had all seven shots by now," the nurse said after a brief interval of this. And then everything cleared up again for me. The time for reason was long past. This was my kid, not hers. I asked her to let us be alone for a while. My son pulled his T-shirt over his knees and curled into a ball.

I went to speak to the doctor. I reminded her that my son has Asperger's Syndrome and that the testing no longer could work. What did she suggest we do? Finally, she agreed that she could mix the serum by an educated guess without more tests. As so many times before, I had advocated for my son and I had gotten accommodations.

My son's recovery, which might have taken days in the past, only took about an hour. All he needed was to lose the nurse and to have a juice smoothie and a pastry. He was content to go to his art camp in the afternoon.

But as he gets older I am grappling with another phase of parenthood – what if I'm not always there? This question is especially poignant for a parent with a child who has Asperger's Syndrome. Their troubles, such as asking for help, or finding out someone's expectations of them, make growing up and becoming independent all the more challenging than usual.

Here his father is a great support. After all, my husband made a good life for himself with far less understanding or intervention than our child has had. He found me, didn't he?

Summary

This chapter has shown that there are many different feelings parents may experience when coming to terms with a diagnosis like Asperger's Syndrome. Coupled with these feelings are the behaviors and actions parents take to help themselves, their family, and the child. Though no two journeys are exactly alike, there are common themes and struggles that many parents experience. The stages outlined in this chapter can help normalize the wide range of emotions and feelings that surface for parents whose child is newly diagnosed. It is important to remember that any individual may or may not go through all the different stages and may experience them in a different order. Some parents may even get stuck in one stage due to any one of a number of factors. As demonstrated in many of the case examples, it is common for mothers and fathers to be at different stages of acceptance and this difference can in some cases lead to marital stress. It can be very difficult for parents to analyze and deal effectively with the stresses when they are so fully immersed in the immediate situation. Knowing where and when to turn for help and having the support and acknowledgment that their experience is valid are critical parts of what the parents need to "refuel" and keep moving forward.

We hope that the stories shared in this chapter can help remind parents that they are not alone. Others have and will continue to grapple with similar issues and strive to do their very best for their child despite the many challenges they face. Normalizing these struggles and accepting that the road to understanding the complexities of a child with Asperger's Syndrome is ongoing and takes a new turn with each developmental stage is the task of every parent. In fact, adjusting to the changes and growth in one's child is often the greatest challenge for all parents.

Part Two

Interventions

CHAPTER 6

Paths of Intervention

From Traditional to Alternative

The most common question from parents of children with Asperger's Syndrome is whether they are doing everything they possibly can to help their child. In this chapter we will explore a wide range of interventions that both parents and professionals may consider at different points in the child's development. The chapter does not focus on interventions targeted specifically at young children with Asperger's Syndrome since those interventions are discussed in greater detail throughout the remainder of this book. Instead, the chapter examines the ways in which more traditional and alternative interventions may be helpful for a child with Asperger's Syndrome and his family at different stages of his development, and provides some information about the growing body of alternative interventions. The chapter also contains a section on when medication may be helpful. Since the authors are not physicians, and the practice of medication therapy is changing rapidly, we will not recommend specific drugs but rather we will explore what to think about when determining if one should see a child psychiatrist for a medication consultation.

Individual psychotherapy for children with Asperger's Syndrome

Individual play therapy is a form of treatment that is familiar to many parents. Some may feel that there is a stigma to having a child in therapy but many are relieved to have a professional involved, someone who they believe can play a significant role in furthering their child's development. Therefore, an important question for parents of children with Asperger's Syndrome is whether they should be seeking such services for their child. Most experts in the field have concluded that traditional, intensive, insight-oriented psychotherapy is not that helpful for children with Asperger's Syndrome (Klin and Volkmar 2000; Palombo 2001). The first reason is that traditional psychotherapy is based on the assumption that the child's difficulties are due in part to early childhood experiences in which the child's basic needs were not met. The goal of therapy would be to provide the child with a nurturing relationship in which earlier issues regarding safety, security, mastery, and attachment could be played out with a therapist who would help him recreate a better sense of self and thereby enhance his relationships with others. However, as we have discussed throughout the book, the difficulties in communication and social interactions that are experienced by a child with Asperger's Syndrome are caused by predetermined neurodevelopmental differences, not by early childhood experiences.

The second reason why this modality has limited effectiveness with this group is that the difficulties that the children have with pragmatic language and their inability to view themselves in relationship to others are barriers to effective psychotherapy. Traditional insight therapy is dependent on the child's ability to express to the clinician his thoughts and experiences through play, verbalizations, and the expressions of emotions. When a child with Asperger's Syndrome tells a story it is often a reenactment of a segment of a previous event, favorite movie, or book rather than an expression of a particular conflict or issue the child is dealing with. Also, he is often unable to provide the listener with any reference to the context of the narrative, and may recount it in a rather fragmented and incongruous way. The child's discon-nected stories or facts could easily be misunderstood by a clinician who is not experienced with children with Asperger's Syndrome as signs of a very disturbed thought process. Similarly, if the clinician is not familiar with the inability of the child with Asperger's Syndrome to understand or express feelings easily, he or she might interpret his lack of expression as a sign of conflict about his primary relationships.

With that said, individual therapy may be helpful for school age children when the therapist is attuned to how children with AS experience the world differently and can provide structured support to the child, utilizing concrete, visual help to understand his social world. The school age child may feel over-whelmed by feelings of frustration at not being able to do an activity "perfectly," or provide the answer to a worldwide problem like air pollution. He may have feelings of loneliness and depression over feeling rejected by peers he thinks do not want to be with him. The therapist can help the child learn more productive ways to express what he is experiencing rather than

throwing tantrums, isolating himself, and finding ways to avoid any poten-
tially stressful situations.

The individual therapist can also provide a valuable role in helping the
parents understand, monitor, advocate for, and meet the special needs of their
child. Therapists can also learn from the parents, since no one has a better
sense of the child's daily stresses and pleasures. The clinician also needs to be
aware of the other modalities the child may benefit from and be willing to
help the parents prioritize these interventions. A therapist attuned to the
needs of a child with Asperger's Syndrome realizes that collaboration with
teachers and other professionals is essential because the child is not always an
accurate reporter of his daily experiences, nor can he easily generalize what he
has learned across settings. He may be great at reporting why he thinks a
teacher is unfair but leave out of his story what he did to push away children
he thought were staring at him in the classroom. The more *collaborative* the
therapist is with the individuals involved in the child's education, the more
likely it is that the child will receive consistent messages across environments.
It is our hope that as more child therapists develop a working understanding
of Asperger's Syndrome they will take a more active role in serving this
population and responding to the needs of both the child and his family.

When might it be helpful for the parents to see a therapist?

Families cope with having a child with special needs in many different ways.
Many factors can contribute to how parents cope with these demands and
impact their decision to seek outside help. Thus, answering this complicated
question varies from parent to parent and from family to family. It is helpful
for all parents to understand some of the common stresses of raising a child
with Asperger's Syndrome. These stresses may lead a family to pursue a
support group or a counselor for help with parenting in areas that can be challenging to all parents, but may be intensified in a child with Asperger's
Syndrome, such as toilet training, sleep behavior, safety issues, or limit setting.
Parents may also want help in understanding and gaining perspective on the
stress that having a child with AS may place on the child's siblings, the family,
and the parents' relationship as a couple. There can be many aspects of their
child that they adore and cherish, but having these feelings does not negate
the feelings of frustration they may experience on a daily basis or the stresses
and demands that having a child with AS can place on the family. A clinician
that has had experience working with young children with Asperger's

Syndrome and/or their families can be a very helpful resource as the parents travel this journey.

Research confirms the significant stress experienced by parents of children with Autistic Spectrum Disorders. In addition to the stresses associated with parenting all children they feel that they have the additional demands of being their child's teacher and advocate (Dunst 1999; Gallagher 1992; Seligman and Darling 1997). If the child is going to different interventions outside of the school it is the parents who have to take the child to these services which occur at the same time as their paid jobs or when their other children need to be cared for. They also are in charge of implementing the behavioral interventions the child's teachers or clinicians have recommended. Parents may experience incredible anxiety if they feel they must intervene with their young child every waking moment because if they don't they will be passing up a critical period in their child's development.

Not surprisingly, most of the research on parents of children with Autistic Spectrum Disorders has found the impact to be greater on mothers than on fathers (National Research Council 2001). The mothers report feeling more responsible for the child's problems, more stressed by the task of balancing the daily demands of the child with the demands of the family, and more anxious about what lies ahead in their child's future (Bristol, Gallagher and Schopler 1988; Koegel *et al.* 1992). Research on fathers of children who are on the autistic spectrum found that, in contrast to fathers of neurotypical children, they experienced stress not in relationship to how they viewed themselves as fathers or partners but rather in regard to their ability to financially support their child's care. The fathers also reported frustration regarding the limits that their child placed on their ability to participate in family social events (Rodrigue, Geffken and Morgan 1992).

Knowing that mothers and fathers often experience stress in different areas, it is easy to imagine the additional strain on a couple when a parent feels unsupported by their partner emotionally and/or concretely in the care of their child. Not surprisingly, Milgram and Atzil (1988) found in couples with autistic spectrum children that those parents who felt that they shared responsibility for their child reported higher marital satisfaction. In the OASIS survey of 327 parents of children with Asperger's Syndrome regarding their relationship, 70 percent of the parents felt that having a child with Asperger's Syndrome placed additional stress on their relationship. The parents were split 50–50 in response to the question of whether or not their relationship had grown stronger or weaker following their child's diagnosis (Bashe and Kirby 2001).

Couples therapy may provide parents with a safe and supportive setting to explore what they are experiencing both as parents and as a couple, and develop more adaptive ways to communicate as a couple; it also provides an opportunity for them to practice these skills without being critical of their partner. (This goal can be a little trickier when one of the parents has Asperger's Syndrome as well.) Parents have to decide who will take on the various responsibilities of taking the child to his ongoing appointments, supervising play dates, fighting over health insurance bills, and researching new programs. The couples with the highest ratings of marital satisfaction are those who feel the most supported for their family roles, whatever those roles are.

One finding that is very common in the families we have worked with is the eventual recognition that one parent may have similar qualities as the child with Asperger's Syndrome. In the OASIS survey of parents of children with Asperger's Syndrome, over a third reported that one of the parents had been diagnosed with a range of disorders – for example, depression, ADHD, OCD, or Asperger's Syndrome (Bashe and Kirby 2001). Having a partner with undiagnosed Asperger's Syndrome can challenge a couple's relationship and parenting. These challenges are vividly described in the growing body of first-person accounts. In Liane Holliday Willey's book *Pretending to be Normal* (1999), she shares with the reader how her daughter's diagnosis of Asperger's Syndrome shed light on her own AS. In her more recent book *Asperger Syndrome in the Family: Redefining Normal*, she paints a picture of what it is like for a partner and parent who has Asperger's Syndrome herself to have children who range on the spectrum from neurotypical development to AS. Similarly, in Gisela and Christopher Slater-Walker's book *An Asperger Marriage* (2002) and Maxine Aston's *The Other Half of Asperger Syndrome*, the authors explore the challenges and gifts that Asperger's Syndrome poses for their partners and their roles as parents.

Should a parent recognize that they too share characteristics of AS, then some of the same roadblocks we spoke about in terms of individual psychotherapy for children have the potential of occurring in adult therapy or in couple therapy. For example, if the therapist is not able to assess how each partner's strengths and difficulties in relating and communicating contribute to their relationship as a couple and their capacity to parent, overinterpretations or misinterpretations of behavior and communication can occur. Similarly, the therapist may expect the parent with AS traits to be able to interpret and be insightful to the emotional world of the spouse when they also have lots of difficulty doing just that.

Many parents appear to go through the same stages of denial, grief, coping, and adaptation on learning that their partner has AS as they did when they learned of their child's diagnosis. However, this situation feels like a double whammy – more than they can sometimes handle. They may be exhausted and feel extremely frustrated about having to put as much effort into communicating with their partner as they do with their child. As one parent put it:

> It just doesn't seem fair. At least my child is getting the early intervention which I see making a difference. My husband has had no help and I feel like it's up to me to constantly have to facilitate his roles as a husband, parent, professional, and friend, leaving no time to take care of my own needs.

They may initially lose sight of what attracted them to their partners, now that they are seeing them through the lens of Asperger's Syndrome. If a parent experiences any of the feelings described here, it can be very helpful to have a therapist to support and sort through the complexity of the situation.

Is family therapy something we should be considering?

The literature has addressed the need to be attuned to the impact that having a child with Autistic Spectrum Disorders may have on the child's siblings. Research has reported that siblings' lives can be disrupted in various ways. Siblings may have a wide range of feelings including sadness, anger, and concern but this stress does not appear to reflect any serious psychiatric problem, and the children can even benefit from their experiences (Konidaris 1997). The key thing to remember is that the situation may change depending on the developmental level and issues of both the child and his or her sibling (Glasberg 2000). For example, a younger brother's skill in reciting Monty Python may be funny to an older sister when she is ten but terribly embarrassing when she is 13. On the other hand, a child with Asperger's Syndrome may be incredibly affectionate and nurturing to a younger sibling, but things often begin to change when the younger sibling stops being the trustworthy follower and starts expressing her own view about what she wants to play with and how. For many parents, the differences in children with Asperger's Syndrome become most evident when younger siblings' capacity to engage in conversation and play surpasses that of the older sibling.

A family therapist attuned to Asperger's Syndrome may be helpful if you feel conflicted over whether to tell your other children about AS, if you feel that the demands of having a child with AS results in short-changing the rest of the family, or if you feel like these issues are becoming a never-ending source of conflict within the family. A family therapist with a working understanding of AS can help you decide when the issues you are struggling with are related to your child's special needs or when they may be a signal of other underlying family system issues. The therapist may be very helpful in fostering the sibling's ability to talk with family members and friends about AS and help normalize some of the feelings the sibling may have. Insight from someone other than the parent can really help the child understand the issues instead of thinking that the parent is just trying to "make excuses" or "play favorites" on behalf of the child with AS.

Where else might one look for support?

What we know from research about stress and coping in families of children with medical and developmental problems is that the more satisfied families are with the support they receive from family members, friends, and professionals the less stressed they feel in their role as parents (Shonkoff *et al.* 1992). We have found that parents turn to different sources for support at different times. Some parents have found informal community based support groups to be very helpful. These groups have been started in clinics that specialize in AS, in the special education department of the local school district, and in community based organizations for parents of children with special needs in general and Asperger's Syndrome specifically. Most of the groups for parents of children with Asperger's Syndrome are targeted at school age children. While some parents of younger children find it helpful to hear about different interventions and school based programs, others find it overwhelming to listen to some of the challenges of older children. Other potential sources of support are the programs for children through the school district, or from OT, speech and language, and mental health professionals. Many of these programs do not have an inbuilt, routine parent component, therefore a parent may need to solicit information or suggest that this be included. Some clinicians have come up with creative ways to serve parents when it is brought to their attention that the parents are seeking these kind of services. Many of the parent support groups begin from the informal discussions between parents that regularly take place in the waiting rooms of their children's therapists.

Other parents have found the online chat rooms, such as those found through OASIS, to be very helpful. Most of the parents who we have worked with talk about a process in which they initially immerse themselves for hours reviewing the literature, signing on to chat rooms, and searching libraries for the newest article or book about Asperger's Syndrome. At some point they identify the need to take a break, stop losing sleep looking for the "right answer," and focus on what they and their children need to make it through the week. As they become more comfortable with the diagnosis and their child's current needs they may return to these web sites for information and feedback from fellow parents about a specific topic. With time they begin to realize how different two children with Asperger's Syndrome can be from each other and how different their family's needs may be from those who offer on-line advice.

What about an individual therapist for me, the parent? I feel like I am taking care of everyone else's needs but my own

Many of the mothers in our group program have found individual therapy to be a very helpful source of support, especially when they cannot turn to their partner for empathy for their parenting role because he too has traits that resemble Asperger's Syndrome. As we have said, having a child is both a rewarding and stressful experience for all parents. All parents experience at some point or another what Selma Fraiberg (1980) called the "Ghost in the Nursery," negative parts of one's own childhood being replayed in the ways one interacts with one's own children. This process is especially challenging when one has a child who responds to a parent's attempt to be a "good" parent with responses that could be easily misunderstood as being rejecting, disrespectful, or embarrassing. As one mother put it:

> I can't believe how much I sound like my mother when I blow up at my child for not saying "please" and "thank you." It's as if it's O.K. that he doesn't make eye contact or have a friend to play with as long as he's polite.

Another parent was reminded of her own childhood when she began to list all of the different activities that she had enrolled her child in. As she began to describe her week, she had an instant flash of how much she resented her mother for making her take so many after-school classes when what she wanted most to do was hang around at their house, play with the animals, and read. For the first time she understood how her mother must have felt, trying to do what she thought was best for her child yet receiving only feelings of anger and rejection in return. In the following scenario it is the father who was replaying his childhood issues with his AS daughter. He was a very competitive swimmer throughout college and wanted to be able to share his love of swimming with his daughter. He could not see that even though she enjoyed swimming and was very good at it, the competitive focus of swim team made it an extremely stressful and anxiety provoking experience for her. She would repeatedly end up getting sick in the pool or refuse to dive in when the gun went off. Not until the daughter began to stay home from school complaining of stomach aches was the father willing to explore this issue with his child's therapist. With the support of the therapist he was able to accept his wife's observation that he was unwilling to hear his daughter telling them that she hated participating in swim team. She especially hated going to competitions where she felt very confused by the different style swimming pools and club settings. He had thought that he was finding something that she could feel proud about. The father was giving his daughter the same lectures he dreaded hearing from his father about the value of working hard and being competitive. It took months of therapy before he could see that even though he found the swim team to be a wonderful source of support, exercise, and structure, it was having just the opposite effect on his daughter. The family finally came up with a compromise in which the daughter found a swim club in which the children swam for pleasure but did not participate in any competitions. "Miraculously," once the competitive pressure was dropped, she began to explore new strokes and excelled in diving. What the father had to work on was not seeing her progress as a sign that she should return to the competitive track.

An individual psychotherapist who is experienced with Asperger's Syndrome can help a parent understand why they have such strong negative reactions towards some of their child's behaviors while being oblivious to others. Individual therapy may also provide parents with a special time in which the attention is directed towards what they would like to see in their own development and what needs to happen for that to occur. It may help the parent refocus on the ongoing challenge of finding a way to address the needs of the family without losing sight of their own needs in the process. As discussed throughout the book, parenting a child with AS can be overwhelming and can impact the parent's sense of efficacy. Parents may find individual therapy a helpful place to discuss their feelings of depression, anxiety, and self-worth.

What about medication for Asperger's Syndrome?

All you need do is watch late night television and you will be flooded with advertisements for different medications that seem like they could be helpful for everyone! Yet there is no medication that has been developed, tested, and recommended specifically for the treatment of children with Asperger's Syndrome. When you consider that children with Asperger's Syndrome can look so different from each other it is not surprising that no single treatment exists. What does exist are medications for specific symptoms that can seriously impact the child's capacity to function both at home and in the school, such as impulsivity, attention difficulties, anxiety, and explosive behavior. For example, a child with Asperger's Syndrome, whose impulsive behavior makes it difficult for him to sit still for longer than five minutes in a classroom, may see a child psychiatrist to determine if a medication is appropriate for his attention difficulties. Another child who has trouble sleeping at night because of obsessive fears of being bitten by a poisonous spider, or a compulsive need to check all of the locks on the door several times throughout the night, might benefit from a medication to reduce his anxiety or compulsive behaviors. Medication may also be helpful for the child who overreacts with explosive behavior to events that are different from what he expected. One key prerequisite in determining if your child should be referred for medication is to have clear documentation of the efforts made at the school or at home to change the behaviors. If you feel that steps have been taken to address your child's special needs and the child continues to exhibit the behavior of concern despite these efforts, then a referral to a child psychiatrist may be warranted. You want to make sure that the child psychiatrist or developmental pediatrician has experience working with young children with Asperger's Syndrome so that your child's behaviors can be understood and treated appropriately.

The child psychiatrist should be able to clearly express which behaviors the medication is expected to help, which it will not effect, and possible side effects. The child psychiatrist will take a thorough developmental and medical history, review past assessments, and may require certain blood or cardiac tests to establish a baseline of the child prior to taking the medication. We strongly recommend that parents sharpen their observation skills so that they can report on their child's behavior prior to taking the medication and once on medication. We believe that it is prudent to make only one major therapeutic change at a time in the child's life. For example, if the child begins occupational therapy, starts a therapeutic group, receives an aide in the classroom, goes on a special diet, and begins a new medication it will be impossible to know which factor contributed to any observed change in the child. Some parents have told us that they don't care what the specific beneficial modality was because they are so relieved to see any progress with their child. They are not willing to forgo an intervention as long as it doesn't exacerbate their child's difficulties. The only caution we give is that if you start four interventions at the same time and have a negative reaction you will not know what to attribute it to and how to change things. Similarly if you have a good response you will not know what contributed to it and what to continue or focus your efforts on.

The other issue you should be aware of is that there are very few standardized studies on any medications for young children. Not surprisingly, it is hard to get parents interested in volunteering their children and difficult to find university ethics committees willing to run such studies. This is not to deny that there is a growing body of clinical reports on specific types of medication that have been helpful for certain behaviors in school age children. Like all of the interventions we have explored in this book, prescribing medication is not a pure science but often a trial and error process that works to varying degrees for different children and for varying periods of time. Some good news: due to the increase in the number of children with Autistic Spectrum Disorders being prescribed medications, the National Institute of Mental Health has identified this as a high priority and initiated large scale, multisite collaborative investigations to look more closely at this issue (Martin, Patzer and Volkmar 2000). Since medication typically is not recommended as a first step in intervention for young children with Asperger's Syndrome, we have chosen not to review the wide range of medications prescribed for older children with Autistic Spectrum Disorders. *The OASIS Guide to Asperger Syndrome* provides a good review of this subject (Bashe and Kirby 2001).

Dietary interventions

Many parents have heard or shared anecdotes about vitamin and mineral supplements improving the symptoms of Autistic Spectrum Disorders. There are anecdotal reports describing positive changes in specific behavior problems such as attention difficulties, disrupted sleep, asthma, or allergies which, when they occur, can exacerbate the child's already existing behavioral difficulties. We are not suggesting that you follow any of these dietary changes. But if you do look into them we want you to be sure to do it under the guidance of a medical professional attuned to your child's nutritional needs as well as the current body of knowledge of the positive and/or negative effects of such intervention, such as a developmental pediatrician, an allergist, or a pediatric gastrointestinal specialist. The specialist will review your child's diet and may conduct a laboratory assessment of your child's vitamin and mineral levels. The Defeat Autism Now! (DAN) Consensus Report (Baker and Pangborn 1999) provides a good review of the current hypotheses in this area and ongoing research on these issues.

Vitamins and Minerals: One of the most widely explored hypotheses pertains to malabsorption problems and nutritional deficiencies. These studies suggest that intestinal disorders and chronic gastrointestinal inflammation may reduce the child's ability to absorb some essential nutrients. They propose that this may be of special importance to children with Autistic Spectrum Disorders because of the role that these nutrients play in the brain's development. The most common vitamin supplement used by children with autism is vitamin B-complex and magnesium (which is needed to make these vitamins effective) because of the role that the B-complex vitamins play in creating enzymes needed for the brain. Other studies have suggested that cod liver supplements, because they are rich in vitamins A and D, have resulted in improvements in eye contact and behavior of children with autism.

Peptides: Individuals with autism have also been found to have a high level of allergies to certain types of foods or chemicals. While allergies alone are not seen as a cause of autism they may exacerbate a child's behavioral problems. Studies conducted in both the United States and England have shown that children with autism have elevated levels of peptides in their urine, suggesting an inability to break down peptides from food that contains gluten and casein. Gluten is found in wheat, oats, and rye and casein is in dairy products. The theory is that incomplete breakdown of the peptides causes disruption in the biochemical processes of the brain, affecting the brain's function. As with vitamin intervention, it is crucial that parents consult with a physician who can discuss with them the type of behavioral changes they may expect to see, how to implement such a diet, and how to make sure that their child gets the nutrition he needs. We want to remind you that the goals of these dietary changes have not been presented as able to alter the diagnosis but to help reduce behaviors that are creating additional challenges and stresses for the child and his family.

Secretin: The last intervention we will review involves Secretin, which is a hormone produced by the small intestine to aid in the digestion process. In 1996, following a case study of a young boy who was given Secretin for a gastrointestinal test and showed improvement in some of his autistic symptoms, a slew of cases reported similar findings. These reports led the National Institute of Child and Human Development (NICHD) to conduct a multisite study on this intervention. The study has reported no significant improvements in the core diagnostic areas compared with children who received a placebo. It is also important to remember that the FDA has only approved Secretin for a single dose; there is no literature on the safety of repeated doses over time (Autism Society of America 1993).

Conclusion

The number of different therapies and interventions available these days to families who are in need is quite large. The few presented in this chapter are certainly not an exhaustive list but an attempt to introduce some of the more common therapies that we have found helpful to parents and school age children. We strongly recommend that parents become advocates for themselves and their families and develop a relationship with the care provider that feels trusting and safe. Sometimes a person must interview several clinicians before they find someone who is a good fit for their family. When parents are feeling particularly vulnerable about their child or their situation, it is hard to advocate and do the research to find the help they need. Support from family, pediatricians, other clinicians, and teachers can make the difference in directing parents to the best resources. It is also incredibly important that parents prioritize their needs and do not overload themselves by seeking too many different interventions at once, possibly getting contradictory messages and making it hard to know what is responsible for any observed change. A very wise parent once told us that in order to determine what to do next she would evaluate where her child's greatest source of distress was and then focus the interventions on this area. Parents similarly need to care for their own needs and the stress on other family members. We hope this chapter has elucidated some of the possible forms of support available.

The next part of the book will take a closer look at interventions we feel are attuned to the developmental needs of the young child with Asperger's Syndrome and his family.

CHAPTER 7

Parent–Child Therapy

An Intervention for Building Relationships

Lori Bond

When parents learn that their child has a diagnosis of Asperger's Syndrome they may have many questions and concerns. Parent–child therapy, the topic of this chapter, can be a helpful intervention to parents as they try to make sense of all of the new information that they have just received from an evaluation. Through parent–child therapy, the therapist and parents work together to understand the child's challenges and explore ways to facilitate the child's social, communication, and play abilities. The goal of parent–child therapy is to provide a setting for parents to enhance their understanding of their child and to gain support. Parent–child therapy is sometimes referred to as dyadic therapy because the therapist might meet with the parent(s) or with the parent(s) and child together.

Overview of parent–child dyadic therapy

The first goal of dyadic therapy is to provide emotional support to parents who are trying to understand the meaning of the diagnosis and the myriad of feelings that can occur when the diagnosis has been made. Parents might express confusion regarding different clinical terms they heard during a conference with a diagnostician, or they feel unsure about what to do next in terms of therapies that were suggested. The second goal of parent–child therapy is to create pleasurable opportunities for the parent and child to play together, thereby facilitating the parent's understanding of his/her child. Play provides the context for dyadic work because it is through play that children develop reasoning skills, flexible thinking, emotional understanding, and perspective taking (Leslie 1987; Piaget 1962). While children with AS may show disorganized or rigid play (as described in Chapter 2), they do like to play and can enjoy doing so with others. Finally, the third goal is for the parent(s) and therapist to identify and practice ways to develop the child's play, and relational and communication skills. These are often the skills that do not come as easily to the child with AS, and parent–child therapy offers a structured setting for the child to practice these skills.

Who provides parent–child therapy?

Parent–child therapy is most often conducted by a child psychologist, clinical social worker, licensed marriage and family therapist, or child psychiatrist. Parents will want to choose a clinician who has a good understanding of AS and knowledge of what is typical for young children in their play, behavior, and emotional development. The therapist can help parents understand what behaviors might be typical for their child's age and temperament and what behaviors might be related to the diagnosis. The therapist and parents will pull together all of the information that they have about the child and explore what strategies might be helpful to support the child's play and social adaptability. Choosing a therapist is always a personal decision and finding someone who you feel you can trust or has a good understanding of your child and who will advocate for you is essential.

When would a family benefit from parent–child therapy?

Parent–child therapy is often helpful following a diagnostic evaluation. Parents can have many emotional reactions to the diagnosis and questions about diagnostic terms (much of the diagnostic information can seem complicated). Parents might read about AS once they hear this diagnosis and then feel disheartened by the information or puzzled by the ways that their child does not fit what is in the books. Furthermore, an evaluation can generate many different recommendations, as is often the case when several different disciplines were involved in the diagnostic process, and parents may feel confused about what direction to take. Parents may have questions about which therapies should take priority, how many times a week particular therapies are needed, and who should provide the services. Or the child might participate in several different interventions, and parents find it helpful to talk with someone who is knowledgeable about the needs of the child with AS and can think more broadly about "the big picture," and how to assess the child's response to different interventions. Importantly, the therapist should develop an understanding of the unique needs of each child in planning for and monitoring treatment.

Additionally, parents often have specific behavioral concerns, such as how to intervene when their child struggles with transitions, seems rigid, or acts out in a social situation. While a diagnostic evaluation can provide the framework for parents to begin to understand the reasons for these behaviors, the ongoing relationship with the therapist helps parents identify specific strategies to use with their child to support coping.

Sometimes following a diagnosis, parents can have conflicted feelings about whether they want to share the diagnosis with family members or friends. The therapist and parents can identify ways to describe the child's difficulties to others and respond to questions that others may have. This can be a scary, painful experience and having a safe place to explore these feelings and have these feelings normalized is important.

Parent–child therapy can also be helpful down the road after a family has digested the diagnosis and when the child is at a new point in his development. Parents might have questions about the meaning of new behaviors they observe in their child and there may be new transitions in the child's life, such as kindergarten entry. For example, there may be questions about what type of setting is best for the child, how the child will handle unstructured playground time, and what resources to request from a school district. Parents might also observe their child's developing interest in pretend play and increasing enthusiasm for bringing the parent into his play, and want to expand upon it. In addition, some parents may read about play based interventions and wish to learn more about it. As described earlier in this book, Stanley Greenspan and Serena Wieder (1998) describe "circles of communication," which is the child's ability to engage in extended back and forth interactions with another person. The field is evolving and many parents have found this work valuable as they think about what skills they would like their child to develop.

What are the roles of the therapist?

The therapist has multiple roles, including support, collaborator, model, facilitator, and advocate. The therapist provides *support* as she listens to the parents describe many different feelings about the child's behaviors and experiences. Perhaps there are uncertainties and fears about their child's development and future. Parents might worry about how their child's difficulties will affect his ability to have friends, be accepted, and develop a positive self-esteem. Parents might observe how their child appears no different from any other child, yet at other times the child's challenges seem so apparent. As therapy progresses, parents may want to talk about how the child's difficulties affect other children in the family. For example, parents might feel unsure about setting different expectations and making different accommodations for their child with AS. Often it can seem overwhelming for parents to take in all the new information about their child with AS, plan for and schedule therapies, and then find the energy and time to meet the individual and changing needs of other children in the family. Each of these issues can surface at different times during the therapy.

As *collaborators* and *shared observers*, the therapist and parents are developing an understanding of the child and together identifying goals for intervention. They may share their observations of the child and find ways to intervene with challenging behaviors or provide predictability that helps the child feel calm. For example, a child who is having difficulty separating from a parent when taken to preschool might benefit from a Social Story that includes pictures and a simple narrative of a consistent separation routine (Social Stories were developed by Carol Gray for use with older children with AS and recently adapted to address the needs of younger children). A child who tantrums when he cannot view a favorite video may respond positively to an activity board that provides a schedule for the day and several options for favorite activities. As another example, a parent may read about behavior modification techniques and have questions about how these techniques might be used with their child. Finally, the therapist and parent might identify what to do during a play date or outing with friends when the child acts out.

As a *model* for the parent, the therapist works with the child to develop different strategies that facilitate the child's relational and play skills. At times, the therapist might describe to the parent what has been helpful for the child. For example, the therapist might say, "I think I am talking too fast to Sam. I am going to pause, speak more slowly, and use fewer words." Another example might be, "He seems better able to play with us when we build on an experience that is known to him, like going to a carwash." These reflections can help the parent begin making sense of what they are observing as well as provide helpful interventions for use at home. This process provides parents with concrete strategies to practice with the child. In subsequent meetings with the therapist, the parent shares his/her perceptions of the effectiveness of these strategies.

As a *facilitator*, the therapist supports the parents as they play with their child and fosters mutual pleasure in doing an activity together. The therapist can identify what the parent is doing that facilitates the child's sustained engagement and reciprocity, and offers suggestions to move the play along and help the parent and child converse. The clinician encourages the parents to share their observations of the child during play. It is useful to set time aside during the session to share these observations. This shared communication creates a process for building play and interaction skills.

As an *advocate* (resource), the therapist can help the parents determine which services may be most helpful, their availability, and ways to obtain them. The therapist may also consult with school staff and/or other professionals to develop a shared understanding of the child and implement consistent interventions. For example, the therapist can educate a teacher about the child's tendency to feel anxious when there is unstructured time or when routines change.

Table 7.1 Role of the therapist in parent–child therapy

- Support: clarify the diagnosis; explore parents' questions, concerns, and feelings about the news
- Collaborator and shared observer: develop understanding of the child's individual needs and challenges and identify interventions that are helpful to the child
- Model: therapist interacts with the child to identify strategies that facilitate the child's relational and play skills
- Facilitator: foster attunement to the child and sustained engagement in play
- Advocate/resource: referral to specialists in the area of Asperger's Syndrome in young children and build rapport with other clinicians/teachers involved in the child's care (provide consultation to schools as needed)

To illustrate these multiple roles, let's look at this example of a therapist beginning to work with a family in the context of parent–child therapy. Brice, age three-and-a-half years, and his parents were referred following a diagnostic evaluation that showed that Brice had good cognitive abilities but difficulties initiating social interactions with peers and using language in a conversational manner, and some rigid routines with play. He was scheduled to enter a regular preschool program several mornings per week as well as a communication based preschool program to provide more focused attention to his needs. His parents had requested assistance with behavioral issues, and strategies to support Brice's play and interaction skills. They had observed that he had lately seemed irritable and easily frustrated and while he sought them out for play, they felt uncertain as to how to play with him. As a first step in the therapy, information was gathered about these issues and ongoing questions about Brice's diagnosis were explored with the parents. Together, the therapist and parents observed Brice's play to learn more about his strengths and challenges. Dyadic sessions were scheduled once every other week. The therapist observed Brice in his preschool and met with his teachers to learn more about what they needed help with. The teachers requested help understanding the meaning of his screaming behavior and how to intervene; they were concerned when he wandered in and out of the classroom and had observed that he did not play with other children. After getting to know Brice and his family the therapist was able to assist the teachers to develop strategies to engage him and decrease negative behaviors.

As the facilitator, the therapist worked with Brice and his parents to develop his joint attention, communication, and pretend play skills (e.g. using toys to develop a story). The therapist modeled how to match Brice's pace and provide structure when he seemed not to know what to do next. When Brice was frustrated and screamed the therapist and parents could discuss reasons for this behavior, how it also occurred in other settings, and ways to intervene. The therapist provided support to the parents when they expressed how helpless and distressed they sometimes felt when he screamed. For example, in one session Brice neatly arranged a set of animals in a line on a table, with each animal facing forward and equally spaced. The therapist, as facilitator, suggested to the father that he and Brice offer each animal a piece of food on a plate. He removed one of the animals from the line in order to find some "food" and Brice shrieked and stomped his feet. When his father reported that he had seen this type of play before, the therapist suggested how hard it was for him to be flexible in taking in new play ideas. Sometimes even slight variations were so troubling to Brice that he reacted by screaming. Through experiences like this one the therapist and parents began to understand also that Brice did not always have the verbal abilities to manage his anxiety and negotiate a solution. The father gently wrapped his arms around Brice and simply returned the animal to its original location and offered it a piece of food. Brice visibly calmed and then repeated his father's actions with a piece of food.

Brice then moved away from the table to resume a familiar activity of putting cars into a garage and his father followed, stating that Brice had found the cars to play with again. Brice's father had intuitively recognized that Brice needed the familiar and comforting rhythm of the cars to reorganize, and perhaps to have time to assimilate what had just happened. As shared observer, the therapist and Brice's father learned the value of giving Brice the freedom to protest, time with safe limits to regain control, and permission to use comforting routines to reorganize. The challenging next step would be to develop these skills in the context of interactions with peers. This type of parent–child work lays the foundation for social interactions with peers.

As you can see the role of the therapist is multifaceted, as is the role of the parent in the work. The work together can empower parents to not only understand their child but also learn ways to foster their relationship.

The nuts and bolts of parent–child therapy

With a picture now of what parent–child (dyadic) therapy can look like, this section identifies more specifically some of the issues which the parent and therapist explore within the parent–child therapy. As noted, the first goal is for the therapist and parent to develop a shared understanding of the child in the following areas:

1. The child's language use in terms of complexity (sentence structure, vocabulary), range of ideas, and communicative intentions (share information, ask questions, express intentions, invite, show).

2. Language processing capabilities.

3. Use of nonverbal behaviors for social referencing purposes.

4. Level of symbolic play, thematic organization and capacity for representation.

5. Ability to initiate and participate in turn taking routines; complexity of turn taking routines.

6. Emotional expression (expressed pleasure in shared activity).

For example, some children will have strong expressive language skills, but the ability to participate in turn taking play might be an area of difficulty. Another child might use language for a variety of purposes, but then insist, for example, that he always be the "chef" in a restaurant and the partner is always the "patron." The child then proceeds with his plan to be the "chef," not really attending to the partner's responses to guide what he should do next. As another example, the child might respond with interest to what the partner suggests in play, but then when the partner waits for the child to carry the idea further, the child continues alone with the same play ideas but does not actively engage the partner. During a session with the parents alone or at the end of a session with the child, the therapist might describe what these different concepts mean, why they are important, and how they take on different characteristics at different stages of the child's development.

In addition, the therapist and parent may explore when the child appears confused or disorganized (which often presents as unrelated statements, phrases from a favorite video, increased motor activity, and "crashing" of toys). Together they try to assess what factors might be contributing to the child's confusion. As the therapist and parent work together at interpreting the child's behaviors they may begin to explore some of the following questions: Is the adult speaking too quickly? Is the adult allowing adequate time for the child to process the verbal input and respond? Is the adult introducing play that is too complicated for the child to grasp? Is the adult introducing too many new ideas into the play? Is the adult asking too many questions? Might the adult be more intrusive than facilitative? In sum, these questions guide the therapist and parent to consider how the child is processing information and responding in both negative and positive ways. The therapist and parent can discuss their responses to these questions to develop a working understanding of why and how the child gets stuck. In this way the therapist and parent can think together about the next step, helping the child reconnect and re-organize.

It is also important for the therapist and parent to consider the underlying meaning of the child's behavior so that the parent can anticipate what situations might be difficult for the child. For example, the child who runs into other children in the play yard might be expressing confusion about how to join a group of peers; a child who fails to comply with the teacher's directions to "clean up" may be distracted by the noise and activity of busy classroom clean-up time or not know what is expected by "clean up." A child who rarely initiates play or conversation with another child might be confused by the unpredictable social world. The therapist and parent can discuss ways to reduce the child's confusion in these situations and provide an environment that supports self-control and development of important social skills.

Table 7.2 summarizes the goals of parent–child play that will be explored in more detail in the next few sections of this chapter.

Table 7.2 Goals of parent–child play

- Develop an understanding of the child's capabilities and challenges
- Develop child's capacity for bringing ideas into the world of play and interactions with the parent
- Foster mutual pleasure in playing together
- Foster communication skills and emotional expression
- Parents learn how to interpret child's behavior (confusion, rigidity) and develop ways to cope with this behavior during play together

---

Strategies for helping children with beginning stages of play

There are many approaches to engaging children in play, and dyadic therapy creates an opportunity to explore different ways to engage your child and help him expand and elaborate his play skills. Since the focus of intervention is helping with play skills, the therapy also helps parents begin to understand the frustrations peers may feel when trying to engage their child. The experience parents have trying to "play" with their child will ultimately help them to figure out what the child will need from other care providers when looking for support for the child. A good starting point for some children is to allow the child to choose a toy and observe the child for a few moments to get a sense for what ideas he expresses and how he uses the materials (e.g. pretend play, or scripted activities such as replaying scenes from a video). The therapist may join the child by offering a simple comment about what the child is doing or imitating the child's action in some way. Sometimes it is helpful to tell the child "I am going to play with you. Let me see what you are doing" so that the child is prepared for the therapist's participation (simply sitting down next to the child may be too subtle, or immediately directing the child to perform a specific action may silence the child). Another strategy that can be helpful for some children is to offer a choice of two activities. This can sometimes help to focus a child who seems overwhelmed by too many appealing items or not quite sure how to begin. The next steps, then, are to elaborate and expand the child's play by adding a new, but related, idea to what the child has introduced. Others have written about this strategy in the areas of special education, language development, and general child psychology (Greenspan and Wieder 1998; Kohlberg and Fein 1987; McDonald 1989). Elaboration often takes the form of slight variations, and the most helpful interventions for the child with AS are those that do not aim to do too much at once. While expanding the child's play it is important to maintain attention to simplicity, structure, and pace. The following case illustrates how elaboration and expanding a child's play might occur in the context of parent–child therapy.

Timothy was a five-and-a-half-year-old boy who had been identified by the school psychologist as having features of AS. His mother was interested in more information about this diagnosis, his development, and interventions that would be most appropriate for him. She was particularly concerned about his disruptive behavior in the kindergarten classroom (such as hiding under tables and refusing certain tasks) and socialization difficulties. She was referred to parent–child therapy to help her address these concerns. During a play session together, Timothy chose a set of plastic bugs to label and move along the floor in a somewhat repetitive manner. His mother observed that he typically played in this way which was making it difficult for him to play with peers who were more interested in creative play. Since he had earlier shown interest in putting cars down a Fisher Price slide, the therapist suggested that the bugs might like to go down the slide. He smiled at this slightly silly idea, seemed to consider it for a moment, and then readily participated. The therapist counted "one, two, three" for each bug as it went down the slide and then ended with a "hooray!" He smiled broadly and joined in by handing bugs to the therapist and waiting for her to repeat the routine. This routine is fairly simplistic for a five-year-old, but the predictable and familiar scenario and salient verbal cues provided a comfortable starting point. The therapist continued the session by using the same set of bugs to act in different ways with other toys, such as going for a ride in a car and playing hide and seek. The goal was to expand Timothy's play repertoire by introducing one new idea at a time and assessing his responsiveness to these small shifts. Later in the session, when the therapist paused to see what Timothy might come up with next, he suggested that the bugs again go in the cars. The therapist playfully suggested that the bugs seem to have fun in the cars and readily joined in (rather than redirect to something new because they had done the same sequence earlier), but again added a slight variation to the theme (it had begun to "rain" and the bugs were getting "wet"). Timothy appeared confused when the therapist altered the scenario, as his verbal responses to the therapist were unrelated to the therapist's questions. The therapist concluded that perhaps her suggestions were more abstract than Timothy could assimilate and that he needed more practice with simpler themes and interaction demands.

During a subsequent individual session with mother, the therapist talked about the information gathered about Timothy after several sessions with him (specifically noting his responsiveness to structure and play that incorporated his interests). They began to understand better his world of play and the ways that they found play with others pleasurable. They also began to identify why he might be disruptive or uncertain about how to respond to the other children in the classroom. Timothy's case is a good example of how parent–child therapy can assist parents in finding ways to develop these important skills.

The important role pace plays for building play skills

Young children with Asperger's Syndrome are confused in peer group settings, often because other children play and interact at a fast pace.

The child with AS often needs the parent and therapist to start at a slow pace as they begin to guide the play and simplify for the child what the child can do to follow. The following example shows how the therapist models this technique for the parent. An almost five-year-old boy, Brian, and the therapist were "heating" a small plastic doughnut in a stove over and over again, when Brian commented that the doughnut did not seem to stay "warm." The therapist suggested that the stove (which in this case was a chair) was broken and they needed to come up with a way to "fix it." Together the therapist and Brian fixed the stove (using small tools that Brian had located nearby) and again "heated" the doughnuts, but without success. Brian and the therapist repeated their frustrating attempts to heat the doughnut in the stove that seemed always to "break." Brian appeared to take genuine pleasure in solving the problem together (he and the therapist each took a turn to call a "repairman," and then a second "repairman" when the first seemed unable to fix the stove). The play continued in this way for quite a while, with numerous repetitions of the same idea and then slight variations (need more "nails"). This child, who had attachments to unusual objects and seemingly little imagination, could readily participate in mutual problem solving and joint attention (fixing the stove together), shared emotion (frustration when the efforts were unsuccessful), and interest in a new idea. For this child, there were several key factors that allowed him to maintain shared interest, take turns, and enjoy creativity in play. The therapist did not rush him, remained comfortable with his pace, and allowed for repetition. Not all sessions can go this smoothly but they are rewarding when they do!

What happens when the child gets stuck?

As noted, it is common for the child with Asperger's Syndrome to develop an obsessive interest in a television character, video program, or ritualized way of playing with certain toys. The child's play may consist of replications of parts of these programs, but these are often not spontaneous and the child may not add their own ideas. The parent might misconstrue the child's play as imaginative when in fact it is a reenactment of a story plot or theme. It is easy to understand how a parent or a teacher might have this point of view, as it is typical for children to incorporate popular characters into their play (e.g. Cinderella, Darth Vader). There are several ways to work with the child on these issues. First, the therapist can help the parent observe and understand the differences in how the play carries out for the child with AS. Then, to begin to broaden the child's repertoire, it is helpful to avoid providing the child with the commercial props and products that accompany a particular character or movie. Second, the therapist and parent create opportunities for other types of play by introducing experiences that are familiar to and enjoyable for the child, such as family outings (visit to an ice cream parlor, visit to a zoo). The child may require explicit cues and more active structuring from the therapist/parent to know what to do. Explicit cues might include props that give meaning to the scenario, such as a cardboard box labeled as an ice cream store and empty ice cream sandwich cartons. Blocks can be used to build a "zoo." Sometimes it is helpful to focus on the constructive aspects of play such as placement of figures and blocks (careful attention given to where the zoo "entrance" might be or where the "lion's den" is), as this is often easier for the child with AS to do. Immediate demands for novelty and true make-believe may be too difficult. In this way the therapist/parent establishes a common focus of attention with the child, partnership in play, and enjoyment in doing a new activity together. These are the core principles of parent–child therapy.

What happens if my child acts like he does not want to play with me?

The child's movement away from the parent or therapist might be his way of expressing confusion about how to create a play theme and share ideas about a new story. We sometimes observe that the child with AS turns his back on the parent and plays alone. A child named Todd had a tendency to separate from his mother and "crash" toys together or repeat the same actions when he was confused by the social interaction demands of play. Todd's mother was perplexed by these behaviors and would attempt to help him by making many different suggestions or asking questions, which seemed too overwhelming for Todd. To reengage him, the therapist coached Todd's mother to offer two simple suggestions for the toys that he was using. With the therapist's guidance, Todd's mother helped him create a "library" (out of blocks) for small figures, and she encouraged him to decide where the "doors" and "book-shelves" should go. Todd's mother reported that going to the library was a favorite activity that they shared together and the therapist encouraged her to bring those experiences into his play. Todd's mother helped him identify which "videos" the figures might want to check out from the library and view at "home." As Todd used these toys to play out scenarios that were familiar to him, his mother introduced several new elements to the play to vary this familiar theme in small ways. With the therapist's support, she provided structure for Todd (such as clear cues for turn taking, rephrasing Todd's statements, pausing) that helped him remain engaged with her. She also practiced how to maintain a balance between allowing Todd to direct the play and follow some of her suggestions.

At a subsequent session, Todd began to throw dinosaurs on the floor and disengage from his mother. Todd's mother saw that he needed help to develop an idea and she suggested that there was a "terrible storm" that had knocked the animals over. She provided animated gestures to show her excitement at what might happen and Todd decided that he needed to "hide" the animals from the storm. Over these two sessions, Todd enthusiastically joined into this play scenario and practiced critical aspects of interactive play: monitoring a partner, reciprocal play (first you do, then I do, then you do it a little bit differently and I do it a little bit differently), and maintaining interaction.

Parent concerns that commonly surface during parent–child therapy

The work that the therapist and parents do together with the child can yield new knowledge about the child's challenges and insights into avenues for intervention. Through the dyadic work, parents can begin to feel some control over what was previously so perplexing. At the same time, there are many feelings about the child and the experience of parenting a child with unique needs that will surface in the process of the dyadic work. Understanding your child's diagnosis requires patience and reflection, a process that can sometimes seem overwhelming. All of these responses can be explored with the therapist. The therapist may also suggest individual or couples therapy as a way for parents to gain additional support for themselves as individuals and as a couple. Individual therapy can help parents explore feelings that might surface about their own childhood and identity as a parent. Talking with someone about these complicated feelings can be empowering. Likewise, couples therapy offers a setting to clarify different perceptions and needs and identify ways for parents to support and understand one another.

How long might parent–child therapy continue?

There is no specified period for parent–child therapy to occur. The duration can vary according to what questions parents have and what they find helpful for themselves and their child with AS. As noted previously, it is often helpful for parents to have an ongoing relationship with a therapist who can observe and get to know the child over time so as to identify changing needs and adjust intervention plans. For example, following the initial diagnosis, parents might meet once a week or once every other week with the therapist to clarify diagnostic information, discuss parents' behavioral and school related concerns, and begin to address the specifics of parent–child play. In some cases, the diagnosis is not new, the child has received several interventions (occupational therapy, specialized preschool program), and the parents are interested in pursuing parent–child therapy as a way to help the child with this (in many cases) unexplored area of the child's development. Regular sessions are helpful to maintain continuity as the parent pursues new ways of thinking about the child and a different way of relating to the child (through play). There are other factors to consider when setting up a therapy schedule and the parents should feel comfortable to discuss these with the therapist. These might include the child's daily school and therapy routine, cost of the therapy, and parents' availability when there are other children in the home or both parents work outside of the home. Sessions might taper to once per month, or once every six months, to monitor the child and provide ongoing support to the parents.

How do I know if parent–child therapy is helpful?

This question is an important one as you initiate any type of therapy with your child. One aspect of parent–child therapy is ongoing discussion with the therapist of the child's strengths and challenges, what new skills are emerging, and where help is needed. You can ask yourself several questions to determine if the therapy is helpful to you: Do I feel supported in the process of understanding my child's diagnosis and needs? Am I learning how to support my child's development? Is my child developing important skills in play and communication? Importantly, parents may find different aspects of the therapy helpful at different times.

What if it feels too overwhelming to be in the same room with my child and the therapist?

Sometimes parents may feel overwhelmed by the challenges that can arise when playing with their child, or parents may feel that they do not know how to play. It may sometimes seem like the therapist knows exactly what to do. It is important for the parent to feel comfortable to express his/her reluctance to remain in the room. Most likely the therapist experiences the same challenges with the child and a discussion of these challenges can bring new insights into the child. Parents may also find it helpful to talk with the therapist about what it is like for the parent to have these feelings.

Conclusion

Parent–child therapy provides a place for parents to sort out their confusions about their child's challenges and uniqueness, receive support for the many different issues that arise, express worries, and, importantly, share hope for what their child can accomplish and take pride in who their child is. This author's work with children and parents has brought to life the many positive steps that young children with AS can take in learning important social and play skills. Through ongoing dialogue between the therapist and the parent and shared observation of the child, parents gain knowledge about their child and learn ways to facilitate their child's development. This process can be very rewarding to the parent who often asks the question, "What can I do to help my child?"

CHAPTER 8

Building Connections with Peers

Therapeutic Groups

As many parents have discovered, almost every assessment of Asperger's Syndrome comes with a recommendation that the child participate in a social skills group. Yet one soon finds out that this is easier said than done, especially for children between the ages of three and six. The first thing one needs to know is that the term *social skills group* may be used to describe a wide range of programs depending on the orientation of the clinician who is running the group. For example, it may be called a "pragmatic language group" if taught by a speech and language therapist, a "language and motion group" if directed by occupational therapists and speech and language therapists, or a "therapeutic play-group" when run by mental health professionals. While these professionals from different disciplines may not share a common approach to intervening or vocabulary to describe their interventions they do share the goal of enhancing the child's social and communication skills (Klin and Volkmar 2000). Before thinking about what we should consider when looking for a social skills group, we will define some of the terms used across settings.

> SOCIAL SKILLS refers to the skills needed to engage with a peer in *reciprocal* social interactions and interpret social situations using both verbal and nonverbal communication.

Young children master these skills at different ages. By three-and-a-half years of age many children can maintain several circles of communication about a shared topic of interest, are able to judge how much information their friend wants to hear, ask their peer direct questions, listen to their response, and read their facial expressions. The three-year-old child loves having a "friend" with whom he or she can share similar interests, such as searching for wet worms, hiding from pirates, or creating and serving delicious mud cakes, to list a few.

By the age of four, the playground becomes the social stage of the children's explorations, activities, and symbolic play. One can reliably observe the complex social steps that young children engage in as they enter into cooperative play. First they have to get their peer's attention, next they need to ask them to play, and then be able to read their verbal and nonverbal responses to tell if the other child wants to play. If the peer says "yes," they need to share or come up with an idea together and then develop a flexible plan for how they are going to carry out their idea. The social and symbolic play provides the young child with a chance to practice and develop skills that they will need both in and outside of the classroom. Since our world is such a social one and children and adults alike need to navigate the complex relationships they will encounter, a priority is placed on the child's world of social play in most preschools.

One doesn't ordinarily think of these skills as requiring a lot of direct instruction since most people are born with the foundations of these social skills which are then fine-tuned over time, aided by the cues received both directly and indirectly from family members, teachers, and peers. As we have described in Chapter 2, core aspects of communication, social interaction, and symbolic play present challenges for children with Asperger's Syndrome (Klin and Volkmar 2000). Some of these core skills include the ability to come up with original ideas in play and to expand these ideas in a mutually pleasurable interaction with a peer. In order to do this, the child must be able to *"read" and deliver nonverbal social cues* as well as *gestures and facial expressions.* Children with Asperger's Syndrome often give a blank grin when they are feeling anxious. This grin can be misinterpreted as being happy, and results in the child getting in trouble for appearing to enjoy being aggressive towards another child when in fact he is often confused and terrified. Other nonverbal skills are the awareness of the messages we give to others by *the tone and volume of our voice,* our *proximity* in standing next to others, and the *eye contact* we maintain during a conversation.

The children also need help in areas of *pragmatic language* (see Chapters 2 and 9). Small group settings provide a wonderful opportunity to practice *conversational skills* such as *turn taking, staying on topic,* finding areas of *shared interest,* and learning ways to *enter into play or a conversation topic with a peer.* Small groups also help children learn ways to *self-monitor.* For example, the child who shouts when a peer does anything that is out of sync with his plan may need to learn how to regulate his voice and verbalize his ideas to peers.

Eventually, the child will learn that his shouting makes his friends mad or frustrated.

Given the need for a young child with Asperger's Syndrome to develop these skills, how do you, as a parent, know if your child might benefit from a social skills group? We will begin by answering some of the questions most commonly asked by parents when deciding if a group program would be helpful for their child.

Who runs social skills groups, do they all focus on the same things, and where are they found?

As discussed above, the therapist's orientation (training) will influence what they focus on, but there may be a blend of styles, especially if they have worked collaboratively with professionals from other disciplines. For example, a speech and language therapist in a group may focus on facilitating the children's pragmatic language during free play, structured activities, and imaginary play. He or she may work with the children sitting around a table, focusing on the children making eye contact, and initiating and maintaining circles of communication. He or she may also use scripts to help the children answer who, what, where, and why questions, those questions that give children with Asperger's Syndrome difficulty because they are abstract, not concrete. In contrast, a group run by occupational therapists may begin with the children doing motor activities, the assumption being that once the children are getting the extra sensory stimuli that they need they will be better able to focus on the social cues they need to read during interactions. Many parents have found that their children can concentrate better on social activities if they do an intense sensorimotor activity like jumping on a trampoline, riding a bike, or swimming before they go to a social activity like school or a play group.

What the mental health professional contributes, in addition to a focus on the child's social communication and interaction, is attention to facilitating the child's awareness of his own feelings and the feelings of others, as well as making links between behavior and underlying feelings. They may also place a greater focus on the level of the child's play: is he playing primarily by himself (solitary); next to other children but not with them (parallel); or with other children, sharing a common interest, developing ideas, and acting out the themes socially (reciprocal)? The "nuts and bolts" of the therapy centers on helping the child move from solitary to social/reciprocal play with his peers. In other words, the therapist aims to foster the child's ability to communicate with his peers by modeling, scaffolding (giving the child the words he needs to communicate his ideas to his peers), and providing visual maps for the play. Another key component of the work is helping the child identify his feelings, express these feelings, recognize the feelings of others, and develop more adaptive ways of managing his frustration. (See the "Curriculum" section of "The Friends' Program" for examples.)

There will also be a wide range of parental involvement in the programs. Most of the programs that we are aware of do not have a parent support group component or professionally guided observations, but may have routine parent conferences. Other groups may have parent participation in the group much like a cooperative preschool, where the parent has the opportunity to observe the strategies the clinicians are using.

As for where these groups can be found, the best place to start is by asking clinicians involved in the assessment process. These clinicians may be found in the Department of Child Psychiatry and Psychology, the Division of Developmental Pediatrics, the Department of Occupational Therapy, or the Department of Speech and Language at university based medical centers. There may also be programs in community based mental health centers and developmental clinics as well as in the school district's Department of Special Education – Early Intervention Programs. Lastly, one may want to look for behavioral specialists who have experience working with children with Autistic Spectrum Disorders. Historically, the focus of these specialists has been more on fostering adaptive behaviors (such as toilet training) with less attention on the child's social interactions with peers, but this is changing and a larger number are doing more work with the children in the context of their classrooms.

If a child is already receiving speech therapy and/or occupational therapy do they also need a social skills group?

The question to raise with the child's therapists is how much attention is given to the child's social communication, interaction, and imaginary play with peers. One would guess that if the therapist is seeing the child alone then they will work on developing skills that will foster the child's communication and ability to engage in play, but they still will benefit from the opportunity to practice these skills in a therapeutic group setting. Another option might be that the therapist puts a group of children with similar strengths and needs together so that they can also have the group experience. Once again, one can only do so much in an hour or two so you want to make sure that structured and unstructured social play is on their agenda.

What might a parent expect to see the children do in a social skills/therapeutic play group?

Groups for young children are often structured to replicate a preschool setting with group time, table activities, motor activities, free play, and snack time. What one needs to remember is that the core of the Asperger's Syndrome diagnosis is difficulty in social communication and interactions with peers, so you want to make sure that the group makes time for adult-guided social interactions and free play with peers. The goal should not be interactions confined to structured table activities that result in nice projects, but rather increased social interactions and communication.

Will my child learn negative behavior from other children in the group?

One of the biggest fears all parents have, regardless of the child's age, is that their child is going to learn bad behaviors from the other children participating in the group. This is an understandable fear. It is important to remember that the reason for a group is that your child is not connecting with other children, following their ideas, or imitating their behaviors. On rare occasions a child may imitate another child's exaggerated behaviors such as a karate kick or a silly rhyme in an attempt to make a connection. What you should look for is a clinician that can tell a child to stop an inappropriate behavior and provide him with a more adaptive way to connect with his peers. Some clinicians may use a behavioral reward system if necessary to change a behavior. It is also important to have adults reinforcing positive behaviors and not giving power to the more negative ones. In the history of our program it was rare for a parent to report that a child was imitating negative behaviors that they observed in-group and acting them out at home or at school. If the children could easily imitate a peer and generalize the behavior across settings after one observation, then they would probably not belong in a group for children with AS.

How helpful is it to observe the child in a therapeutic group setting?

Many parents often wonder what goes on in a group setting and would like the opportunity to observe their child in the group. Some programs can adapt to this request while others don't have the facilities and/or other parents consent to do so. Either way, when an opportunity arises to observe your child's program, we strongly recommend parents to do so. Furthermore, having the opportunity to observe on an ongoing basis provides insight that may not be achieved in other settings. It is not uncommon for a parent to initially be concerned by what they observe when they watch their child's behavior in the group. They describe it as being much worse than anything they had ever seen at home and worry that the group is hindering rather than helping their child. It is important to remember that this situation is very different from what occurs when the child is interacting with an adult or with one other child who follows the child's plans or allows him to play by himself following his own agenda. A play based social skills group places demands on a child with Asperger's Syndrome in the areas where they feel the most anxious and vulnerable – communicating, interacting, and playing with peers for an extended period of time.

Wouldn't it be better yet to have a group with "normal" children so that the child with Asperger's Syndrome could learn more appropriate social behavior from his peers?

Many young children with Asperger's Syndrome have the opportunity to play with other children either at school or in the neighborhood. However, these opportunities to naturally connect with other children don't always go smoothly. As we have discussed, the young child with Asperger's Syndrome may need to feel in control or appear aloof and his behavior may be misinterpreted. Because of the difficulties young children with AS have in recognizing and responding to nonverbal and verbal cues, it has been our experience that in the beginning phases of intervention these children benefit from being with other children who need a similar structure and coaching in order to engage others successfully. That is not to say that it is not helpful for your children to have play dates with "normal" children outside of the group, particularly when there is an adult who can facilitate the interactions and help the child when needed. The children may also benefit from participation in social activities such as swimming, art classes, or nature camp, as long as the teacher is willing to serve as an interpreter in the unstructured social aspects of the activity.

How might a group for young children differ from the programs one reads about for school age children?

The short answer is *play*. As the book has emphasized, the young child's social world centers on their play; thus the group may use different types of play (art, science, manipulative toys, symbolic play, outdoor play, and games) as the context for the child's social interactions. Also the groups for young children usually have a snack time since it is an activity that naturally brings the children together with a shared interest and goal. It is astonishing how often this is the time when the children are the most social with each other, make the most eye contact, and have the most reciprocal conversations.

How does one know if the therapist is skilled in working with children with Asperger's Syndrome?

The best way to start is by asking the therapist about his or her experience working with children with Asperger's Syndrome, both individually and in groups. One could also ask if there is a parent in the program who would be willing to talk about their experiences. Next, ask about the goals they have for the group and see if these are goals that you share. One should ask about parent involvement in the program. Is there an associated parent group, do the therapists give the parents regular feedback, are the parents able to observe the group, and how do the clinicians see their role in regards to collaboration with the child's teacher and other professionals involved in the child's care? Parents want to make sure that the people involved in their child's care are able to learn from each other and give the child consistent messages.

To fully understand the answers to the above questions, let us now turn to a group therapy model that will bring to life the concepts that we have been discussing. It is difficult to describe all the different models of intervention because clinicians are just starting to write about their specific programs. However, we hope that this chapter will provide you with a better under-standing of what you might expect in a group by hearing about a model program that we have found to be effective in helping young children with Asperger's Syndrome and their families. The program's goals are to develop social skills with peers as well as foster the parents' understanding of Asperger's Syndrome, which in turn enhances their relationship with their child and empowers them to be advocates for their child. We will now introduce the Friends' Group Program, a therapeutic child–parent group program for young children with Asperger's Syndrome and PDD-NOS. In the process of describing this model, many different interventions will be introduced. A chart of interventions used in the program and the targeted social skills can be found following the description of the Friends' Program.

The Friends' Program – A model program

The history

The program evolved from our early attempts to develop effective therapies for an increasing number of referrals of young children having social skills difficulties. The group provided an effective setting for understanding these children. The diagnosis of Asperger's Syndrome had not yet come out in DSM-IV so most of the children were being referred to rule out ADHD, Disruptive Behavior, PTSD, PDD-NOS, or Anxiety Disorders. The group also gave us a chance to explore interventions that might help these children both at home and at their school.

For many of the parents, the group was their first step in seeking professional help. These early groups were structured to include a children's group, parents' group, and parent–child time that took place within the parameters of the children's group. One can imagine how loud, visually stimulating, and chaotic a room filled with five children, five parents, and three clinicians could seem to any child, but especially to a child who had sensory regulatory difficulties. To make things even more complicated, we had children who coped with the challenge of being in a group in very different ways. For some, the strategy of choice was to block out the stimuli by hiding under a table, others focused on their area of special interest. Still others fought their mother's separation tooth and nail, panicked that they would not know what to do without her.

We quickly learned how hard it was for parents to observe their child struggling in the area in which he has the most difficulty – play with peers. The parents who had the most difficulty with this were those whose children had not been evaluated prior to joining the group. Understandably, it was very stressful for them to hear other parents bring up different diagnostic terms and treatment strategies that were foreign to them while at the same time watching their child behave in what they saw as being such an unacceptable manner. For these parents, the focus often ended up being how the diagnosis did or did not fit their child.

The children taught us two things early on in the program. First, how quickly the anxiety of the children with Asperger's Syndrome decreased when they were given visual cues and a sense of predictability in the group activities. Second, we could see how different the quality of the symbolic play of children with Asperger's Syndrome was from that of the children with ADHD or children who had experienced trauma. The children with ADHD would approach their peers and be eager to engage them in an activity, but not be able to wait very long for a response before going off to another activity. The child with Asperger's Syndrome tended to be oblivious to peers' attempts to engage him verbally or nonverbally, either because he did not see or understand the cues, or by the time the child figured things out, the peer was off doing something else. The traumatized child was eager to engage the children in making up a story of the good guys versus the villains. Because the needs of these children with different diagnoses are so different, we decided that it would be more helpful for the children with Asperger's Syndrome to be in a group in which the mechanics of social interactions, communication, and play with peers were more clearly spelled out.

The lessons we learned over the past ten years have led to our most current working model. This model is, in many ways, an ideal. Our groups have the luxury of a two-way mirror, allowing for parent observation; yet such a luxury has not always been available and it is important to know that we have run this group on a playground, inside a transformed storage room, and in a transitional office space. Our groups also have the luxury of experienced staff and good staff-to-child ratios. They have survived many fiscal pressures allowing many families to participate for two to four years. We hope clinicians can take many of the interventions we have found to be helpful and adapt them to their settings. We also hope that parents will gain an understanding of a model that includes their participation in the group interventions. Keep in mind that many of the interventions and activities about to be described can be utilized by parents when facilitating play dates.

The Friends' Group Model

The goal of the Friends' Program is to create a supportive group setting that fosters a positive social experience with peers. The program involves both the parents and the child. The parents in the younger group (three- to four-year-olds) participate in an opening circle with their child, providing them with an opportunity to be part of the child's group and have a shared experience with the child as the leaders review the day's activities and present

a social story with puppets. The parents say goodbye after circle and participate in a parents' group led by a mental health professional. Parents and the
clinician will choose a time to observe the children through a one-way mirror.
Therefore, the parents' group provides not only parent support, but also
ongoing education and opportunity to learn interventions utilized by the
children's group therapists. Parents rejoin the children for closing circle at the
end of the group. The group uses visual cues, table activities, thematic play,
motor activities, and outdoor play to help the children develop social skills,
symbolic play, and social language problem solving.

The goal of the parents' group is to foster the parents' understanding of
their child and offer suggestions for fostering his/her development. The
group also provides an opportunity for parents to receive guidance and
support from both professionals and parents of children with similar strengths
and needs. A portion of each group is spent observing the child in the group
setting and discussing observations with other parents in the group, such as:
why did the therapist let my child stand up at the table, say such silly things, or
not complete an activity? Collaboration with other professionals working
with the child is strongly encouraged. It is not uncommon to have a teacher,
therapist, grandparent, or nanny joining the parent group for the guided
observation time.

Inclusion criteria

Admission into the Friends' Group requires the diagnosis of Asperger's
Syndrome or PDD-NOS (many clinicians do not feel comfortable giving the
diagnosis of Asperger's Syndrome prior to the age of six), and a pre-group
assessment. The pre-group assessment takes place in the playroom with the
main therapists for the parents' group and the children's group, the child, and
his parents. The setting provides a chance for the child therapist to assess the
child's pragmatic language, rigidity, level of play, and ability to handle transitions. If we feel that the child expresses very little or no desire to connect with
the clinician, or has an extreme need to follow his own plan, we may
recommend that they begin with parent–child (dyadic) therapy as the first
step in expanding the child's interests in other people and ideas. At the same
time, the parents' therapist is sitting with the parents at a table answering any
questions that they may have about the children's group, the parents' group,
the parents' feelings about the diagnosis, and the level of comfort they have
discussing these issues with other parents. We have learned over time that
some parents cannot attend the groups because of the demands of their paid

job, while for others it is too painful to view their child's vulnerabilities in a social group or be in a setting in which the term Asperger's Syndrome is openly used by the parents. In these cases we recommend that they begin with dyadic therapy. We also want to make sure that the parent can tolerate hearing different ideas about the diagnosis, and is able to provide other parents with support even if they have different perspectives. For some parents we recommend individual therapy as well as the group. We have learned that it is very difficult for most parents to be seeing the same therapist for the group as well as individual or dyadic therapy – thus we recommend that they see someone outside of the group for therapy. We strongly encourage maintaining a collaborative relationship in which there is ongoing communication between all of the clinicians involved in the family's care.

The setting

The group takes place in a therapeutic playroom that has a large observation room. It is designed to look like a "typical" playroom setting with a carpeted area that can be used for circle time, free play, and dramatic play, an art/snack table, a bathroom, and an outdoor play area.

Staffing

The children's group is staffed by two clinicians. There is always one mental health professional (a social worker, psychologist, or psychiatrist) or a speech and language therapist who has experience working with young children with Asperger's Syndrome. The other clinician is either a mental health professional, an early childhood specialist, or a trainee. It is important to have two staff members for the children's group in case one child needs to be taken out of the group or if we want to divide children into smaller groups for play activities. The parents' group is run by a licensed mental health clinician who is also a parent. It is our belief that not until an adult experiences, as a parent, the social world of the young child can one imagine the inherent complexities and pressures that occur in the child's world at home, the playground, school, and the larger community. Each group has between four and six children. The problem with having such a highly educated large staff and small number of children is that the program is very costly.

Children's group structure

The program was designed to mirror a typical school day. The session begins with the parents bringing the children into the room and sitting with them at circle time. If the children are older, parents may just drop them off. Circle time is when the clinicians and children greet each other, go over the day's schedule, use puppets to act out a social or communication skills issue, and say goodbye to the parents. Next, the children go to the table for an art activity or game and the parents go to the observation room with their therapist to observe the group. After the table activity the clinicians prepare the children for the symbolic play activity, which includes a wide range of activities, from building houses, making zoo cages, preparing a space voyage, to going on a pretend overnight fishing trip. All of these play themes have a visual guide that provides a structure, shared props, and shared meaning for the story. We learned very early on that if the children were given the opportunity to use the materials in their own way, they tended to exclude other children from play. Having visual guides for the play and defined roles ensures more cooperation. For all of our children, having to participate in play that accommodates another child is hard work for both the children and the staff but it is very rewarding when it happens. It can also be very hard for the parents to watch.

After structured social play time the children have outdoor play in which they have the opportunity to engage in gross motor activities, group games such as "duck-duck-goose" and tag, as well as manipulative activities in sand and water. It was striking to us just how paralyzed these children could be by these games. Many of these games are learned by observation and practice; but a child who has a hard time picking up subtle verbal and nonverbal cues may be confused by the nuances of "freezer tag," "wall ball," or "dodge ball." However, as we have learned, once the game was broken down and explained, with visual cues and time to practice aspects of the game with a clinician, many of the children began to be eager to play the group games.

After outdoor time the children come in for a snack. Not surprisingly, after the intense sensory workout the children do a better job sitting in their chairs and engaging in conversations about shared topics such as the day's events, a book that was just read, or a peer's ideas. The snack time is also used as a time to tell a social story related to a conflict that may have come up during the day, or work on social skills such as asking a friend if they would like a cookie before giving them one. This is also a time when the therapists reflect to each other about a child's actions or affect. The parents join the children at the end of each group for a circle time in which the therapist reviews the day's events, shares some experiences with the parents, and gives each child positive reinforcement for participating in the group.

While the children are participating in their group, the parents meet in a separate room where they have a chance to have a cup of coffee and take a moment to relax. The group provides a safe place for the parents to talk about what they observed in the children's group, discuss issues that may have come up during the week, and, if time allows, review an article the therapist or a parent brought for the group. With Asperger's Syndrome being such a hot topic, there are always articles promoting a new type of intervention, hopes for future treatments, and hypotheses about possible causes.

For many of these parents, it is very difficult to watch the child who they view as being creative, bright, and sophisticated physically bar another child from entering "their" space, or grabbing a toy from another child's hand. If the therapist handles the situation differently than the parent, for example the therapist doesn't express disapproval about a behavior but redirects the behavior instead, parents can sometimes become concerned that the group may not be the best setting for their child. Guided observations help the parents reflect on these differences in managing behaviors as well as begin to reflect on why the child's behavior seems to be so different with them at home than in the group. The parents can also learn strategies that can promote their child's capacity for social interactions with peers (see Chapter 5 – "The Parents' Journey" – for an in-depth description of the path parents of children with Asperger's Syndrome often travel).

Curriculum

Curriculums are used to structure different activities such as table time and interactive play. We try to use themes that are typically integrated into a young child's school curriculum such as seasons, friends, transportation, nature, space, communities, or camping to create a shared interest that the children can use in their social interactions and play with their peers. The challenge for the clinicians is to not become focused on the end product of an art project or expanding the child's wealth of information, and thereby lose sight of the main goal, which is to facilitate the children's social and communication skills. (It is very easy to get waylaid listening to four different experts telling them about trains while they ignore the child sitting next to them.) We attempt to limit the time children spend sharing a favored toy or "fact book," since this tends to restrict rather than expand or stimulate the children's interactions and play. The group also made a choice not to focus on holidays, since they are given so much attention in the schools and are celebrated so differently in the homes, often causing anxiety in the child who is fixated on there being a right and wrong way.

We have also learned that the children did better when a theme or symbolic play activity was repeated for several weeks in a row. When changing a theme we always needed to assess whether it was because we were bored or because the children seemed to lose interest. The parents became keenly aware of the same process taking place in their home. Together we worked on differentiating when a child was repeating a topic in a perseverative manner and when they were able to use the familiar topic to integrate new ideas and connect with a peer.

The last point we want to make about curriculum is the need for *flexibility*. Many times we thought we had come up with a great theme and set of projects, only to have it flop five minutes into the group, often because it was too abstract and too dependent on verbal instructions. For example, we had been playing with sea animals in the water table and had just finished reading a book about homes for the animals in the ocean. We covered the table with a sheet of white butcher paper and gave the children finger paint to create a picture of the ocean, an animal, and their home. For some of the children the sensation of finger paint absorbed all of their attention. For another child the thought of touching the paint panicked them and they insisted on washing their hands numerous times as soon as the paint touched their finger tips. All of the children were confused by the image of making the paper into one large picture of the ocean rather than five separate pictures, and were baffled by the concept of making a picture on top of the paint with their fingers or a stick. Shortly into the project we decided to drop the idea of the fish and focus on what it feels like to finger paint, and the different ways that the picture may change by adding different colors and finger movements. The children enjoyed the process so much that they all wanted their own paper so that they could take their pictures home. One could imagine the tantrums and fleeing which would have occurred if we had insisted that they paint one joint picture of the ocean and a picture of a fish for the class mural. Over the years we have learned to always have a back-up activity such as clay, since many of the children avoid any of the drawing activities because they are keenly aware of the difficulties they have drawing or cannot tolerate the messiness of the project. We have also learned not to see one activity "disaster" as cause for abandoning the activity but rather a cue for taking it back to the drawing board and finding a way to introduce it in a more simple and clearer way. It is easy to fall into the trap of exuberantly giving the children a lengthy verbal explanation, only to realize they had no idea what we were talking about!

The next section outlines the group activities and typical interventions utilized during the group. A list of common behavioral challenges will be depicted in a chart following the group activities. The chart will include intervention strategies that can be adapted for use in other groups and, it is hoped, in the classroom as well as at home.

Overview of group activities

Activity: Circle Time

GOAL: ORIENT CHILD AND PARENT ABOUT THE GROUP ACTIVITIES AND ISSUES

Intervention	Strategies
Leader wheel	A visual cue that provides children with a concrete way to see when and what they are going to be first at. It is striking how much more relaxed the children become when they know they will have a chance to be first at least once during the group, and it is not based on who gets in line first or some other random method.

Intervention	Strategies
Visual chart daily schedule with pictures and words	The chart provides a visual reference for the child about the day's activities, reducing the anxiety that occurs when they feel confused about what is going on in the group. It is not uncommon to see a child refer back to the chart throughout the day. It is helpful to have both written words and visual icons to help nonreaders.

Intervention	Strategies
Carpet square name	The carpet provides the child with visual boundaries to define their physical space. Having carpet squares of different colors also helps those children who don't recognize their name recognize their carpet square. Placing the carpets in the same place every week serves to help define the child's spot. The continuity also helps reduce anxiety. The carpets can also provide some children with the needed tactile stimulation achieved by rolling the carpet around the legs or pulling tightly on the carpet's edges. And like all other interventions, when we feel that the children are becoming too dependent on the routine, and rigid, we will introduce a change such as moving the squares around or eliminating them all together.

Intervention	Strategies
Puppet show Hi, my name is George the monkey. What's yours?	Puppets provide the visual stimuli that bring the stories and social scripts to life for the children. It is amazing how quickly the children's attention moves from themselves to the front of the circle as soon as a puppet begins to talk in an exaggerated tone of voice. The puppets are used to act out communication skills such as using names, or social issues such as sharing, following another child's ideas, and expressing feelings, to list a few.

Intervention	Strategies
Social Stories	With young children, the puppets usually are the narrators of a social story designed to represent a current issue in the group, such as not being first or losing a game. The parents are given a copy of the story so that it can be repeated and applied to similar situations that arise at home and in school. You can also supplement puppets with a visual version of the story that the children can follow. Leaving the poster of the story available during the group helps children reference back to it when the social issues surface. Keeping stories simple and very concrete is important. Parents can help by volunteering a situation that occurred during the week, which can then be adapted for a social story for the group.

Activity: Table Time
GOAL: FOSTER SHARED EXPERIENCES, FINE MOTOR, AND VISUAL-MOTOR SKILLS

Intervention	Strategies
Board games	Provides practice with an activity that the child can replicate with peers. Many children can easily be fixated on winning or may not have practice focusing their attention on a shared interest. The game becomes a tool for practicing taking turns, tolerating losing, acknowledging a peer's cues, and following the game's rules (not one's own rules). Favorite games have included animal bingo, "Candyland," "Snail's Pace," and other visual matching games. When the children are ready, groups can develop their own games – for example, making a bingo game of faces/expressions that the children match and then identify the feeling. Incorporating a situation that identifies the feeling can be added after much practice.

Intervention	Strategies
Clay	Homemade play dough is a favorite activity for all of the children. The clay is a fun way to get tactile stimuli from rolling, pounding, and cutting. It is often a safe activity to begin with since minimal interaction is initially required. As the group begins to solidify, the task moves from fostering individual creations to finding ways to have the children connect their creations with others – for example, via water, bridges, transportation, animals, and human figures. Limiting the number of available clay tools also encourages the children to ask to borrow a tool.
Intervention	**Strategies**
Group drawings	There are several ways to conduct a group drawing exercise. A large piece of paper can be introduced to the group with a theme or task that is completed by them. For example, a road is drawn down the page and children draw individual houses, zoo cages, or stores. The drawing then becomes the visual setting for their symbolic play with manipulative objects. Children can also be given a piece of paper on which they are asked to draw something simple, leaving space for friends to add. Then they pass the picture around with each child adding something different to the picture. Ultimately the child should end up with the picture he or she began with. This activity gets children to think about differences in ideas and tolerate others joining in their artwork. Drawing often is a very difficult activity, primarily because the children have such a wide range of fine motor skills and narrow range of subjects they like to draw. Since many of these children have delayed fine motor skills, providing alternatives to drawing such as stickers, magazine pictures, and finger paint can assist their participation. The important thing to remember is that the focus is on the children's social interactions, not the end product. To avoid the pressures children can feel to perform a certain way, keep the themes and designs simple.

Intervention	Strategies
Manipulative figures	Children are much more attentive to animal, people, car, and block figures which they can manipulate with their hands when they have a visual guide. For example, providing a road that runs between children's spots at the table helps children use their figure to connect with others. One always wants to prevent children from spending long periods of time absorbed in their own figures without acknowledging or attempting to interact with peers. Therapists often need to play an active role in helping make the connections between the peers' play by making observations about the other child, noting the similarities in their play, or modeling ways the children can connect with each other.

Activity: Social Play

GOAL: HELP THE CHILDREN DEVELOP THE SKILLS NEEDED TO ENGAGE IN SYMBOLIC PLAY WITH ANOTHER CHILD

Intervention	Strategies
Social Stories	Initially, when beginning a group, free play tends to be at the parallel play level. Children will often have a difficult time coming up with original ideas and allowing others to contribute to their ideas. Therefore, providing concrete directions and themes can help children at least begin to get involved. For example, each child can be given a set of blocks to create his own home. It is likely that little effort to connect with peers occurs without a clinician's assistance. As with all of the table activities, the goal of the clinician is to find ways that the children can interact, develop shared interest, experience mutual pleasure, and reciprocate in their symbolic play. For example, the clinician may write a script that entails the children taking a train to each other's home and playing a game, or joining their trains to make one big train. Children often feel safer when they are provided with their own space – for example, having boxes which each child sits in and pretends is their own train car allows the child the personal space they need in order not to be tactilely and spatially overwhelmed. The next two interventions take a closer look at this process.

Intervention	Strategies
Stories for play	Since many children have a very difficult time coming up with themes for play that are not a reenactment of a memorized book or tape, utilizing their visual memory can be helpful for stimulating play. By reading a picture book to the children prior to the play-time, the story becomes the shared theme for their play. The children will still need the clinician to assign roles and visual props as they scaffold the children's interactions with their peers. The therapist may read a section, show the children a picture, give them a prop to clarify their role, and then have them act out that section of the story. It is important to select simple stories that have few words and good visual cues.
Intervention	**Strategies**
Symbolic play scripts	Visual play scripts provide a very simplified, illustrative map of the events which make up a theme for pretend play. It always helps to develop a theme that may be of interest to the children and then draw out a simple story that the children can follow. The "map" can be followed along and referenced when a child is either drifting away from the theme or stuck at a certain spot. For example, if the theme is "going fishing" the script will describe a group of sailors getting in a boat, going into the ocean, catching fish, and bringing the fish home. A picture will accompany every statement. Once the children are comfortable with pretend sailing they may end up spending the night on an island, having a barbecue, or sleeping on the beach. The script may be based on a story or a symbolic play theme such as going to the store, putting out a fire, going to the restaurant, camping, or sailing the ocean. These play scripts can provide much pleasure to children who typically have difficulty engaging in a shared theme with other children but so enjoy doing it when they are helped. The theme may be replicated for several weeks or even months. Clinicians can elaborate and add new ideas to the same theme along the way. The familiarity and continuity help the children master the ideas and feel comfortable engaging in a shared experience with their peers.

Activity: Outdoor Play

GOAL: GROSS MOTOR ACTIVITIES, DEVELOPING OUTDOOR PLAY SKILLS, AND RELEASE OF TENSION

Intervention	Strategies
Outdoor free play	After working hard on the symbolic play sequence, children are often tired and need free time to run, swing, jump, ride a tricycle, or lay on the grass. It is helpful to allow some unstructured down time outside followed by an activity. The goal of outdoor time is to help the children negotiate their way through the challenges they encounter daily on the playground such as sharing objects and physical space, and not hurting others in ways that they think are fun, like squeezing another child or splashing them with water. The therapists can organize play in sand, around a water table, or on a play structure. Other structured activities that can be introduced are games the children tend to avoid such as tag, "red rover," "dodge ball," "t-ball," and "duck-duck-goose." Simple explanations of the rules can be reinforced by making a visual outline, walking through the rules, and then creating social stories to help the children better understand the game and conflicts that may or do arise.

Activity: Snack Time

GOAL: CREATE MUTUALLY PLEASURABLE SOCIAL ACTIVITY

Intervention	Strategies
Snack at the table	Snack time is often the time when there is the most shared interest and communication. Snack follows outdoor time, which may help explain why children seem more receptive to communicating with peers. Often after an intense gross motor activity such as swinging or tag the children are better able to concentrate on the social interactions. Snack time is also a time when children are clear about what they need to do (eat!), freeing them to be more relaxed and attentive. Children may be picky eaters, or be on special diets, so it is important to get that information before they join the group. The snack is also an excellent time to reflect about the day's activities, conflicts, and resolutions, as well as positive behaviors that will be shared with parents. As with most activities mentioned, it is helpful to mark the child's spot for snack, either by having placemats with their name or simply by placing a piece of tape with their name on the table.

Activity: Closing Circle Time

GOAL: PARENTS REJOIN THE GROUP AND REVIEW THE DAY'S EVENTS WITH THEIR CHILDREN

Intervention	Strategies
Attendance chart Names and dates attended	Having a chart with all the children's names hanging in the room, with a box for each date of attendance, helps children keep track of their attendance as well as who might be missing. At the end of the month or session the children love receiving the part of the chart that contains their name, and the stickers that marked their attendance, a visual reminder of their participation in the group.
Intervention	**Strategies**
Reward stars Great Sharing!	It is always our preference not to become dependent on concrete awards in the group. If the children are having a difficult time adjusting to the group, little prizes or stickers may be used as positive reinforcement for making it through a session. For example, if there is a maladaptive behavior that the therapist cannot reframe and extinguish then providing the children with a number of stars for positive behaviors which can be cashed in for a prize at the end of group can motivate the child to change his behavior. Over time, the children may not need the toy rewards. A nice substitution is a paper star with a description of a positive social interaction they had with a peer. The star reward provides clear feedback to both the child and the parent about the child's positive behavior so that they can enjoy the experience together; children seem to thrive on the positive feedback. The closing circle is also a time to remind the children about any upcoming changes in the group due to a child's or a therapist's vacation, an upcoming holiday, or a new child. Each session ends with a goodbye song that the children love to sing in many different keys and silly voices.

A note about behavior

The behavioral chart at the end of the chapter outlines behaviors that commonly emerge during particular activities, and strategies for intervening. While the same behavior may be seen at different times in the group, the underlying issue may be different. Understanding the issues is very important when considering the intervention to be used. For example, if a child tends to run around frenetically during circle time and the behavior repeats itself during table time, asking questions about what sets this child off and what could be making him anxious or confused are important. At circle time, the child may be anxious about what is going to happen during circle discussion. The clinician might be using too many words and talking quickly, which in turn makes the child feel anxious. The child may not know how to connect with his peers and the adults. Or perhaps he had some difficulty prior to group that is still making him anxious and he isn't able to settle down. If the behavior repeats itself during table time, all of the previous questions should be revisited. Assessing the specific demands of the activity and the child's capacity to perform or feel comfortable enough to try the activity should be explored.

Many fine motor projects are challenging for children with Asperger's Syndrome. A sensitive child might be distracting himself and others from his difficulty by running about or roaming aimlessly in the room. As one can see, there are many different possible triggers for a given behavior. Realistically, it is impossible to always know and be sure what is driving a particular behavior. The same intervention might be used regardless. However, when the connections between the child's concern and his behavior can be made, beginning groundwork is set for helping the child develop self-awareness. *These connections need to be made over and over again* for the child, given how self-awareness is such a central area of difficulty for the child with Asperger's Syndrome. Parents also benefit from helping themselves, and then their child, make the connection between behavior and what is driving it. Having an understanding of what underlies a certain behavior can help both the parents and the child out of the cycle of feeling helpless, overwhelmed, overly frustrated, and angry with each other. Teachers and clinicians go through a similar process. When behavior is disruptive or at times confusing, they can feel powerless or unsure of how to manage the behavior. When a person feels this way they may be more reactive to a child, viewing the behavior as a personal insult to them, leading them to interventions that might not be the most helpful.

The group therapy chart attempts to illustrate some common problem behaviors, possible causes of such behavior, and interventions that might be useful. The hope is that the chart can get parents, teachers, and clinicians to begin thinking about why a child is presenting specific maladaptive behaviors, and provide some practical suggestions that might help the child cope more adaptively (see Appendix II: Behavioral Strategies Chart for Group Settings). We have learned that many of the children are much more responsive to comments being made indirectly about a maladaptive behavior than directly. Being told directly not to do something sets many children off, either to flee the activity or react aggressively towards the individual they feel is criticizing them. We have often been better able to stay connected with them by either identifying more adaptive solutions in the context of the conversation with another colleague, or suggesting an alternative directly to the child.

There will be times when these strategies may not deter or alter a child's behavior. At this point, more stringent behavioral systems may need to be utilized. An important issue for clinicians in the group is deciding whether to implement a behavioral program for all children or just the child who is having difficulty. Since children with Asperger's Syndrome have difficulty understanding that rules can be different for different people, it appears to be easier on everyone if a system is in place for all of the children. All children seem to enjoy positive feedback and utilizing a behavioral system serves to reinforce the positive behaviors you are working on.

How does one assess the effectiveness of a social skills group?

One must remember from a research perspective that these programs are still in their infancy. Standardized evaluations cannot take place until the interventions are conceptualized, documented, replicated in many places, and compared to a control group. The adolescent age group has been researched the most. Attwood (1998), Klin, Volkmar and Sparrow (2000), and Ozonoff and Miller (1995) have all reported progress in the child's social skills following participation in a social skills group.

The first question that consumes everyone's interest is whether the progress the child makes in the group setting will be generalized to other settings. For that to happen, the child must be able to internalize some of the cues he has been taught and apply them to people and settings which are not identical to the group setting. So, in practical terms, one would think about the behavior problems which triggered the entry into a therapeutic group and see if these problems are still taking place, in what settings, and how frequently they occur.

Next, one might explore whether the child is being provided with interventions that can be replicated in different settings, such as the home and school. The best way we have found to foster generalizations is to share with the child's parents and teachers techniques that we have found helpful in facilitating a child's communication skills and social behaviors. The parents in the program quickly learn by observing their child in a group setting that their child is much more responsive when the adults reduce the amount of verbal requests and use visual cues. When they do make requests they make sure they have the child's attention before talking, speak in a much slower and less complicated manner, and use visual cues to support them. Teachers have found it very useful to observe their student in the group and have a chance to talk with the child's clinician about the most helpful, specific interventions with the child, and how they may be applied at school. We frequently send a clinician to the child's school to consult with the teachers, develop a shared understanding of what they are experiencing, and brainstorm about which of the interventions that have helped in the group may be integrated into the school setting (see Chapter 11 for a more
   detailed look at this issue).

Lastly, one might ask if the child is having more positive experiences with peers both at school and on play dates. We are always surprised to hear how fondly these children, who meet once a week for 90 minutes, talk about each other. For many of the children, this is the first group they describe as being their "friends." After months of practice they use each other's names as they rush into the waiting room to show a new toy they just received, or tell a joke. The children they see in the group are often the same children they ask to have over for play dates or invite to their birthday parties. Still, one must remember that social and emotional difficulties are the core of the Asperger's Syndrome diagnosis. Even though the presenting problems may diminish and the child's interests may change or expand, the child will still have difficulties in the area of social relationships, though they may be subtler. In short, the group program we have presented here has never "cured" a child, but rather we have been able to fine tune our understanding of the child and develop intervention strategies to better fit the child's strengths and needs, fostering his adaptation at home and at school.

How do we communicate with our child's teacher about the strategies that have worked to enhance our child's social development in the group program?

Many teachers are responsive, and welcome reading materials that can help them understand a child's behavior. Our program provides families with a group summary written with the hope that the parents will share it with the child's teachers, clinicians, and childcare providers. The summary has been helpful for both parents and teachers when thinking about how to change certain behaviors and also to understand what underlies the behavior. Table 8.1 is an example of a group summary that can be adapted by either a parent or other professionals.

Table 8.1 An example of a group summary for the school

FRIENDS' GROUP SUMMARY

Name: "Brian"   Parents:

Birthdate: Address:

Dates of Program:

Identifying and Referral Information:

Brian was evaluated at age four and diagnosed with Asperger's Syndrome. He has attended the Friends' Program since the summer of 1999. The group was recommended to help him improve his socialization and communication skills.

Program Description:

The Friends' Group is a therapeutic group program designed to help children who are having difficulty adapting socially in their home, school, or day-care setting. The goal of the group is to provide children with a positive group experience by fostering their ability to develop positive relationships with the therapists and peers and to enhance their communication and socialization skills. There is a parents' component – a weekly parent group that meets in conjunction with the children's group. The group meets once a week for an hour and a half.

Behavioral Observations:

- Brian often needed verbal prompting during circle time in order to help him attend to the topic.
- Brian was eager to connect with other children and responsive to staff support.

- During open-ended conversations with peers, Brian's attention often drifted and he could appear internally distracted.

- Brian initiated play frequently with peers but had difficulty sustaining the interaction for more than a few minutes.

- Brian frequently expressed concern over his friend's feelings and would attempt to find solutions to cheer his friend up.

- Brian expressed his frustrations by withdrawing or giving up on a task. He sometimes would "freeze" when something occurred which he hadn't intended, such as accidentally spilling juice or causing a problem with a friend.

- When Brian was tired or confused, he would begin to wander around the room and needed support to refocus his attention.

- Brian is beginning to identify a wider range of emotions and, with prompting, can express his feelings to peers in an attempt to resolve conflict.

- On occasion, Brian would imitate other children in an attempt to connect with them. The imitation occurred typically when he was unsure of how to engage a child.

Strategies Which Have Been Effective:

- Visual cues to clarify schedule and expectations – when introducing a change in the schedule, it is important to walk through the changes with Brian, providing visual cues when appropriate. He also responds well to simple explanations as to why changes are occurring. If you don't provide the explanation he can become stuck on thinking about it and appear mildly resistant.

- *Verbal rewards and external reinforcements* (e.g. behavioral system) – Brian responds well to corrective feedback and a positive approach. If something is very challenging for him, a reward system can help motivate him to persist at a task.

- *Prompting and modeling appropriate response to peers' initiations* – Brian often misses the cues children provide that suggest they want to interact with him, resulting in his friends at times feeling ignored. That is rarely Brian's intent. Brian responds quickly to a prompt from an adult – for example, "Brian, John is asking you a question. Can you ask John to tell you again what he wants?"

- *Facilitate ongoing social interaction in play by prompting, modeling, structuring the tasks to keep Brian engaged* – Brian is motivated to interact with peers but at times needs to be provided with a suggestion as to how to maintain the theme of play. He has made much improvement in this area when interacting with one other child but groups of children are more difficult for him to navigate.

- *Label his confusion and redirect him back to the situation with a suggestion regarding what he can do* – Brian is a sensitive child who can be confused by social situations or situations where a lot of verbal directions are provided. He will wander off or become distractible in response to his difficulty in processing information. It is helpful to recognize his confusion and help him understand either the situation or the directions and to not interpret his behavior as willful or manipulative.

- *In large group situations, seat Brian near the teacher or near a calm child. Avoid placing him in the middle of the group* – in large groups, Brian can become overly stimulated by too much sensory input – touch, noise, movement; therefore, it is helpful to try to decrease the sensory overload as much as possible.

- *Provide consistent and clear behavioral expectations. Outline consequences for behavior that is not acceptable* – *Brian is very responsive to rules that are clear and consistent; outlining consequences ahead of time can help him make better decisions for himself.*

- *Cue Brian to use a child's name when he is speaking to them* – Brian can start talking "into the air" and not realize he hasn't gotten anyone's attention. Reminding him to use names improves his chance to make a connection.

- *Help clarify Brian's intent when he "freezes" out of anxiety* – if Brian has accidentally caused a problem, he worries that he is going to get in trouble or be misunderstood. It is important to let him know you recognize he didn't mean to hurt anyone (define the situation) and ask him to see if his friend is O.K. and to verbalize that it was an accident (or ask him to pick up whatever he spilt, etc.).

Areas of Strength:

- Ability to generalize learning
- Polite, generous, eager to please – responsive to adult direction
- Empathy for others and responds to others' distress
- Fairly high frustration tolerance
- Interest in interaction and making friends

Areas of Concern:

- Difficulty reading social cues
- Difficulty recognizing his own feelings, interpreting others' and responding appropriately
- Delayed reciprocal social conversation – trouble following another person's topic of conversation
- "Freezes" when he causes social problems
- Difficulty following complex, multi-step directions – slow verbal processor

Summary:

Brian is a very sweet, generous child with an easy-going temperament who has made significant progress in the last year since he first entered the Friends' Group. His interest and eagerness to interact with children has expanded significantly. His responsiveness to adult support and positive feedback is a significant strength. He continues to need help reading a social situation and incorporating other children's perspectives. Similarly, his pragmatic language (social use of language) is below that of same age peers. He processes verbal information slowly and needs time to integrate multiple pieces of information. Visual cues can help him process the information more quickly. Brian is also a child who interprets the world in concrete, black and white terms. Therefore, changes in the routine that are made unexpectedly will not always make sense to him and he will become anxious if the changes are not outlined ahead of time. Similarly, more abstract verbal information may initially be confusing to him. The most challenging social situations for Brian are large group, unstructured, and minimally supervised times (e.g. recess). He may not always know how to handle the social demands made by peers and will tend to imitate or follow the other children's behavior (good and bad). With support and understanding of his needs, one can help predict and prepare Brian for such situations. Because Brian isn't prone to behavioral problems, should they arise for Brian (resistance, aggressiveness, hyperactivity), the environment and the support he is receiving should be closely evaluated.

Recommendations:

1. Begin using a daily schedule to reduce confusion (e.g. sequence of events, time, etc.).
2. Develop a collaborative relationship with teachers and other professionals working with Brian.
3. Encourage play dates and provide facilitation when needed.
4. Continue in the Friends' Group Program to foster communication and social skills.

Conclusion

Group therapy interventions are powerful tools that can empower not only parents but also teachers and other care providers working with a child with Asperger's Syndrome. The many interventions and strategies introduced in this chapter are intended to be a starting point for those working with children in a group setting. Much of the information presented can be adapted to fit with other therapeutic modalities and should not be seen as limited to the intensive parent–child model of the Friends' Program. Some of the interventions can also be easily utilized in a classroom or day-care setting. For example, the noise thermometer, a visual aid to help children control their voices, was eagerly adopted by many teachers who found it helpful for their entire class. Many of the speech and language pathologists involved in the children's care have found that observing them in the group gives them ideas for interventions that they can apply to their therapy sessions, such as writing a social story to help the child cope with not being first in every activity. The group observation also allows them to observe the quality of the children's pragmatic language with both adults and with peers. This is especially helpful if they typically see them only in individual sessions. The collaborative relationship between parents, teachers, childcare providers, clinicians, and the group therapists is essential to ensure the continuity of goals, a shared understanding of the child, and to provide the best chance at generalizing new, more adaptive, behaviors.

The Friends' Group Model has the luxury of providing parents with an ongoing opportunity to observe their child with a therapist trained to interpret the child's responses and the strategies being utilized by the child therapist. The luxury of being able to work with the same small group of families for an extended period of time provides both the therapists and parents with those powerful memories of what a child was like when they first entered the group. It is striking how quickly a parent can forget how their child initially refused to participate in any group activity, and hid under the table. All they can think about now is how to get their child to do a better job at regulating his enthusiasm towards seeing his friends, and not hug them too hard or yell their name out across the room. Over and over again, parents report the power of these observations and how the insight they gained has enabled them to become better advocates for their child, accepting and understanding certain behaviors that they may have previously viewed as being puzzling, frightening, or simply annoying.

Many clinicians may feel as if they do not have the facilities or the resources to provide such an intervention. However, parents and therapists can be creative in finding different ways to try to create similar opportunities. For example, a parent may go with the therapist to the child's school or daycare setting so that they can conduct an observation together. Similarly, parents being able to share their stories with other parents going through similar difficulties is a powerful intervention that can take place in a doctor's waiting room, a therapist's office, the playground, or an empty classroom in a school. What is important here is that the parents and professionals become partners in advocating for this type of intervention and the building of collaborative relationships with the shared goal of helping the child.

CHAPTER 9

Enhancing Relationships through Speech and Language Intervention

Christine Bate

The first two chapters of the book illustrated the central role of comm-unciation in all aspects of the child's life. Both spoken language and nonverbal language such as facial expression and body language are essential elements of our ability to function in our society. Since difficulty with the social use of language is one of the defining characteristics of Asperger's Syndrome, this chapter will focus on ways of helping the child use language to communicate with others and engage in social interactions.

During the diagnostic process, parents' attention is drawn to the way their child communicates. A thorough evaluation will have included observation of the child's use of language to communicate in various settings, in addition to the parent and teacher checklists that are used. A test of pragmatic skills may also have been administered, although these are not as informative as observa-tion of the child in real life situations, especially with the younger children in the age range we are addressing. A standardized test presents the child with a situation that involves the social use of language and asks what he would or should do. The situation is described either verbally or in a picture and, for the purposes of scoring the child's response, it has to be a single isolated event. This leads to a stimulus sentence such as "Arturo didn't like the sandwich his mother had made for him. What should he say?" or, while being shown a picture of a group of children playing a ball game and a boy approaching them with a bat, "Jimmy wants to join the game. What should he say?" The social situations that children with AS have difficulty negotiating are usually more complex than this and they occur while other activities are going on, as in a preschool setting. Frequently the children with AS have already been taught scripts to use, and in a quiet testing situation can give an appropriate response. Because of this, scores from a test of pragmatic skills should always be supplemented with observation in various settings.

After the evaluation is finished, there are two questions that are frequently asked by parents, teachers, and clinicians when the child has been given a diagnosis of language disorder, or a diagnosis such as AS where the language disorder is part of the syndrome.

We were told that the child's language was different as well as delayed. What does this mean and will he catch up?

One important distinction to be made when looking at delayed language development is whether the language is only delayed, or delayed and different. In the case of delayed language, a child aged five years may have the language of a normally developing three-year-old. When language is delayed and different, a five-year-old may have the vocabulary and sentence structure of a three-year-old, but will also have unusual language features, such as inability to maintain a conversation, poor eye contact, or echolalia. In the case of children with AS, their language is different in that, although they appear to understand and use age-appropriate sentences and frequently have a large vocabulary, they do not use their language successfully in turn-taking communication with others, either socially or to share information. When language is different as well as delayed, this requires a treatment program that is likely to be much longer in duration. It can take a long time to teach children the social uses of language.

Why does the child need a hearing evaluation? He seems to hear well enough in many situations but he doesn't always pay attention to what I say

It is very common for parents and preschool teachers to have concerns about the listening skills of young children. These concerns are magnified for good reason when a child is experiencing behavioral and communication problems. This is why a hearing evaluation is generally suggested following a speech and language or a team evaluation where a diagnosis is made.

A *hearing evaluation* determines whether a hearing loss is present – that is, whether sounds and words at a normal level of loudness are received by the hearing mechanism. However, once the sounds have reached the brain, they have to be interpreted or processed for any message to be meaningful. A loud bang does not need much interpretation, but a string of instructions puts more strain on the system. This phase of listening is referred to as *Central Auditory Processing* (CAP), and it is an area where many children with diverse diagnoses have difficulty. CAP occurs frequently in children with AS. There are tests of auditory processing that can be administered, but generally they are not suitable for young children. There are also therapeutic programs for children with auditory processing problems, called *Auditory Training*. In these, different aspects of listening are addressed. For instance, to help a child focus on spoken language, he may wear a headset and hear a recording of someone speaking in one ear while he hears the noise of a busy street in the other earpiece. In early childhood these programs are not to be recommended, because at this age young children learn better from real experiences. If parents or clinicians are interested in exploring the use of these programs later, information may be obtained from therapists and on the web. The usefulness of the diagnosis of CAP and treatment programs is still being debated among professionals (Cacace and McFarland 1998).

Children on the autistic spectrum may also experience *sensitivity to noises* that do not bother most people. Sometimes unusual sensitivity to high frequencies can be detected in a hearing evaluation; however, more frequently the problem is noticed with noises such as loud machinery or another child's block structure falling. An understanding of the child's real discomfort enables one to accept his behavior and make accommodations. For example, it is disappointing to find that Susan is not enjoying the brass band performance in the park; she had looked forward to it, but is now covering her ears. A parent or teacher might find a space to watch where there is enough room to step back safely with her. Interestingly, Susan probably makes plenty of noise herself in her daily activities, but this does not bother her.

Overview to speech and language intervention

This section will look at how difficulties with the pragmatics of language impair a child with AS and explore interventions that can be applied both at home and in the classroom to address these issues.

The following terms are the cornerstones of the difficulties seen in the child. The *pragmatics of language* concerns how all the skills involved with receptive and expressive language are put to use in communicating with others. Broadly, it means the use of language to have one's needs met, to find out about the world, and to be appropriately social. Speech and language pathologists look at two major aspects of pragmatics when evaluating children's language. The first one is their *intent to communicate*: what functions they want their language to accomplish; and the second is their understanding of *discourse skills*. *Communicative intent* refers to the purposes for which a person interacts with someone else. Early developing examples are seeking attention or making a request. These intents remain remarkably similar from the preverbal action of a toddler who tugs on a caregiver's pants to an adult saying "Hey!" or "Excuse me" to get someone's attention. It is the way the communication is encoded that changes. *Discourse skills* are the conventions for carrying on a communicative interaction in the culture to which the speakers belong; they are the social rules that define our social roles in all the different settings we encounter. Typically when two people interact, there is an exchange of greetings, a topic is introduced and discussed, with each person taking turns in the conversation and reading the clues that indicate when it is their turn to speak. A change in topic is signaled, perhaps by saying "Oh, by the way…," and an agreement to end the conversation is reached by exchanging comments such as "Well, I'd better be going" and "O.K. See you later." There is much more to discourse skills, for instance reading facial and gestural language, inferring meanings, and knowing what form of address is appropriate in different situations. Yet it is usual for everyone to observe these rules in social interactions, and when someone violates them, that person is perceived as rude or odd.

A child with AS has problems with discourse skills both with peers and adults. In a group setting, he may find it difficult to make and keep friends. For example, one morning Peter interrupted a group of children who were feeding the guinea pigs to show them the racing car from his collection that he had brought to playgroup. He continued to point out the car's features even when the children turned back to the guinea pigs. Loretta said "Go away" and blocked his way into the area. He left and ran his racing car by himself, away from any other children. His behavior showed that he did not understand that he should join the group and talk about the animals before showing his racing car. He did not read the signals given by the group, such as not responding to his comments about his car and turning their backs, that indicated that they wanted to continue their activity. The next day Peter did not want to go to playgroup. He said he had no friends. But his mother understood that he had misinterpreted his peers' cues and felt rejected. She persuaded him to go to the playgroup by suggesting that they could drive past the car showroom on the way to the group. Once they arived, she asked the teacher with Peter when it would be a good time to tell his friends about the new cars that he had seen and was very exicted about. The teacher supported his mother for her attempts to set up a successful interaction and told Peter that she was sure that his friends would like to hear two things he liked about the cars at circle time. If they had more questions, they could ask him on the playground.

Just as there are many variations in behaviors and skills among children who are diagnosed with AS, there are many variations in the kind of intervention programs, or combination of communication based programs, that are appropriate. As described in other chapters, these children can be helped by consultation, by individual, dyadic, or group programs, or a combination of them. Since difficulties with the pragmatics of language are common among children with AS, a speech and language pathologist should always be involved in decisions about treatment plans and how to carry them out.

In a program such as the Friends' Group Program described in Chapter 8, it is always ideal to have a speech and language clinician as one of the therapists. When this is not possible, there should be ongoing consultation with the group leaders to discuss each child and make recommendations, for him and for the whole program, in order to facilitate communication skills.

Other ways in which a speech and language clinician can be involved are through individual therapy and consultation. As a rule, individual speech and language therapy is not the chosen intervention for a child with AS because his difficulties are predominantly with the social use of language that are best addressed in a group situation, among other children. A child with AS may have the same communication problems in interacting with both adults and children, but an adult makes allowances and adapts to the poor communication skills, whereas children do not. Young children benefit from guided experiences in real situations rather than relating to an adult clinician, or acting out pretend situations and then being expected to transfer the information to real situations outside the therapy room. Having said this, there are times when individual therapy is beneficial both to the child and to the parent. In these sessions, the speech and language pathologist can demonstrate and teach interactive language strategies that will improve communication and make it easier for parents to understand and help their child with interpersonal relationships, both at home and out in the community. It is not suggested that this should be long-term therapy but rather that, following this period of direct intervention, the speech and langauge clinician should continue to act as consultant to parents and other professionals providing services.

An alternative to a social skills group is a small group program of six to eight children with a speech and language therapist, often called a language group. There is usually an assistant who may be an early childhood educator or a speech and language intern. The session typically resembles a preschool session with free play, art projects, fine motor activities, snack time, and gross motor activities. The language teaching occurs as the children are engaged in activities and interactions that are natural and provide teachable moments. Another combination of services is provided in a language-motor group with a speech and language pathologist and an occupational therapist. Again, the sessions will resemble a preschool program but both motor and language activities are chosen to meet the specific needs of the children enrolled in the program.

Sometimes, preschool teachers or other therapists suggest that a child with AS should have an aide, or "shadow," at preschool to help promote better communication with the other children. This can be very effective when the person is chosen carefully and receives training. There has to be an understanding that the "shadow" is not a friend to play with, or an individual teacher. The challenge in providing a "shadow" is that it takes a knowledge of the dynamics of play and activities among young children and a sensitivity to language to be able to support tactfully when a child needs support and to know when to withdraw because the child is managing a situation on his own.

Play-based therapy

A play-based program is often recommended for speech and language intervention with young children. It is based on the philosophy that the optimal way to enhance children's capacity to communicate is respectful of the child as he engages in age-appropriate activities in a naturalistic environment.

Some of the strategies that will be described are useful for enhancing language development for all children and can also be used to remediate delays in receptive and expressive language development as well as difficulties in the use of language to communicate. The emphasis in the later part of this chapter is upon the particular difficulties that children with AS experience in the use of social language. The methods described can be used at home or in group situations as presented here, but there may be times when the expertise of a speech and language pathologist can be helpful.

The information in this chapter is based on the INter-REActive Learning (INREAL) program (Weiss 1981) but in addition embodies best practice approach to early childhood communication development and enhancement. The philosophy and strategies described here can be used at home or in a group setting by parents, caregivers, and teachers. There are other language

programs for young children that are based on play in a naturalistic environment and there is a great deal of overlap among them. The Hanen program, for
instance, is a widely used parent–child communication program that trains
parents, caregivers, and teachers. The program has been adapted to the needs
of parents of children with Autistic Spectrum Disorders in the book *It Takes
Two to Talk* (Manolson 1992). *Also Working with Pragmatics* by Anderson-Wood and Smith (1997) explains the pragmatics of language and
describes informal assessment and intervention based on the authors' philosophy of using a naturalistic approach in everyday communication situations.
There are many similarities between these approaches to the remediation of
communication difficulties in children with AS, and the Floor Time model
developed by Stanley Greenspan for the treatment of children on the autistic
spectrum (Greenspan 1992). Twatchman (1995) describes an intervention
program for school age children that includes some strategies and methods
that may be useful in group situations for young children. The activities are
generally more structured than in play-based therapy.

The INREAL program emphasizes the importance of using age-
appropriate activities in a naturalistic environment. This method is easily
adapted to interactions between caregivers and the child at home, and its use
provides consistency in dealing with the child. The child plays either with a
clinician or in a group, choosing the activities that he will engage in during
free time, and engaging with others in group time or snack time with support.
As in individual therapy, materials and activities are available for the child to
choose from. The room looks very much like a good preschool setting but the
environment, either a preschool type setting or a clinic room with toys and
materials available, is carefully planned in order to foster and elicit the kinds
of communication that are felt to be appropriate for that particular group of
children. The activities and materials are a specialized selection from good
practice in early childhood education. In this environment, the child makes
his own choices; it is a planned but unprogrammed environment.

INREAL emphasizes the importance of the parent or clinician respecting
the child, which means being genuine with him. Authenticity is an attitude
that leads to avoiding talking down to the child, using normal intonation
rather than the higher pitch and sing-song voice that is used with infants,
listening to his ideas, and giving him choices. It requires adults to be aware of
how they are communicating with a child or with the children in a group at
the same time as they are talking to them. This is not easy and, at the
beginning, parents and teachers are advised to choose only one strategy, for

instance active listening, and focus on it for a set period of time each day, perhaps ten minutes, then add another strategy, or focus on a different one. Soon, it becomes second nature to be aware of how you are communicating, as well as what you are communicating, and you begin to wonder why others are not so aware of just what they are doing when engaging a child in conversation. The answer is that most children "pick up" all the aspects of language – pronunciation, vocabulary, grammar, meanings, and social conventions – with only a little help from those around them. Most parents are unaware of how they communicate; they do not teach their child to talk: the child learns. Parents and teachers of an AS child find that they need to teach him *the social use of language and the finer meanings of words and sentences.* In order to do this, they need to understand what the child's areas of need are and find a way of helping him learn. Thinking about what is said to the child as well as why it is said is empowering.

In using the INREAL model, adults desiring to enhance and improve a child's language skills can learn how to make their interaction with a child more useful. A self-awareness of how they are reacting and responding to what the child is doing and saying is developed, enabling them to apply the child centered philosophy and strategies of the program. The child centered philosophy is embodied in the ways in which authenticity or respect for the child is implemented. There are some broad guidelines for laying the groundwork for successful interactions by *setting the inter-reactive scene,* and there are *strategies* for using the interactions to enhance the child's language development and teach the social use of language.

Setting the inter-reactive scene

There are four general categories that help increase one's awareness of how to communicate respectfully with a child: *pace, positioning, preparation,* and the *use of questions* (Table 9.1). You can think of these as minding your Ps and Qs! An understanding of these enables you to set the stage for a meaningful interaction in both clinical and home settings.

Table 9.1 Setting the inter-reactive scene

- Pace
- Positioning
- Preparation
- Use of questions

Pace refers to the rate at which you talk, the time you leave between conversational turns, your tolerance for silence, and your body language. All of these factors make a noticeable difference in the attitude you project to the person you are communicating with. Whether you are a parent or professional, being aware of your pace really encourages a genuine relationship. Unless someone draws your attention to it, you tend to be unaware of the rate at which you talk, and everyone has times when they talk faster in excitement, anger, or irritation, and the pressure mounts. A way of monitoring pace in a therapeutic setting is to set an audiotape recorder going and leave it to run for a period of time.

Many children with AS are slow to respond when they are absorbed in a favorite activity. One can be pleasantly surprised by the quality of the response and the ideas that are expressed when time is taken to wait for a response. Be aware that body language – facial expressions and gestures such as tapping a finger or twisting a ring – can send the message to the child that you have something else to do.

Positioning refers to setting the scene for a conversation. Most of the time, we keep talking to members of the family as we go about our business and even move around the house, without even thinking about it. In a preschool setting, teachers may begin to talk to a child from across the room and walk past other children before being face to face with him. On the other hand, there are times when we really want to drive home a point, for instance when a child has just started to run into the street, we stop him, take his face in our hands, look him in the eye, and say, "That's not O.K. Stay with me and hold my hand!" Somewhere between these two situations is where we want to be when communicating with a child whose language skills we are trying to improve. To position yourself well before speaking to your child, get down to his level, keep a comfortable distance so that you are not in his "bubble," make eye contact, and then you are ready to make sure he is paying attention by using an alerting word or gesture. Now is the time to say, "Juan is asking if you would like to play spaceman with him. Please answer him." This is particularly important when you have a child who may not be hearing you, may have "selective hearing," or has auditory processing difficulties.

What is important to remember about these children is that they are frequently not going to be attentive to your auditory cues. Therefore in order to get their attention it is helpful not to speak across the room, especially when another person is speaking or in group situations. Approach the child, check on your positioning, and remember about pace.

These children also often need extra time to make transitions. This is when *preparation* can help avoid a frustrating interaction. On a small scale, this can mean getting a child's attention before giving the important part of your message. This is especially useful for a child with AS who has auditory processing problems.

On a larger scale, verbal preparation for a transition is essential for all children with AS. It is helpful for parents and teachers to remember that the first step is to get the child's attention. This can then be followed by introducing the topic in a clear way to pave the way for better understanding, for example saying, "We said we'd go to the library after lunch." This may not be enough, so then build in a short sequence of events that lead up to departure, such as "Finish your milk," "Now wash your hands," "Collect your books," before finally the message that you have led up to, "It's time to go."

The last area in setting the inter-reactive scene, understanding the *use of questions*, is very helpful in increasing spontaneous conversational language. The use of too many questions can lead to an adult- rather than a child-oriented conversation. Also, an understanding of the use of open and closed questions can help the adult extend conversational interactions.

Looking in more detail at the use of questions by one of the participants in a conversation provides an opportunity to examine these rules in use. For instance, an adult who sees a neighbor child with his mother in the store and wants to engage him in conversation may focus on a toy that he is carrying. She asks, "What's that you have there?"; by saying that, she establishes the topic of conversation. The child may reply "A space ship," and that constitutes his turn. She takes the next turn and says, "Where did you get it?" – thus continuing the topic and asking another question that leads to the child's response, "The toy store." So far, the adult has controlled the topic by asking questions that require an answer and can be answered in one word. She could at this point leave a few moments of silence to allow the child to make a comment of his own, either on the same topic or another one if he would prefer to talk about something other than his space ship. Then it would become a true turn-taking conversation.

Questions that can be answered with one word are referred to as closed questions and there are many times when it is appropriate and useful to use them – for instance, "Is that your library book?"; "Do you want milk or juice?" However, when a child needs help in learning to express his own ideas and to carry on a reciprocal, turn-taking conversation, the use of open-ended questions is beneficial. A question such as "What happened?" or "How did you make that?" elicits phrases or sentences that express the child's own ideas. As was suggested in the above example, pausing before taking another turn also could encourage the other participant to add his own ideas to the conversation. A useful strategy for parents and teachers is to make a statement rather than asking a question. The adult in the example could have said "You brought your space ship to the store" or "I saw you at the pool yesterday." If there is no response after a pause, move to a "wh" question.

Now that the inter-reactive scene has been set, it is time to talk about strategies for enhancing and remediating communication skills.

Strategies

The strategies from the INREAL program begin with *SOUL – Silence, Observation, Understanding, Listening.* The first word, *silence*, gives the parent, teacher, or clinician permission to take time before engaging in communication. This may mean that a teacher approaches a child at play with some blocks and watches for a time before speaking. A parent may enter a room and watch a child quietly to tune into his activity, or a clinician may point to a garage and figures and say "See what we have here," and then watch without making suggestions as to what to do with the toys, in order to observe the spontaneous play that the child engages in. Frequently, the child will begin to talk about what he is doing and the conversation can go on from there. If he does not even talk to himself out loud about what he is doing, joining him in parallel play without speaking gives a situation where there is togetherness without intrusiveness. This is called mirroring and will be discussed later.

During the silence, *observation* can take place and this leads to an *understanding* of what the child is doing and perhaps pretending. This avoids the intrusion of an adult to change a child's agenda and therefore leads to genuine communication about what the child is really interested in rather than the adult directing the topic of conversation.

Finally, *listening* enables the child to express the thoughts that he has about the situation, whether it is pretend play, functional play, or large motor play. Active listening occurs when a person gives his whole attention to the speaker, gives eye contact, and encourages the speaker by making appropriate comments that demonstrate the listener's true interest. This verbal and nonverbal engagement in the interaction assures the speaker that the information being given in each turn is being processed.

SOUL is a good foundation for communicative interaction with a child. Other strategies can be used to build on this engagement with a child in order to enhance, expand, and remediate language development. Table 9.2 presents common strategies as defined in the INREAL program. They offer a way for a clinician or parent to join in a natural conversation and model appropriate social interaction. At the same time, grammatical or pronunciation mistakes are remediated and new or better ways to express thoughts are demonstrated.

Table 9.2 Ways to encourage language development
• Mirroring
• Self-talk
• Vocal reflecting
• Expansion
• Modeling

The following text includes strategies for expanding the child's language development.

Mirroring:	Imitation of actions, movements, and facial expressions without speaking.
Goal:	Joining a child without getting in his way.
Example:	Move to the child slowly and watch for a time before mirroring a small action. The child is running a small car. Slowly begin to do the same beside him.
Self-talk:	Talking aloud about what you are doing while you are with a child.

Goal: Modeling how to express emotions and expanding language without the child feeling confronted.

Example: "I'll finish washing this lettuce, then I'll phone Maria. She's sad because she lost her purse."

Vocal reflecting: Saying a child's words or sounds right back to him.

Goal: Showing that you are interested and are listening and want to know more while correcting pronunciation or grammatical errors without comment.

Example: The child says "Cesar bringed him boat today" and you reply, "Cesar brought his boat?"

Expansion: Repeating what a child just said and adding new information.

Goal: Encouraging turn-taking conversational skills by saying more about a topic while correcting pronunciation and grammar and modeling social skills.

Example: The child is playing with dinosaurs and says, "He's hitting him." You reply, "Yes, the blue dinosaur is hitting the red one and it really hurts."

Modeling A: Taking a turn in a conversation without using the child's words but staying on the same topic.

Goal: To demonstrate new and varied use of language on a topic.

Example: Leroy says "This playdoh makes my hands yucky" and the teacher replies, "You can wash your hands at the sink."

Modeling B: Providing a demonstration of a desired response (McCormick and Schiefelbusch 1990).

Goal: To provide a script that a child can use, often in a social situation.

Example: Lavonne says "Carmen won't let me have the big dinosaur" and the teacher replies, "You can say, 'I'd like a turn with the dinosaur when you've finished.'"

The above strategies are very helpful for children with AS. However, the overriding characteristic children with AS have is difficulty in developing and maintaining social relationships and reciprocal communication with their peers (Attwood 1998) – in other words, social language. Table 9.3 outlines areas of difficulty with social language. Examples of each of the areas and ways of dealing with them will be presented and then three typical situations that arise with children with AS will be described and discussed. The examples may not apply to every child with AS. However, they may be helpful when thinking about how to analyze the communication problems that we see and deciding which of the strategies suggested would be helpful in either resolving the problem, or supporting the child as he struggles to understand the complexities of social language.

Table 9.3 Areas of difficulty with social language

- Joint attention
- Eye contact
- Being a partner in conversations
- Providing too little or too much information
- Polite forms
- Understanding and use of facial expressions and gestures
- Understanding and expressing emotions
- Speech melody
- Sifting information in interactions
- Literal interpretations
- Symbol use and pretend play

The following text takes a closer look at specific areas of pragmatic language which are often difficult for children with Asperger's Syndrome, and examples of intervention strategies targeted at them.

Joint attention: The child is sharing in an experience by looking at an object or event another person is looking at or pointing to. He shifts between looking at the object or event and looking back to the person. At times it is the child who initiates the joint interest.

Example: Charlene continues to hug her favorite toy dog when you draw her attention to a dish the dog could eat out of and thus extend her pretend play. You repeat her name, move to her with the dish, and tap on it as you say, "Look at this."

Eye contact: Connecting with you by looking at you at times but not always. This is an important way of showing social connection. It usually occurs at the beginning of an interaction, and then at times during the interaction, but is not normally continuous.

Example: "Alfredo, look at me just a minute so that I'm sure that you and I are understanding each other."

Being a partner in conversations:

Staying on the topic of conversation and taking turns, opening a topic, closing a topic and giving warning of a shift of topic.

Examples: Debby starts to talk about an incident in *Beauty and the Beast* during a group discussion of tomorrow's picnic. The teacher says, "We're talking about the picnic now."

Billy interrupts and the adult says, "It's Sarah's turn now."

Jim says "Now I'm coming to gobble you up" and his teacher asks key questions and then says, "Oh, you're talking about *The Billy Goat's Gruff* that we read yesterday."

A teacher joins Michelle in the housekeeping area and picks up another phone when Michelle dials. The teacher models opening and closing a conversation.

Providing too little or too much information:

Failing to introduce a new topic so that others can follow, or continuing to talk on a topic when the conversation has shifted.

Example:	Alex and his mother meet Tom in the store. When Alex is introduced, he asks whether Tom's car has a stick shift or automatic transmission. He continues to talk about cars. Alex's mother suggests that Tom would like to hear about their recent visit to the skating rink.
Polite forms:	Using language that is appropriate to a situation and will lead to a successful outcome for an interaction. Children with AS may be surprised and need support and an explanation when they use a "polite script" they have learned, and it is not successful.
Examples:	Roberto pushes Jason away from the table because he put his reptile into Roberto's space station. The teacher says, "You could ask Roberto, 'Can my snake guard your space station doorway?'"
	Carol uses a script and asks Maria, "Please may I play with the tambourine?" Maria says, "No I'm using it." The teacher says to Carol, "Thank you for asking politely. Maria is busy with the tambourine. Ask her if you could have the next turn."

Understanding and use of facial expressions and gestures:

	Interpreting someone's feelings or mood by observing facial expression and body language, both while listening to their words and also without spoken communication.
Examples:	The child does not understand the difference between "This room is a mess" said with a smile or a serious expression and with different body postures. Monitor the child's reaction and supply a clarifying sentence.
	Jenny hits out at Clayton with a smile on her face. The teacher comforts Clayton and tells Jenny "I think that you were angry, but it doesn't look that way when you smile," then she models a fierce expression.

Understanding and expressing emotions:

Being aware of how someone else is feeling or being able to analyze and express one's own state of mind.

Examples: It is Sean's turn to help with a cooking project and he indignantly repeats "It's my turn to stir" while the teacher is comforting Frank, who has fallen off his chair. The teacher may explain to Sean, "Frank is hurt and I need to help him before we continue cooking."

Nate pushes Serena down because she takes his place in the line. The teacher tells Nate, "You can say 'I don't like it when you cut in line,' but it's not O.K. to push her."

Speech melody: Also called *prosody*, means the patterns of stress, intonation, and rhythm of speech.

Examples: Ben exclaims "To infinity and beyond!" exactly the way it is said by the movie character Buzz Lightyear, as he builds with blocks. He may also have been having an internal conversation and this one phrase was spoken out loud. His parent says, "You were thinking about Buzz."

Raymundo speaks in a flat tone as he talks about his favorite topic, earthmoving equipment. His teacher reflects and expands what he says, using an animated way of speaking.

Sifting information in interactions:

Noting all the useful information in an interaction and ignoring sounds and sights that are not important.

Examples: Nahom misunderstands "What are you laughing at?" from a teacher who is looking stern and is meaning "Stop laughing," when a group of children is being silly.

Kyoshi focuses on the page numbers in the story book rather than listen to what his father is reading.

Literal interpretations:

Lack of awareness that figures of speech are not to be taken literally.

Example: The teacher says "Timmy let the cat out of the bag" and Cesar says, "I don't see a cat." The teacher explains that she meant he had told about a secret.

Symbol use and pretend play:

The use of conventional gestures to convey a meaning and the acting out of pretend situations.

Examples: Gerald has never waved goodbye as someone leaves the house, although he dragged his mother to the refrigerator when he wanted a snack from an early age. His mother continues to model the social "goodbye" behavior.

Matthew uses pretend play with his trucks and a garage, but the events are predictable and unvaried. His parents join him in his play, extend the sequences of events with the trucks and garage, and model events that bring in other vehicles and buildings.

As you probably know only too well, this list of difficulties may tap into some of the difficulties a child has, but not all. Let us look at some very common questions asked by parents and teachers of young children with AS and use these examples to illustrate how the information about language in this chapter can be adapted to helping a child with his communicative problems.

What do I do when a child interrupts me all the time and doesn't stop talking?

Poor joint attention is at the bottom of this problem and this leads to trouble with being a partner in conversations. When a child interrupts he is not taking turns in the conversation; he is not watching for visual clues or listening for a tone of voice that signals that it is now his turn. When he keeps on talking on his own topic, he is taking too many turns and is probably providing too much information, something that he has difficulty monitoring. You may find that it is helpful to teach him the rules of conversation openly; as with many children with AS, he is not "picking them up." For example, say "It's my turn" when he begins to take two turns in the conversation at circle time. In addition to modeling good conversational behavior, it can be helpful to interject comments that give him information about how to converse. For example, say "You look as if you're ready to go outside now, so I'll read you the rest later," or "I know you want to tell your dad about your game, but you need to wait until your sister has finished talking."

How do I handle arguments with a child who doesn't seem to have a sense of my perspective?

Children with AS are often rigid and have difficulty with changes of rules and exceptions (Bashe and Kirby 2001), and there may also be times when a child continues to keep you talking with comments like "You promised" and "Just one more time." In this case, prolonging the conversation and reasoning with him is not working. Normal conversational turn-taking is not helping to resolve this situation because with each response the child is given the opportunity to take the next turn and continue the argument.

This situation can be handled in two ways. You can take a turn after each comment but give no new information – simply repeat the first response in this argument, such as "We are going to the park on Tuesday." This is often called the "broken record" approach. Otherwise, withdraw from the conversation as you take the next turn by saying "I'm happy to talk with you but I'm tired of this conversation," or "I don't want to talk about this any more," and then remain silent or leave the room or area. With some children it is useful to role play a similar conflict later, using puppets and exaggerating the other person's perspective.

What should I do when a child ignores what I say?

Parents and teachers often wonder whether a child has *selective hearing*, and it is true that we all have selective hearing at times. The concerns about the presence of selective hearing and whether or not a child with AS has *Central Auditory Processing* problems are both difficult to resolve in young children. In both these cases, naturalistic strategies that modify the listening environment of the child are recommended. Table 9.4 presents a list of ways to help a child with poor listening skills.

Table 9.4 Ways to help a child with poor listening skills

- Gain his attention: say his name and perhaps touch him
- Use an alerting phrase: "Listen to this"; "I've got something to tell you"
- Approach him: avoid shouting across a room
- Be at his eye level so that eye contact is comfortable
- Break up instructions: name one unit at a time
- Use short sentences that you know he can understand
- In groups, place him near you where he can see your face
- Be aware of the general level of noise: notice noise in the room and outside

Is it possible to have a conversation with a child with AS?

Many children with AS like to spend a lot of time at their own activities, and when they are ready to interact, they choose the topic of conversation, do not follow turn-taking rules, and do not respond to a change of topic from their conversational partner. It is not easy for children with AS to develop the skill of conversing; it is a complex activity that they have to learn, and patience and consistency are necessary when helping them to make changes.

The art of conversation is complex, and there are many ways to help a child improve his conversational skills and move towards engaging in reciprocal conversation. A brief outline of a suggested sequence of interactive approaches follows:

- The first step is to set the inter-reactional scene; use SOUL and the strategies for establishing joint attention.
- Join the child at his activity, mirror his actions, and use self-talk.
- Stay with his topic, take short turns, and give clear signals at the end of each turn, both with voice and nonverbal signals such as eye-contact and gesture.
- Be satisfied with a short sequence of turns or circles of communication (Greenspan 1992).
- Engage the child in a short conversation on his topic, then introduce an extension of his topic.

- To introduce a new topic – for instance, asking him what he would like for lunch and naming two choices – use the alerting strategies for children with poor listening skills listed in Table 9.4, and be satisfied at first with a minimal number of turns rather than a discussion of the menu.

It is helpful for parents and teachers to work on one area at a time and continue to focus on that area for brief periods until they feel comfortable using the suggested strategies. Ten minutes of focussed interaction at a time is a good place to start. Other areas can be addressed as the adult feels ready to move on, either by starting on a new conversational task or adding one.

Conclusion

This chapter has presented information about the treatment of speech and language problems relevant to young children with AS. It is hoped that the examples provided throughout the chapter will help the reader better understand the child's communication difficulties, and provide them with strategies to address these issues. Clearly, speech and language is not the only area that concerns the reader and some overlap of information among the chapters will occur. Language permeates all the situations that a child experiences and it is hoped that an understanding of the processes of listening and speaking will enhance the ability to communicate with young children in a way that helps them enjoy satisfying relationships and supports them in their interactions at home, at school, and in the community.

As children with AS progress through school and then move towards adulthood, their difficulties with verbal and nonverbal communication will change. More sensitivity and understanding will be expected of them in interactive situations and, although their expressive and receptive language skills and understanding of the world will likely have kept pace with that of their peers, there may still be aspects of social communication that pose challenges for the child or adult.

Occasional consultation with a speech and language pathologist may be helpful in supporting the child and adult with social communication difficulties. Speech and language intervention provides a safe and supportive setting to explore, understand, and find solutions to the challenges and barriers that communication can pose for them.

CHAPTER 10

Building Connections through Sensory and Motor Pathways

Occupational Therapy

Teri Wiss

As has been described throughout this book, young children take many developmental leaps. Central to the world of the young child is the ability to move, navigate, and regulate one's own body through the multitude of new experiences that young children have. Young children with Asperger's Syndrome (AS) often have challenges in these skills which can impact many aspects of the child's life. These children are often described as clumsy and many avoid fine motor activities. Many of these children seem overly sensitive to noise, touch, and movement, all aspects of sensory modulation. Researchers have documented that children with Autistic Spectrum Disorders score significantly lower in sensory-motor and motor coordination tasks than peers with similar IQ scores (Dunn 1999; Dunn, Myles and Orr 2002; Iwanaga, Kawasaki and Tsuchida 2000). This chapter will provide more detail about sensory and motor functions and their impact on the child's "occupational performance." Occupational therapists (OTs) can help us understand these challenges. Interventions to support the child's participation in meaningful daily life activities, such as getting dressed and eating, interacting with other children, participating in group activities, and developing school readiness skills, will be explored. Before discussing the various sensory systems, let us first discuss how to begin deciding whether a child needs intervention for sensory and motor issues.

When would a child benefit from intervention for sensory and motor issues?

Determining whether OT is needed to address a child's sensory or motor issues depends on many factors. If a child is able to seek and participate in satisfying interactions and appropriate experiences for developing mastery, then the child does not need therapy (Ayres 1979). However, if needs exist, family resources (including both time and money) will be important. The child's sensory and motor needs will have to be prioritized relative to other areas of difficulty. *Safety* is a major priority. Does the child's level of attention, activity level, or lack of motor control threaten his ability to safely meet the demands of his environment? Another factor to consider is the child's current level of progress, as measured by developmental gains. Are the child's sensory and motor needs interfering with his ability to benefit from opportunities that are being provided, such as group programs, physical activities, and attention to tasks? At times, decisions are made when looking at future needs of the child. Parents may be able to modify experiences at home to limit the sensory and motor challenges and allow the child to function, but will the child be equipped to meet the demands that will be placed on him at school? Will the school have the resources to modify demands to meet the abilities of the child? While some children with AS may have only subtle difficulties in processing sensory input and motor skills, they may have more obvious difficulty in self-regulation or praxis. These terms will be further discussed later in this chapter.

In general, if a child has been struggling with skills related to sensory and motor functioning despite attempts by parents, care providers, and teachers to help him adapt to the day-to-day demands, then occupational therapy to address these issues may be an important intervention to pursue. As described in Chapter 3, an evaluation by an OT will determine if intervention is needed and what type of intervention may be most useful. Let us now discuss the types of interventions available.

Overview of interventions

Occupational therapy often consists of a combination of direct and consulta-tive (indirect) services. Therapy utilizing a frame of reference focusing on "sensory integration" (the ability to integrate sensory experiences) is typically provided in conjunction with other approaches, including developmental, sensorimotor, behavioral, or learning, and coping strategies (Anzalone and Murray 2002). As part of occupational therapy, the child, environment, and context in which the task must be performed are important in improving the child's performance and life satisfaction.

Occupational therapy may be provided on an individual basis, since the activity is adjusted moment to moment, depending on the child's responses. Every child is different and the specific activities used may vary from one child to the next. While the therapist may include activities that teach specific skills designed to improve day-to-day skills, such as dressing, activities may also be included that assist in integrating sensory experiences. For example, in order to help prepare a child to focus, a therapist might provide a climbing activity which may help organize the sensory systems just prior to, and as a part of, working on skills. Difficulties in sensory integration can make it difficult for a child to play, just as play can also build sensory integrative abilities. Occupational therapists utilizing a sensory integrative approach have often used play and work on developing play as a part of their therapy sessions (Bundy 1991; Ewald and Parham 1997; Lindquist, Mack and Parham 1982; Mailloux and Burke 1997; Parham and Primeau 1997). "By matching the child's sensory thresholds and needs, the therapist can successfully engage the child, sustain the child's effort, maintain the child's attention, and promote new developmental skills" (Case-Smith 1997, p.498). Examples of therapy activities might include:

- swinging on a variety of swings, using different body positions to experience specific movement sensations, develop an understanding of body in space, and develop postural control

- finding toys hidden in putty or a large container of beans or balls to develop tactile discrimination and decrease tactile sensitivities

- picking up or tossing bean bags or toys while swinging, to improve timing and motor planning of movements while addressing control of eye movements

- creating and moving through obstacle courses to develop ideation, motor planning, and body awareness.

Effective therapy focuses on the "inner drive" of the child, and uses the active participation of the child, with the therapist balancing between providing structure and allowing the child freedom to explore, try things, and make choices (Parham and Mailloux 1996). As much as possible, the child should be involved in the planning of the session, with the therapist guiding and adapting the activities for a "just right" challenge (Ayres 1972).

The OT may provide intervention to children in a group program. In this case, the goals of the group may be different than individual treatment, since the needs of all the children will have to be balanced. The program would tend to have more structure than an individual session. In such a program, general sensory and motor goals could be combined with goals for developing social skills and participation in functional living skills. A cooking activity or snack time could require children to wash hands before snack time, manipulate utensils, take turns, share, request what they need, use a napkin, taste new foods, and clean up. A gross motor activity with a ball could require the children to work on their arousal levels while in close physical contact, receiving sensory input, eye–hand coordination, and coping with frustration if they miss the ball. If the individual child's needs match with the goals of the group, this could be an appropriate intervention.

Communication with parents and teachers is imperative for addressing difficulties that interfere with the child's full participation in daily activities and life satisfaction. Regardless of other occupational therapy interventions provided, the OT should consult with the child's family and teacher. The therapist can recommend strategies to help modify the demands of home or school so that there is a better fit between the child's abilities and environmental demands, and work within the context in which the skills are needed. Parents and teachers can learn how to meet the child's sensory needs in ways that improve attention, behavior, and participation for the child with AS.

As one can tell by reading this description of the types of interventions available, there are a number of terms that must be defined in order to better understand the sensory and motor challenges of young children with Asperger's Syndrome. These terms are frequently used when discussing the ability to take in and interpret sensory experiences.

Overview of sensory integration

In elementary school, we learned that there are five senses: touch, sight, sound, smell, and taste. However, there are actually more forms of sensory input. Information from touch and other senses that provide input from muscles and joints and respond to movement is critical to our basic understanding of our bodies and our world. Occupational therapist and psychologist Dr. A. Jean Ayres first developed the theory of sensory integration (Ayres 1972). *Sensory integration* refers to "the organization of sensory input for use" (Ayres 1979, p.184). It is a neurobiological process that is a part of normal development. The ability to perceive and integrate basic sensations or sensory input appears to be mainly processed within lower, non-thinking areas of the brain, but with influence from the higher, cortical centers. Likewise, the higher centers, responsible for perception, language, and learning, are influenced by the lower centers. The ability to process this sensory input is not an all or nothing process, but is on a continuum.

Children with AS tend to respond too much and too little to different sensory experiences (Dunn, Myles and Orr 2002), suggesting inefficient "modulation" of sensory input. Poor processing may be demonstrated by:

- seeking sensory input
- avoiding sensory input
- becoming easily over-excited by sensory input
- inability to appropriately use the sensory information.

A child's response to sensory stimuli in the environment depends on many factors and can be affected by the sensory systems involved, stressors, time of day, and the environment (Miller and Summers 2001).

Some children may demonstrate difficulty in only one area, while others may have multiple areas of difficulty. Daily experiences consist of multi-sensory input and sensory processing is complex. In order to understand the sensory systems and their influence, each system will be discussed individually, followed by guidelines to interventions.

Tactile processing – touch

The tactile system relies on receptors in the skin to receive information about touch from the environment. The brain then processes the input, which contributes to an awareness of where the body ends and the outside world begins. The tactile system includes information both for protection of the individual (pain, temperature) and detailed information about the stimulus (size, form, texture). When there is too much or too little inhibition from higher brain centers, the ability to perceive and interpret tactile and other sensory input is affected. When less than typical inhibitory signals are provided, ordinary experiences may be interpreted as a threat. This part of the tactile system contributes to emotional responses, alerting and arousal level, and body awareness. If you have ever had a stray hair land on your face that felt like a bug crawling on you, you have experienced this. Because you were unable to immediately determine what was there, you had to quickly try to brush it away. This "fight or flight," or freeze, response to non-threatening tactile input is called *tactile defensiveness*. The mouth, face, palms and soles of the feet are particularly sensitive and more likely to result in a defensive response than other areas of the body. The memory of these experiences can even result in behavioral responses to the mere thought that the experience *might* occur. For example, David has a crying meltdown every time his mother asks him to put on his shoes and socks. Because he has severe tactile sensitivities to the seams in his socks, the behavioral response occurs before he puts the socks on, before the sensory input has even occurred.

Children with tactile defensiveness may avoid group activities and tactile-based activities such as messy play. Unstructured activities, which are typical on the playground, often provide more inadvertent tactile input (e.g. children bumping into each other), and therefore are often particularly difficult for children with tactile defensiveness. When a child is under stress, the child may act more defensively, assuming, for example, that his peer intentionally bumped into him while standing in line. The stress can be the result of a "good" stress, such as a visit from a favorite relative or friend, or as "bad" stress, such as having a cold, poor sleep, or a parent being out of town.

Children with extreme levels of tactile defensiveness tend to have more rigid or inflexible behaviors (Baranek, Foster and Berkson 1997). Many children with AS demonstrate extreme levels of tactile defensiveness. Table 10.1 lists some possible signs of tactile defensiveness. Because typical experiences may be avoided, specific motor control issues often arise (Paris 2000).

Table 10.1 Possible signs of tactile defensiveness

- Discomfort with the feeling of sock seams, tags in clothing
- Resists having face or hair washed or cut
- Objects to having teeth and hair brushed
- Picky about food, especially foods with lumps or multiple textures
- Avoids getting hands dirty or wants them washed immediately
- Responds aggressively to touch (or possible touch) from others

---

The tactile system also includes the ability to discriminate (interpret) tactile input and provides a foundation for visual-spatial understanding, planning body movements, and fine motor control (Paris 2000). Many children with AS demonstrate decreased ability to interpret tactile input. For example, they may not notice when their hands or face are dirty or their clothing twisted. They may appear "lost" in their own world or seek additional tactile input, such as excessive touching of others or objects.

Proprioceptive processing – input from muscles and joints

The tactile system is closely related to the proprioceptive system which perceives input from muscles and joints. This sensory system contributes to knowing what the body is doing and the amount of force needed to complete tasks. This input tends to be calming to the nervous system. Children with AS tend to seek proprioceptive input, like jumping, climbing, and crashing. Table 10.2 provides some possible signs of difficulty in processing proprioceptive input.

Table 10.2 Possible signs of difficulty in processing proprioceptive input

- Use of inadequate or excess force in completing tasks
- Difficulty judging the direction to apply force (pushes the wrong way)
- Excess jumping, crashing, bouncing, and toe-walking
- Chewing on clothing or prolonged thumb sucking

Inefficient processing of proprioceptive input can be seen in a variety of motor and social tasks, with difficulty knowing the amount and direction of force needed to complete a task. A very loose or very tight grasp on a pencil or marker may be seen. In social situations, some children with AS demonstrate behaviors that are seen as "aggressive." For example, Samuel's parents reported that he is unaware that his hugs are so tight that it is painful for his siblings and peers. Reliance on physical ways of interacting (due to limited social language skills) and difficulty in grading the force of movements may result in an attempt to gain a peer's attention that is interpreted by a peer as grabbing and hitting.

Vestibular processing – movement

The proprioceptive system is also closely related to the vestibular system. The vestibular system provides information about gravity (Am I upside down or right side up?) and movement of the head (forward, backwards, sideways, and around in circles). Vestibular input combines with proprioceptive input to provide for motor control, balance, spatial awareness, and eye movements for visual skills. Ineffective processing of vestibular input can contribute to a child easily becoming over-stimulated and having difficulty regulating sleep and wake cycles. Indicators of possible difficulty processing vestibular input can be seen in Table 10.3.

Table 10.3 Inefficient vestibular processing
Vestibular system is under-responsive
• Frequent seeking of fast swinging, spinning, moving • Difficulty sitting still
Vestibular system is poorly inhibited
• Becomes over-excited with movement • Difficulty with calming and attention after movement activities
Vestibular system is over-responsive
• Avoidance or fear of movement • Fear of having the head out of the vertical position/feet off the ground • Easily becomes motion sick
Vestibular influence on motor control
• Low muscle tone – "floppy" appearance, flat hands and feet (poor definition of muscles), locking of joints for stability, w-sitting • May have a fear of falling • Decreased strength or endurance • Inefficient balance responses, clumsiness • Lack of hand dominance for tool use (marker, pencil, scissors, utensils) • Poor bilateral coordination (use of right and left side simultaneously) – riding a tricycle/bike, cutting shapes with scissors, manipulation of buttons/zippers

Many children with AS also demonstrate poor processing of vestibular input (Dunn *et al.* 2002). They may seek activities that provide movement even though they may not be safe, such as standing on a swing. When someone attempts to impose movement (pushing the child on a swing), the child may become angry. For example, John initially resisted swinging because he was afraid he would fall. He would only swing when being held by his mom and would yell at his mom every time she suggested he swing by himself. However, once he gained the physical control to keep his balance, he wanted to swing and spin all of the time. While he demonstrated progress in his processing abilities (i.e. improved balance and tolerating experiences to work on more improvement), he still demonstrated processing difficulties (i.e. seeking excessive spinning).

While children with AS may seek movement, they may become easily over-excited by the input. This was the case for Virginia, who loved to swing and run during outdoor play but then had difficulty calming down when it was time to go inside. While less common in children with AS, some children have difficulty tolerating any movement and avoid movement activities.

For some children with AS, inefficiencies in processing combined vestibular and proprioceptive input affect their motor coordination (Paris 2000), making them *appear clumsy*. When the child is young and the issues are subtle, the difficulties may be seen in *how* the child completes a task. For example, the child may lock joints (knees, elbows) or use objects in the environment to lean against. The child may show poor sitting endurance, leaning against furniture, propping up the head with a hand, wrapping legs around the legs of a chair, or fidgeting in the chair. Even mild inefficiencies can impact visual and visual-motor skills like handwriting (Burpee 1997; Kawar 2002; Okoye 1997). Decreased control of muscles of the mouth and tongue can combine with tactile sensitivities in the mouth and contribute to difficulties with eating.

Other sensory systems

Some children with AS may demonstrate a defensive response not only to tactile input, but also to other sensory experiences (such as auditory, visual, and olfactory), indicating a global "sensory defensiveness." For example, some children find the sound of the blender, electric razor, or coffee grinder intolerable. The mother of a three-year-old reported her son's sensitivity to smells resulted in a gagging response to the smell of his dad's shaving cream.

Difficulties in sensory integration may also impact processing of auditory and visual input. If a child spends much of the time in an over-aroused state and is unable to attend to important stimuli, they may be unable to develop the auditory and visual skills they need. In addition, vestibular processing has been hypothesized to have complex neurological influences on auditory processing abilities (Ayres 1979; Ayres and Mailloux 1981; Frick 2002; Frick and Hacker 2001; Lane 2002). Similarly, vestibular processing may impact visual skills due to the vestibular influence on muscles and motor control impacting the eye muscles necessary for visual skills (Ayres 1979; Kawar 2002; Lane 2002).

Praxis

Our ability to utilize sensory input to interact with our environment is much more complex than the ability to process input from each sensory system. Praxis refers to the ability to visualize and plan out unfamiliar tasks. The first step is ideation – that is, to form an idea about an action or thought. Once we have an idea, we must organize a plan of how to carry this out. This is the motor plan. This requires timing of movements and understanding the spatial demands of the task (Blanche and Parham 2001). As seen in children with autism (Parham, Mailloux and Roley 2000), many children with AS appear to have difficulty in both ideation and motor planning. These difficulties are often reflected in clumsiness, resistance to tasks that they are uncertain about, and rigidity in doing things the same way. See Table 10.4 for elements of praxis.

Table 10.4 Praxis

Ideation – form the idea

- Ability to develop an idea of how to use an unfamiliar toy
- Ability to tolerate changes in routine or an activity

Motor planning – organize a plan of action

- Ability to imitate body postures
- Ability to copy 2-D and 3-D constructions (drawing, building)
- Ability to time body movements in relation to movements of objects
- Ability to interpret spatial relations of body to environment and objects to each other

---

While visual skills are generally thought to be a relative strength for most children with AS, that strength is in using visual stimuli that have been presented to them. In contrast, some children have difficulty in ideation: developing and visualizing a concept of interacting with objects and how to achieve it, a complex concept that is not yet completely understood. Individuals with AS often use routines because novelty is intolerable (Attwood 1998; Williams 1992). It is often easier to keep things the same rather than risk something new. This may explain why children with AS do well with clear, predictable routines.

Once an individual "knows" what they want to do, a plan is still required. We see this when some children with AS have difficulty imitating body positions (Attwood 1998). When participating in novel tasks, they may need to "feel" what the body is supposed to do before they can perform the task. Some children with AS have difficulty with the timing of their movements (Asperger 1991) and spatial elements of a task (Iwanaga *et al.* 2000), seen in a lack of smoothness or fluidity of movements and poor ability to catch a ball (Attwood 1998). You can imagine how confusing a soccer game would be for a young child with AS, since the body positions and strategies required are constantly changing.

Sensory modulation abilities

When a child is over- or under-responding to sensory experiences, it may affect behavioral responses, including arousal, attention, affect, and organized action (Williamson and Anzalone 2001). Many children with AS demonstrate sensory excitability which results in difficulties staying calm (Dunn *et al.* 2002). The greatest challenge to sensory modulation generally occurs in unstructured, non-routine situations and therefore may interfere with effective social skills and emotional responses. For example, Zach had difficulty processing vestibular and tactile input and became over-excited when playing outside. He loved playing tag, but if another child bumped into him, he responded as if the bump was on purpose and usually hit the other child. Nothing can be more frustrating for both a parent and child than for the child to get so over-excited about being part of an activity that the child must be removed from the activity because following the rules is too difficult.

Helping children learn strategies

We teach young children to understand their body and its needs, including when they are hot, cold, hungry, thirsty, and tired. We also need to teach young children with difficulty in regulating their arousal state to identify their arousal level and what can help them achieve and maintain a calm, alert state (Williams and Shellenberger 1994). Often a combination of strategies will be required. Not only does this mean a combination of sensory strategies, but also a combination of sensory and behavioral strategies (Trott 2002). Often it is most productive for the needs to be addressed from collaborative work of the multidisciplinary team (Miller and Summers 2001).

As a word of caution, some children may attempt to use these strategies in ways other than to assist them in their arousal level. To get a friend's attention, a child may attempt to throw a toy which was provided to feel and fidget with during circle time. Another child may request a favorite food because they like it and want it, not because of the effect on their arousal. If a strategy is being abused, then it is probably not the best strategy for that child.

Another caution is that signs of sensory overload may appear if you have attempted to alter the sensory input provided and provided too much stimulation, or the wrong type of input for the child. A decrease in attention, more difficulty with arousal level, and "negative" behaviors may be seen. This is not uncommon during a first attempt to manipulate sensory experiences. An adjustment in the input provided may then result in success. If your own attempts to adjust the sensory input have still been unsuccessful, consultation with an occupational therapist may assist you in finding the appropriate sensory strategies for your child.

Williams and Shellenberger (1994) provide a checklist to assist in helping adults to identify their own sensory strategies. In better understanding your own sensory strategies and preferences, you may be better able to find what is organizing for your child. (Additional resources for strategies include: Anderson 1998; Frick *et al.* 1996; Henry Occupational Therapy Services 1998, 2001; Kranowitz *et al.* 2001; Oetter, Richter and Frick 1995; Williams and Shellenberger 1994; and Williamson and Anzalone 2001.)

Providing assistance for difficulty in processing tactile input

Table 10.5 lists strategies that may be helpful for a child with difficulty in processing tactile input. For a child with "tactile defensiveness," the first step is for parents and other adults to understand that the defensive responses are part of the difficulty in processing sensory input and not a "willful" behavior. The expectations and ways of helping the child through difficulties are different. While a child should be made aware of when a behavior is inappropriate, *intervention should focus on learning appropriate ways to respond rather than expecting the child to repress a neurological response that they cannot control.*

Table 10.5 Addressing tactile processing difficulties

Understand that defensive responses have a neurological base (not just "behavior")

Limit extraneous and unexpected light tactile input:

- child should sit at the edge of a group (rather than the middle)
- child should stand at the beginning or end of the line
- others should approach the child from the front (rather than the back) and provide verbal cues ("Let me help you")
- others should use firm (not light) touch

Encourage tactile-based play and tactile discrimination:

- shaving cream, water, finger painting, tub of balls/beans, textured toys
- object identification without vision

Provide deep pressure and "heavy work" input:

- consider deep-touch pressure brushing

Limiting the amount of unexpected light touch can be helpful in allowing the child with tactile defensiveness to function in everyday life. For example, if the child can anticipate the touch and is provided firm input (rather than light touch), it may elicit less (number and severity) of a defensive response.

Encouraging (but not forcing) tactile-based play (e.g. water, sand, finger paint), within the child's tolerance, can also be helpful. Some activities can be just for the sensory experience; others can require more precise tactile processing, to discriminate and identify objects/small toys in a bag, without using vision.

Activities providing deep pressure and proprioceptive (muscles and joints) input (discussed below; see Table 10.7) tend to decrease the negative response to tactile experiences and therefore may be helpful. Some OTs recommend a specific deep-touch pressure "brushing" to the skin, also referred to as the

"Wilbarger Protocol," named for the developers of the technique (Wilbarger and Wilbarger 1991). In this technique, deep pressure brushing, followed by input to the joints, is designed to broaden the child's tolerance of touch. This intervention is controversial even among OTs. For some children, this input can be too stimulating, resulting in disorganized behavior (e.g. increased activity level, decreased attention and focus). Consultation with a therapist trained in this technique may help to determine if this is an appropriate intervention for a specific child.

Children who seek touch (rather than avoid it) for their hands by constantly touching people and objects may benefit from having a small textured toy (e.g. mini-koosh ball, stress ball) or resistive putty to fidget with. This may allow for the child to demonstrate more socially accepted behaviors.

Providing assistance for the picky eater

Children with tactile sensitivities in and around the mouth may be picky about foods that they will eat. Generally, oral proprioceptive input may be beneficial. In the infant, the input they need may be provided when sucking on a bottle, pacifier, thumb, or when breast-feeding. However, dentists have found that sucking a thumb or pacifier past the age of two or three years of age places the child at a greater risk of later problems with alignment of teeth (Warren *et al.* 2001). Other ways of obtaining this input could include activities for resistive sucking, chewing, and blowing.

Motor inefficiencies may combine with tactile sensitivities, resulting in the child avoiding foods that are more challenging to chew. Cleo is a good example of a child who is unable to handle resistive foods. She refuses meats, with the exception of "easy" meats like "Chicken McNuggets" and processed "fish sticks." She eats yogurt, but refuses yogurt with fruit pieces mixed in. Food tolerances, preferences, and refusals should be carefully analyzed. Increasing a child's food tolerance usually requires a combined behavioral and sensory approach. See Table 10.6 for strategies that may be helpful with picky eaters.

If safe eating (i.e. avoidance of choking) is a concern, an immediate evaluation should be sought from an occupational, physical, or speech therapist that specializes in feeding issues. Mental health concerns may also relate to feeding issues such as when food is used manipulatively by the child to maintain a parent's attention, or by a parent to get the child's cooperation. Previous publications have addressed specific treatment strategies

Table 10.6 Addressing the needs of the picky eater

Encourage oral tactile-based input and play:

- textured rubber toys/teething toys
- washcloth
- Nuk toothbrush
- battery-operated toothbrush

Provide oral "heavy work":

- blowing whistles, beginning musical instruments
- sucking on a popsicle
- drinking from a straw, juice box, sports water bottle
- chewing resistive foods: dried fruit, bagel
- chewing crunchy foods: fat pretzels, dried cereal, baby carrots
- chewing on aquarium or therapy tubing

Slowly broaden the sensory properties of foods tolerated

(Case-Smith and Humphry 1996; Morris and Klein 1987, 1999; Murray-Slutsky 2000).

Providing assistance for difficulty in processing proprioceptive input (input to muscles and joints)

Children with poor processing of proprioceptive input tend to benefit from activities that provide additional proprioceptive input. Additional input can be achieved by having the child work against increased resistance by adding weight, working against gravity, or using heavier objects. Table 10.7 provides ideas for addressing difficulties in processing proprioceptive input.

"Heavy work" activities can be used for chores and play, such as emptying the trash, stacking chairs, or playing tug-of-war. Deep pressure input can be provided by a weighted or neoprene pressure vest or a large bean bag placed in the child's lap while sitting. These strategies can be particularly helpful for completion of table work (at school, home) since they can be used when seated and have been found to improve attention during a fine motor task (Fertel-Daly, Bedell and Hinojosa 2001).

Table 10.7 Addressing proprioceptive processing difficulties

Participate in activities that provide proprioceptive and deep pressure input

Work against resistance (weight of task, add weights, or work against gravity):

- carrying laundry, unbreakable groceries, move furniture
- lying on stomach on the floor for playing, watching videos
- climbing, tug-of-war, wheelbarrow/animal walks
- manipulating play-dough/clay/bread dough, "stress" ball, a spray bottle with water to "draw" on the sidewalk or chalkboard

Provide deep pressure input:

- weighted vest
- neoprene pressure vest
- long bean bag
- being sandwiched in pillows, rolled up in a blanket

Practice using muscle control-targets for throwing objects or where the body should land

---

When a child has difficulty in regulating the force used, likes to crash, and has not developed controlled use of the body, precision motor skills may be limited. "Practice" using controlled movements should focus on the quality of movement. For example, Susan tended to move very quickly, with very poor accuracy for throwing a ball. While the practice session for using control had to be short, she was able to stop and use control for throwing three bean bags into a target and then allowed to throw "her way" for three bean bags. Asking a child with AS to meet a challenge for too long might end in refusal or frustration.

Providing assistance for difficulty in processing vestibular input (input related to movement, head position, and motor control)

Children who seek extra movement may benefit from being provided purposeful, productive ways of receiving the input they seek. Many children do well with additional movement input from sitting on an inflated cushion (for example, DynaDisc, Disc'O'Sit, SitFit, Move 'n Sit Cushion, Movin' Sit). Some children find rhythmical, consistent, predictable swinging to be calming and organizing. Moving to a different location in the room or standing rather than sitting may be helpful for a child's attention. The movement break can be combined with proprioceptive input, such as taking books to another teacher or doing some brief exercises. Children who seek input are not always able to perceive when they have had sufficient (or too much) input. Because of the potential for vestibular input to increase arousal level, caution must be taken to avoid *over-stimulation*. See Table 10.8 for possible signs of over-stimulation. If over-stimulation occurs, input should *immediately* be stopped and deep pressure or proprioceptive input should be provided (refer back to Table 10.7) to inhibit the simulating effect of the vestibular input (Fredrickson, Schwartz and Kornhuber 1966). Over-stimulation may be seen during the activity providing the input, immediately after, or even a few hours later.

Table 10.8 Responses that may indicate over-stimulation to vestibular input

- Change in face color (red or white)
- Change in breathing (speed, yawning, hiccups)
- Upset stomach or headache
- Sweating
- Change in attention or activity level (hyperactivity, distractibility, or drowsiness)
- Change in sleeping or eating patterns

(Adapted from Anzalone and Murray 2002)

If coordination difficulties accompany the child's sensory processing difficulties, they can be specifically addressed. In therapy, coordination issues are frequently addressed simultaneously with intervention for sensory processing. When addressing coordination, emphasis is on the quality of the motor performance. Any concerns about the level of the child's abilities, safety, precautions, or appropriate activities can be answered by an evaluation from an occupational or physical therapist. General ideas for coping with difficulty in processing vestibular input can be found in Table 10.9.

Table 10.9 Coping with vestibular processing difficulties

- Discourage "w-sitting" (feet on either side of and behind the bottom)
- Provide supported seating for fine motor work
- Address motor needs: gross, fine, visual, and oral motor; physical education, gymnastics/tumbling, occupational/physical therapy

Any child should be discouraged from remaining in a w-sitting position (sitting on the bottom, with feet on either side of and behind the bottom), although some toddlers may move through this position during play. The w-sitting position is not good for the hips and knees, placing the ligaments on an extreme stretch. In addition, the child does not receive practice and experiences working on subtle balancing reactions and trunk rotation while reaching around for toys as when sitting cross-legged (tailor sitting). If a child has difficulty with trunk control, it is important that, when expecting control for seated tasks using the hands, the child be in a chair which provides adequate support.

While some "typically developing" young children begin to write some letters (particularly those in their name) around four years of age, other writing is not required at this age. However, at a preschool age, most children make significant gains in grasping a pencil and scissors, cutting, stringing beads, managing clothing fasteners, and visual perception skills (Case-Smith *et al.* 1998; Pehoski 1995b). If a child is avoiding these tasks or using atypical patterns of movement, they may not be ready later for the fine motor demands required in school. See Table 10.10 for suggestions for developing pre-writing skills. Additional resources for strategies and activities to improve fine motor coordination include: Benbow (1995, 1999); Bissell *et al.* (1998); Case-Smith (1995); Exner (1995); Levine (1991); Myers (1992); Pehoski (1995a, 1995b); Saunders (2002); and Tobias and Goldkopf (1995). If a child is having problems with fine motor tasks in school, classroom activities can be modified to increase success (Bissell *et al.* 1998).

Table 10.10 Activities for developing pre-writing skills

- Work in the vertical position (easel, chalkboard) or use a slantboard
- Use a formed pencil grip or large diameter tools (thick markers, sidewalk chalk, egg-shaped chalk)
- Wrap pipe cleaners around the thumb hole of scissors to decrease the size of the hole
- "Draw" without paper and pencil (shaving cream, water, chalk, sand, clay)
- Construct letters with wooden (or cardboard) lines and curves (Olsen 1998)
- Manipulate small objects with one hand (coins, pegs, marbles, dice, beads)

Providing assistance for difficulties in other sensory systems

When addressing a child's overall sensory defensiveness, decreasing the defensiveness in one sensory system may have an impact on other sensory systems as well. For example, addressing tactile defensiveness may also decrease the level of *auditory defensiveness*. Specific auditory strategies, using specially recorded CDs, have also been used by some OTs using a sensory integrative approach (Frick 2002; Frick and Hacker 2001).

For some children with vestibular processing difficulties, when intervention is provided utilizing a sensory integration approach, positive changes may be seen in the ability to interpret auditory or visual input. While some therapists may incorporate other strategies to address these needs in a treatment session, a sensory integrative approach does not specifically address improving the ability to discriminate auditory or visual stimuli.

In addition, *auditory and visual input* can be used to facilitate sensory integration and day-to-day functioning. Auditory input (e.g. music) can be calming, alerting, and/or organizing to a person's nervous system. For example, some children benefit from alerting music with a quick tempo in the morning (e.g. "Zip-a-dee-doo-dah" from the Jungle Book or cheerful children's music) to assist with their morning routine. In contrast, music that might be used in the evening, as a part of a bedtime routine, would be a different tempo and quality. Calming nature sounds, soothing classical music, children's bedtime recordings, or chants may be helpful in the evening. Because of the strong beat, some children with a poor internal sense of rhythm benefit from listening to drum music, finding that it provides an external rhythm they can attempt to match.

Visual input may also be increased or decreased to assist with arousal level. Generally, an increase in visual stimuli would be more alerting and would be used for a child with low energy or arousal. If a child is having high arousal or is easily excited, it may be helpful to limit extraneous stimuli or provide slow, predictable input for calming. Examples could include watching fish in an aquarium, a fire in a fireplace, "oil and water" toys, or playing an enclosed water toy game (e.g. shooting the ball into the basket). For individuals with repetitive behaviors, visual input should be carefully monitored to ensure that it is not used as a self-stimulatory behavior.

Providing assistance for difficulty in practic development

As discussed earlier, many children with AS demonstrate limited ability in both ideation (the idea) and motor planning of a novel task. Cognitive strategies and feedback to encourage the child to be actively involved in the session may be helpful (Giuffrida 2001). Ideas for addressing practic development can be seen in Table 10.11.

Table 10.11 Assistance for poor practic development

Ideation

- Assist to develop and follow a plan
- Guide changes within activities: "Let's come up with a new way."
- Support/assistance for beginning tasks, especially novel tasks
- Observation of others in novel tasks before expectation for participation
- Routines for difficult tasks that occur regularly
- Visual schedules for understanding expectations, especially changes in routines
- Assist for transitions: transitional warnings, information about the next task

Motor planning the spatial and temporal demands of the task

- Balloons and beach balls move slower than balls, for greater success
- Obstacle courses for learning about body in space
- Music to develop awareness of a rhythm
- Critical tasks specifically taught (e.g. letter formation for writing)

Children with AS who demonstrate poor ideation benefit from learning to develop and follow a plan. This often requires adding structure to the activity in which they are participating and having the child come up with a plan prior to beginning. If needed, a model can provide specific ideas. The child can create a construction (e.g. Lego, Tinker toys) and then attempt to make a second one that is the same. Similarly, an adult (or peer) can make a model and the child can copy it. More than one photograph or drawing of models can be used to encourage the child to make a choice.

Many children with AS are very rigid in their play. If provided a model, they may feel that it is the *only* way the task can be done; therefore, it is generally best to have more than one model. In order to make and sustain relationships with peers, it may be important to work with such a child on learning that there can be more than one way to play with a toy or solution to a problem. Strategies can include asking, "Can you think of a new way?" Modeling could be used by having a peer (or adult) playing in a parallel manner and demonstrating a new way. Verbal comments about the new way can be made, "I had a different idea," while not initially requiring the child to do the same thing.

Children with AS often have difficulty starting a task. Particularly with novel tasks, emotional support and demonstration may be required. It is helpful to allow the child to observe others in new tasks before being required to perform the task. If it is the first time playing with a new toy, it might be appropriate to state, "I have a great idea. Watch." While a few children with AS may tolerate "hand over hand" assistance to be physically guided through a task, many might find this a threat, due to a loss of control over the situation or the input provided. A child may do better if told "Let me know when you are ready for me to help" or "Try one time and the next time I will help you."

Routines are often helpful for young children (Butterfield 2002; Fiese 2002; Kubicek 2002; Rosenkoetter and Barton 2002) and children with AS tend to do especially well with clear routines. They may benefit from understanding that tasks and play have a beginning (setting up), middle, and end (cleaning up). In particular, novel, challenging, or social situations (Wolfberg, Berry and Fuge 2001) may be made easier if they begin and end with predictable rituals. Due to the tendency of children with AS to have strong visual skills, visual schedules can be helpful for understanding expectations in non-routine situations. Photographs or representational pictures can illustrate the schedule of the day and of the week. A specific schedule can be made to assist with a routine that creates problems, such as getting ready in the morning, getting ready for bed, transitions, or changes in routines. Strategies used with young children (Larson, Henthorne and Plum 1994), such as warnings about an upcoming transition, information about the next task, and use of music and rhythm, frequently assist even older children with AS in making transitions.

Whether or not a child struggles with ideation, he may have difficulty with motor planning. The child may need assistance with motor planning, particularly as tasks become more difficult, requiring timing, spatial under-standing of tasks, and rhythm. For children who are unable to time the movements of their bodies for catching a ball, the use of a balloon or beach ball can be used, since they move more slowly. Whole body physical activities such as tumbling, gymnastics, and obstacle courses can assist in learning about where the body is in space. The use of music with a strong beat during partici-pation in a rhythmic gross motor activity can assist with developing of rhythm.

Due to difficulty with motor planning and tendency toward rigid behaviors, it is often more successful for children with AS to learn critical tasks correctly from the beginning rather than later attempting to change "bad" habits. This is often the case when learning letter formation for writing. While inefficient letter formation may allow short-term success, it may not allow the speed and proficiency needed as writing demands later increase. Inefficient letter formation for printing may also later make learning cursive more difficult.

Providing assistance for difficulty in sensory modulation

For children with AS, over- and under-responding to sensory experiences can contribute to difficulties in attention, arousal, affect, and organized action. Therefore, individualized sensory-based strategies may enhance attention and self-regulation, allowing the child to have better functional skills and more socially acceptable behaviors. A *sensory diet* refers to the sensory input that a child may require throughout the day in order to maintain a more optimal level of arousal (Wilbarger 1984, 1995). Often children will benefit from even slight changes in their sensory diet, even if the "ideal" sensory diet seems impossible to implement. At times, these same strategies may also be helpful when the child is already having difficulty and needs assistance in regaining behavioral self-control.

In a sensory diet, a combination of activities may be included that are 1. like snacks and have a short impact on our behavior and attention, and 2. more substantial input that will have a longer lasting effect (Wilbarger 1995). Individual needs and responses to input may vary according to the task that needs to be performed, time of day, environment, and stress.

In addition to the sensory strategies already provided in this chapter, respiratory strategies to encourage slow, deep breathing can be helpful (Frick *et al.* 1996; Oetter *et al.* 1995). However, young children often do not know how to "take a deep breath." Toys that require sustained blowing (e.g. musical toys, blow "darts," string pipes, bubbles) and singing and humming can be used to assist in improving respiratory patterns.

To help children achieve a calm, alert state, at times the removal of sensory input may be helpful. This can be illustrated by what worked for Kyle. When over-stimulated, Kyle required a "tent," created by placing a sheet over a table, to block some stimuli. He often crawled under pillows in this space. While there, he might drink from a sports water bottle or juice box, crunch on baby carrots, and listen to classical music. If a preschool program is unable to create a tent, a "down time" corner in the "reading" area, partially enclosed by a bookshelf, with a bean bag chair and the child's favorite book, may help calm him when the classroom activities are too stressful or stimulating.

Frequently asked questions

Why is this child giving me mixed messages? At times he is very affectionate and climbs in my lap for cuddling, but if another child gets too close or tries to initiate a hug, he acts as though it's a punishment and he either acts out or runs away instantly

Sensory input can be most easily tolerated if the child has control over the input rather than it being imposed. Similarly, input repeatedly provided by a parent may be better tolerated than the same input provided by another relative, teacher, or peer. The child may have grown accustomed to the way a close family member provides the input, but the input may vary when provided by a different person and then not be tolerated.

Should I encourage this child to participate in a team sport?

Every child is different. If the child is asking to participate and perceives some enjoyment in the activity, then the activity may be beneficial. However, if the activity is too fast, too difficult, or too confusing, the child may not be getting any benefit from the activity and just experiencing frustration or possible failure. While parents and teachers may be looking for a group opportunity for the child to work on motor and social skills simultaneously, most young children with AS do better with participation in individually focused motor activities (e.g. martial arts, tumbling, gymnastics, rock climbing, even bowling or dance) rather than traditional team sports. Some families have found success with providing some initial individual sessions to "pre-teach" the skills that will later be taught in a group class. It is also helpful to try an activity that naturally provides the type of sensory input that the particular child seems to seek. If classes are grouped according to age, it is most likely to be successful if the child is one of the oldest in the class rather than one of the youngest. The child's skills (physical and social) may then be more within the skills of the group and expectations of the instructor. Take care to avoid competitive programs and instead place your child in a program which stresses the improvement of individual abilities and the participation of all children.

The pediatrician never mentioned OT. In fact, (she) he says the child is likely to outgrow these things and we should just wait and see. How long should we wait? Shouldn't the pediatrician be able to tell us if OT would be good for this child?

Depending on their interest and background, pediatricians know childhood diseases, but do not always have in-depth information about developmental issues. If you have read this chapter and feel that OT would be helpful for a particular child, perhaps you could discuss the specific concerns with the parents and pediatrician. You could even loan the pediatrician your copy of this book!

While there is a range of ages at which typically developing children acquire specific motor skills (e.g. walking from 10 to 15 months), other issues (patterns of movements used, sensory and behavioral responses) may provide a more clear red flag. Some of these responses may just be different at any age, *not* like a younger child. All professionals who work with young children agree that intervention is best provided when the child is as young as possible. When intervention and family education is provided early, patterns of behavior can be more easily changed and the functional impact of the difficulties are often lessened.

This child is receiving OT but he seems to be worse (less focused, high energy, and more sensitive) after his therapy sessions than before he goes. Is this supposed to happen?

While this may occasionally happen, it is *not* the plan. First, discuss your observations with the OT. The disorganization may be due to the input received, the transition of leaving OT, or something that happens after the child leaves OT. At times, a child may process sensory input slowly. He may have appeared to have had the correct amount of input during the therapy session, but not completed processing the input until after the session was over. The OT should listen to your observations and may change what is happening during the session (e.g. any arousing input earlier in the session, followed by activities for calming). If the child is having difficulty with the transition leaving the OT session, the OT could problem solve with you about strategies for the final transition. If the difficulty is occurring after the session (the child goes to class immediately after OT and that is where the difficulty is occurring), the OT could help to problem solve the issue and try to develop a plan for a sensory diet to address the child's needs.

How will addressing sensory and motor issues help the child develop better play skills with his peers?

Many skills are involved when two children play. We usually take this for granted, since typically developing children make it look easy. Young children tend to socialize and learn social skills while participating in sensorimotor activities. Therefore, if a child does not have the motor skills or appropriate responses to sensory experiences, it can interfere with learning and practice of social skills. Sensory processing difficulties can impact many of the prerequisites for social skills (Case-Smith 1997). If improvements are made in these component prerequisites, learning social skills may then be much easier to achieve. Some of these improvements may include:

- attention to the task, to the peer, to the activity
- self-regulation to respond to a peer in a more appropriate manner
- understanding of spatial relationships with other people and toys
- organization for beginning and sustaining the activity
- awareness of own body, to then better read the nonverbal body language of others.

A child must be connected to his own body before being able to connect with his environment and peers in his environment. In addition to improving the sensory and motor skills that may allow participation in activities to work on social skills, OTs frequently work on beginning social skills as a part of the occupational therapy session.

What would OT consultation look like?

The form and content of consultation will vary, according to the child's specific needs. Consultation could consist of talking on the telephone to an OT to determine if it would be helpful to arrange for services. For another family, consultation might be a single visit with an OT for ideas related to a very specific issue, such as avoiding fine motor challenges. For yet another family, a number of sessions might be planned with the OT, working with the child to understand some of his sensory needs and develop a sensory diet that can be implemented at home and school.

How can I find an occupational therapist?

Ask people you know. Many families are referred to a therapist by another family or a professional (teacher, speech and language pathologist, psychologist, social worker, pediatrician) who is working with the child. The closest hospital or school may have knowledge about a therapist in your area. If you have a nearby university, check to see if it has an occupational therapy program and can provide a referral. Most developed countries have a national organization of occupational therapists and may have more local, state/providence, or regional organizations, as well. If you are unable to find a place to begin, you could see if your country has an organization that is a member of the World Federation of Occupational Therapists. At this writing, information about member organizations of the World Federation of Occupational Therapists can be found at www.wfot.org.au/.

Conclusion

Occupational therapy for children with Asperger's Syndrome can assist in modifying environmental demands and activities, and facilitating play interactions. Concepts from sensory integration theory can provide an alternative explanation for behaviors, differences in ability to function, and disorganized learning (Spitzer and Roley 2001). For some children, intervention may involve attempting to normalize sensory responses, organizing sustained attention, and promoting self-regulation. Occupational therapists can provide consultation with the family and other professionals to actively guide play, and experiment with strategies for a more optimal sensory diet. Those individuals interested in research on the effectiveness of occupational therapy utilizing a sensory integrative approach are encouraged to read reviews and discussions by Mulligan (2002), Ottenbacher (1991), and Spitzer and Roley (2001). While these strategies will not change the diagnosis of Asperger's Syndrome, they can assist in developing functional performance and the child's ability to make connections both at home and at school.

Recommended next readings

Ayres, A. J. (1979) *Sensory Integration and the Child.* Los Angeles: Western Psychological Services.

Kranowitz, C. S. (1998) *The Out-of-Sync Child: Recognizing and coping with sensory integration dysfunction.* New York: The Berkley Publishing Group.

Kranowitz, C. S. (2003) *The Out-of-Sync Child Has Fun: Activities for kids with sensory integration dysfunction.* New York: The Berkley Publishing Group.

Kranowitz, C. S., Szklut, S., Blazer-Martin, L., Haber, E. and Sava, D. I. (2001) *Answers to Questions Teachers Ask About Sensory Integration: Forms, checklists, and practical tools for teachers and parents, Second Edition.* Las Vegas: Sensory Resources.

Murray-Slutsky, C. and Paris, B. A. (2000) *Exploring the Spectrum of Autism and Pervasive Developmental Disorders: Intervention strategies.* San Antonio: Therapy Skill Builders.

Trott, M. C. (2002) *Oh Behave! Sensory Processing and Behavioral Strategies: A Practical Guide for Clinicians, Teachers, and Parents.* San Antonio: Therapy Skill Builders.

Trott, M. C., Laurel, M. K. and Windeck, S. L. (1993) *SenseAbilities: Understanding Sensory Integration.* San Antonio: Therapy Skill Builders.

Williams, M. S. and Shellenberger, S. (1994) *"How does your engine run?": A leader's guide to the alert program for self-regulation.* Albuquerque, NM: TherapyWorks.

CHAPTER 11

Building Connections with the Child's School

One of the biggest challenges parents face is finding a school environment that will meet the needs of their young child with Asperger's Syndrome. Parents often have many fears about their children making friends and fitting in. They may wonder if they should share the diagnosis or worry that the sharing might bias a school/teacher against their child. Typically it is those schools (teachers) which are willing to work with the parents and support the process of collaboration after they have been informed about the child's diagnosis that best meet the needs of the child. The partnership between home and school is a critical alliance for ensuring the young child with Asperger's Syndrome is understood and interventions are consistent across settings. This chapter will discuss building a home–school partnership as well as the multiple questions that often surface for parents and teachers when thinking about how to best prepare a child for preschool or kindergarten and also how to best prepare the school. Teachers and caregivers go through a process similar to parents as they begin to understand the needs of their young students. This chapter will also emphasize the perspective of the teacher and the importance of making sure that they are provided with support as well.

How do I know if a child is ready for a preschool program?

Most children can benefit from a preschool experience that helps prepare them to be part of a small group, communicate, socialize, follow simple rules, and be comfortable separating from their parent before they enter kindergarten. Because these present special challenges for young children with Asperger's Syndrome, they will very much benefit from some practice in all of these areas. Therefore, finding a good school environment that can support them is the essential task at hand.

Finding the "right" preschool

Most young children with Asperger's Syndrome are likely to attend a regular education school program, not a special school (Attwood 1998). For both parents and professionals, choosing a school that meets the needs of the child can be challenging and at times confusing. They ponder the various questions: Does the child need more structure? Would the Montessori approach be beneficial, or would a more play-based school better serve his needs? How can I tell if the school is/should be play-based versus academic-based? The options are plentiful, and sorting through what each type of program offers takes time, research, and support. For parents with a child with Asperger's Syndrome, the quest to find the best placement can be disheartening. It may feel like each program has some aspect that would be beneficial for the child, but it is often difficult to find a program that feels like it can address all of the needs that you, as informed parents, have learned to look for. This, by the way, is not that dissimilar to what parents go through when searching for a program/school for any child.

The *teacher is key to the success* of any program. What we most strongly advocate for is finding a teacher who is open to working with the child with AS, and who is willing to accommodate and adapt his or her program to fit the needs of the child. Certainly, the structure of the classroom is also important, but it is how the teacher facilitates and supports children within this structure that determines how well the classroom is functioning. It is the teacher's job to ensure that all children in the class are achieving their educational and social goals. To do this, it is necessary to create an environment that encourages and values individuals and recognizes that children have many different learning styles. A teacher who sees the positive attributes of a child and can accommodate the child when needed will have more success than a teacher who is negative or has unrealistic expectations of the child. For example, if a child is having difficulty with all the noise of a music class, then perhaps the teacher can find an alternative activity while the rest of the class participates in music. A teacher who is open to communicating with other professionals involved in the child's care can help ensure that the child is being understood across therapeutic settings and that a consistent approach to managing behavior is implemented.

Other key issues to consider when selecting a preschool may include the following:

- Is there a sense of order and predictability within the environment: for example, toys and materials organized and clearly marked; visual aids to depict the class schedule?

- Are modifications made to incorporate the interests of different children (e.g. developing play themes in the area of interest of the child; a special science section)?

- Are the children helped to understand the routine? Are they provided with supportive prompts and references to visual charts when needed? Or is the teacher willing to implement these strategies in the class?

- Are the demands on the children increased gradually, with particular attention to how each child is accepting the changes?

- Is the children's attention achieved by one-on-one feedback instead of using open cues to the whole group?

- Is the teacher monitoring and evaluating progress as time goes by, adapting new interventions when needed?

- Is there good communication between home and school? Ask about how information is communicated, how frequently, and how parent concerns are addressed.

- Is collaboration valued with other practitioners involved in the child's care? Ask teachers their experience with other children who may have had other professionals involved in their care.

- Is the school open to having an aide (assisting a child) who works closely with the teacher to implement a program for an individual child?

How do I evaluate a teacher's skills?

Parents and professionals are often challenged in knowing how to evaluate if a teacher is able to function in the role described above. Parents may need to observe and talk to several teachers before they find a teacher they are comfortable working with. *The OASIS Guide to Asperger Syndrome* (Bashe and Kirby 2001) and the OASIS website provide helpful information about modifications, adaptations, and support needed for children with AS, which can be

useful to a parent when they go observe a classroom. The following checklist was taken from models designed for teachers by Dalrymple and Ruble (1996) and Ruble and Dalrymple (2002) and then revised by a lawyer for submission to the OASIS website to better describe the modifications that might be needed for a child with Asperger's Syndrome. Both Dalrympl
e and Ruble models and the OASIS example can be used as a guide to help organize both parents' and clinicians' observation of a classroom and the teacher's skills in the following areas:

ENCOURAGING COMMUNICATION WITH STUDENTS

- Pause, listen, and wait.
- Watch and listen to attempts to respond.
- Respond positively to attempts.
- Model correct format without correction.
- Encourage choice and input when possible.

ENVIRONMENT AND ROUTINE

- Provide a predictable and safe environment.
- Minimize transitions.
- Offer consistent routines.
- Avoid surprises, prepare thoroughly and in advance for changes.
- Reduce distractions and sensory overloads.

SOCIAL SUPPORT

- Praise classmates when they act with compassion.
- Decode social conflicts in simple language and prompt student to respond.
- Focus on social process rather than end product.
- Provide developmentally appropriate play activities.
- Specific teaching, rehearsal, practicing, and modeling in natural settings of following skills:
  - turn-taking
  - responding
  - inviting

- waiting
- greeting
- joining others
- following ideas of others
- accepting answers of others.

- Concentrate on changing unacceptable behaviors and ignore those that are simply odd.

For a more comprehensive checklist, we refer readers back to the OASIS online home page – "Specifically Designed Instructions for Educators." Teachers who are responding to *some* of the challenges according to *some* of the suggestions made are likely to have the skills and offer the support you are looking for. It is unrealistic to expect even the most qualified teacher to be attentive to all of these issues all of the time.

Lastly, parents need to trust their intuition and knowledge of their child when looking for an optimum school environment. These guidelines can be helpful to organize one's approach but ultimately knowing your child and finding an environment/teacher that values home–school partnership is one of the key factors to a successful placement.

Advantages to sharing the diagnosis with your school

Once a school placement has been determined, parents often face the question, should we share the diagnosis? We have found that providing information about Asperger's Syndrome to the school is very beneficial in aiding all parties involved (child, parents, teacher, special education staff, and school administrators). Because teachers often personalize their successes and failures just like parents, finding out that the child's poor adaptation to the classroom is not a result of their professional ability can be a great relief. A dedicated teacher may wonder if the child appears lost due to the lack of structure they are providing. They may wonder if he is "acting out" due to the lack of individualized attention he is receiving in the childcare setting, or they may feel like they are not able to provide such a bright student with a stimulating enough setting. Knowing that the child understands things differently can be quite a relief to the teacher who has personally felt they weren't doing enough. Sharing a working understanding of the diagnosis can also help teachers gain a better understanding of what the parents are going through. It also increases their awareness that the goals need to shift from trying to get the child to conform to the classroom, to figuring out how to best connect with the child. Focusing on the positive qualities of the child is important for all involved. However, because the diagnosis of Asperger's Syndrome is still not widely known to teachers and school administrators, teachers are often just as surprised as the parents to hear about it, and they too need time to digest the information and come to terms with the ramifications of the syndrome. Supporting teachers as they learn about developmental issues of Asperger's Syndrome is an important step for building the collaboration between home and school.

Parents may have a similar experience when they inform the school or a teacher about their child's diagnosis at the time of admissions or at the beginning of the school year. The school's first response may be that the parents are making too much out of nothing, the child just needs a little time adjusting to a new classroom, and everything will be fine. As with many parents, it may be hard for them to conceptualize that a child who has so many academic strengths could possibly have a developmental disorder. With time and guidance they should be better able to see both the child's strengths and challenges, and develop strategies to insure the child's success, both in the classroom and in the playground settings.

Building rapport with your school

Whether or not a family has shared the diagnosis, the need for building rapport and developing a collaborative relationship between school and home always exists. Developing a partnership between home and school can vary, depending on the attitudes of both school personnel and the parents.

Table 11.1 Factors influencing parent–teacher communication

- Parents' history of communication with teachers/school
- Teacher's ability to communicate concerns
- Parent's acceptance of child's differences
- Parent's personal history
- Teacher's experience with children with special needs both personally and professionally
- The school's resources and teacher support

However, we have found several key factors which are helpful to think about when you embark on the road towards collaboration.

In the beginning, it may be helpful for families to consider some of the factors outlined in Table 11.1. Parents can begin by identifying their own process (anxieties, fears) and be aware that similar issues may be present for a particular teacher. Teachers are in the position of being responsible for the needs of many children in a short period of time. When a child threatens to upset the equilibrium and general functioning of a classroom, teachers can become quite anxious and unsettled, particularly when many of the principles of behavioral management that have worked in the past aren't effective. As mentioned, they may blame themselves and question how they are doing things. Some may feel they don't have enough experience. Others may externalize the blame and think the difficulties stem from parenting problems. This process is not that different from the parent who begins to feel anxious when they can't impact their child's behavior. Being aware of the similar processes both parents and teachers can go through when investing and dealing day to day with the young child with Asperger's Syndrome is important in establishing empathy and support for one another. When these fears can be discussed, communication often improves and both parties feel better understood.

In the process of developing rapport, it is important to identify the person who will be an advocate at the school (e.g. teacher, principal/director, special education staff, or consultant) and elicit their help in bridging the communication between home and the class. In identifying the advocate, parents often have the opportunity of exploring their concerns and the school's concerns about their child. It is helpful to do so before having a formal meeting where the child's educational plans are being determined.

After the initial efforts at building a dialogue about the child has occurred, it may be helpful to set up a parent–teacher conference with all the key players involved in the child's interventions to discuss results of the evaluation and/or the diagnosis, and to begin brainstorming as to how the child can be best supported in the classroom. Often in the first meeting, everyone is trying to digest information from the child's evaluation and translate it to understand the child's behavior and learning style. A review of the assessment process and how a clinician arrived at their conclusions and recommendations can help demystify the process. Some families and educators find it very helpful to have someone from the assessment team present to support and clarify issues for them, as well as advocate for the child's needs.

Table 11.2 Guidelines for initial meeting with school

1. Consider the history of how communication has evolved between home and school

2. Identify who may be an advocate at school

3. Explore with teacher or advocate both the parent and school's concerns about the child

4. Contact school principal and/or teacher and ask for a meeting

5. Review assessment process and meaning of the diagnosis

6. Explore school and parents' concerns about meeting the child's needs

7. Begin the dialogue about what can be done to mediate the child's experience and provide school with resources (written material, consultation from a mental health specialist)

8. Plan for follow-up meetings to evaluate how things are working

---

Table 11.2 summarizes some of the key points to be considered when arranging a first meeting and some issues that might to be explored in this meeting. You may only be able to address one of these points during this first meeting, such as defining Asperger's Syndrome. Be ready to set up follow-up meetings in a timely fashion should this occur. If communication is breaking down, be open to having a third party (for example, another school administrator, mental health consultant) come in to help facilitate the process. And in all instances, the best interest of the child needs to be the focus of the meeting.

From our experience, teachers are often the parents' best advocates. They understand the child's day to day behavior and often are incredibly intuitive when it comes to knowing what works and doesn't work for a particular child. Empowering teachers for their knowledge and support of the child goes a long way to building a strong relationship between home and school.

It is equally important to understand how overwhelming it can feel for teachers to learn that many of the strategies they have used to communicate with the children and control the class may not work with a child with Asperger's Syndrome. It is natural for teachers to worry that if they make accommodations for one child they will need to make special arrangements for all the children. Yet what often occurs is that the child with Asperger's Syndrome challenges the teacher to develop strategies for him that turn out to be helpful for most of the children in the classroom, such as visual charts for the daily activities and feeling meters such as we described in the group chapter.

Role of a "consultant" to the preschool

As mentioned above, a consultant can play a role in building rapport and connections between school and home. As we have discussed, parents may struggle with determining if the school is meeting the social and developmental needs of their child. Many preschool teachers and administrators struggle to determine if they can deal with a young child's unique needs when that child's behavior is perhaps impacting the equilibrium of the whole group. Or perhaps the child requires so much one-on-one that the teachers feel they are neglecting the rest of their class. These situations arise and are handled differently depending on the school's resources and the teacher's experience. One very useful service available to parents and schools are consultants who are trained to work with both parties and assist in teasing apart the factors influencing a child's behavior. Consultants may have a child development background or a mental health background. Some preschools have their own consultants as part of the staff, or consultants are available on a contract basis. Parents can also hire a consultant to help them understand what the issues are when a conflict or concern arises.

An experienced preschool consultant will observe a child in his school setting with the goal to understand the child's developmental and social and emotional profile, and determine the fit between the child's needs, the teacher, and the program structure. The preschool consultants are often the first people to discuss with the parents the possibility of a more comprehensive assessment, if warranted. They can also help make concrete suggestions to the teacher about how to best support the child. For the consultant to be successful, they must approach the consultation as a collaborator and facilitator for the school and parents. Entering the consultation as the expert, without sensitivity to both parties' needs, may undermine the process and could hinder instead of help build rapport between home and school.

Monica Perez, who is a child consultant specializing in working with young children and their childcare or school setting, has found the following guidelines helpful when preparing for a teacher/school consultation.

A preschool or childcare consultation should include:

- general information of the diagnosis (it is always helpful to bring an article for the staff)

- specific information about the ways in which the disorder presents in the child being observed, with emphasis always being placed on defining the child's strengths and weaknesses in relation to *normal development.*

Teachers value consultations that provide information based on concrete examples from an observation done in the child's residing classroom.

The school based observation might include:

- general information of the observation (activities, transitions, etc.)
- examples of specific situations that capture moments when the child appears to be challenged and successful in the classroom
- what the child was doing
- who was involved in the interaction
- the emotional climate of the classroom, interaction
- what the likely perception of the child was
- what the likely perception of the peer(s) was
- what the likely perception of the teacher(s) was
- what strategies appeared to be working with the child (highlight the teachers' strengths)
- what didn't work regarding the manner of response
- the provision of multiple ideas for intervention
- how to prevent and anticipate certain situations
- facilitating understanding of parents' perspective with the teachers
- suggestions of ways to communicate with the child's parent in order to work toward a collaborative relationship
- the offer of phone follow-up.

Every consultant will have his or her own individual style of working; however, these guidelines can be useful for parents and teachers to keep in mind when discussing how a consultant may go about supporting their family and the school.

To illustrate the process of building rapport we now turn to the case of Steven, the four-year-old boy you read about in Chapter 4 who presented with behavioral problems both at home and at his preschool. This case is a good example of how strong communication between parents and the teachers expedited the evaluation process and facilitated the implementation of interventions. A consultant (the child's therapist) was also instrumental in helping teachers understand Steven's behavior.

Case of Steven

Steven is a four-year-old boy who was referred by his teachers for what were thought to be difficulties with attention and hyperactivity. The teachers' complaints were that Steven couldn't stay at one table activity for more than a few minutes, except for puzzles and the blocks. The teachers were puzzled by how, despite being such a very verbal child, he didn't "try" to communicate with the teachers or engage with his friends in reciprocal play. He was a child who was always eager to participate in a class activity but his focus was more on being first than what the activity entailed. For example, the teachers could always count on him to raise his hand before they had finished the question, knowing that nine times out of ten his response would be a fact related to the weather or nature rather than the question they had asked. Steven was seen as being somewhat of a loner and was often rejecting of peers' efforts at engaging him. The teachers were caring but overwhelmed with Steven's distractibility and noncompliance. They wondered if he was being obstinate and stubborn in his refusal to participate in group activities.

Steven's parents also had concerns about his behavior and, because of the good rapport with his teachers, they were open to seeking an evaluation. Through their insurance company they were referred to a Child Development Clinic where a psychologist evaluated Steven and diagnosed him with Asperger's Syndrome. The psychologist made a school visit and talked with teachers regarding the teachers' concerns and observations. When the parents shared the news that Steven had AS, the teachers were initially relieved that they hadn't been wrong that something was different about Steven. They were provided with a lot of information about AS and were open to trying to make things work for him in their program, despite being quite unsure if they were equipped to handle the needs. They admitted to being a bit over-whelmed by all the reading material and needing help translating the information into practical ways of intervening on Steven's behalf in the classroom. The therapist working with Steven's family was willing to come back to the classroom to both observe Steven and make suggestions as to how the teachers might begin eliciting his cooperation.

The therapist assessed the teachers' strengths during her observation and established some guidelines for intervention based on these strengths. For example, one teacher was very rule oriented and reinforced the rules often during many of the activities. The therapist was able to point this out and validate how comforting it is for many children to have clear expectations of what is expected of them. She then made the suggestion of providing the rules in a visual form so that Steven could process them more easily, since he didn't always pick up on the verbal cue. Again, Steven's teacher was open to the feedback and, despite feeling nervous when the therapist observed, she was able to incorporate the suggestions.

Not every situation can go as smoothly as the case of Steven. Yet this case does illustrate the importance of the working relationship between the parents and the teachers and the tremendous advantage of having teachers who are able to communicate information in a sensitive manner which empowers the parents to get help. In a worse case scenario, Steven's teachers could have been frustrated with him, shared only the negative, and alienated the parents or even asked the child to leave the preschool. In this case, Steven might have to fail several placements before he and his family got the help he needed.

How do parents go about getting special services for a child in their school?

In general, a safe first step is to go to your child's school, or the school you anticipate your child attending in the upcoming school year, and inquire in the office about how parents go about seeking school based services for children with "special needs." In the United States there are national laws regarding the type of services that the public schools are responsible to provide. Since 1975, key federal legislation in the United States (P.L. 94–142, Education of All Handicapped Children) was introduced addressing the needs of children with special learning disabilities who, because of those impairments, need special education and related services. (See Table 11.3 for the list of categories of disabilities which may qualify for special education services.) This legislation has been amended since, and currently is called Disability Education Act (IDEA, P.L. 105–17). As you can see in Table 11.3, children with autism are included in the definition of a "child with a disability" (National Research Council 2001). As a result of this legislature, schools are mandated to provide *free and appropriate education* in the least restrictive environment that meets the child's educational needs. *What is important to remember here is that schools are required to provide the most appropriate program, not the best possible program.* Children with special needs are also guaranteed a nondiscriminatory evaluation prior to being placed in a special education program, with tests that are appropriate to the child's cultural and linguistic background. The law also states that the school must develop an *individualized education plan* (IEP) for each child who qualifies for special education services. The IEP is a plan that describes the child's current functioning, establishes appropriate goals for the school year, and determines particular services to be delivered. Districts may vary in how they categorize the different impairments; for example, some districts use the term autistic-like instead of autistic. But in general, these are the impairments that qualify a child for services. We refer readers to Appendix III for more information regarding IEP procedures.

Table 11.3 Eligibility criteria for special education services in the United States

- Deaf
- Hard of hearing
- Visually impaired
- Specific learning disability
- Orthopedically impaired
- Other health impaired
- Established medical disability (0–5)
- Traumatic brain injury
- Emotionally disturbed
- Cognitively impaired
- Speech and language impairment
- Autistic
- Multiple disability

Should a child be mainstreamed or placed in a therapeutic class?

The most common recommendation is to try to maintain a child with Asperger's Syndrome in a regular classroom setting where stronger models for socialization are available. In a regular classroom setting, the services that may be available are "pull out" services (speech and language therapy, occupational therapy, or resource specialist help). In the case of speech and language therapy, the therapist might meet with the child once weekly in a small group to work on pragmatic language, and also meet with the teacher to assist with ideas of how to help the child within the context of the classroom.

There are times when a child can benefit from a small self-contained classroom designed for children with Asperger's Syndrome or communication difficulties, where his academic, behavioral, and social needs can be addressed. For many of our children, a special class has provided them with a positive experience in which they learned that teachers can be trusted and learning can be fun. There are some school systems that have had such an influx of referrals of children with Asperger's Syndrome that special classes have been developed just to meet the diverse needs of this population. In many of these classes the children are mainstreamed in a regular class for a period of time, starting the first week of school; but to this date, these classes are rare.

A special class for children with Asperger's Syndrome and/or communication difficulties, that has a strong, experienced teacher and an integrated staff, that may include an aide, speech and language pathologist, occupational therapist, and psychologist, can provide a child with the individualized care he needs so that his academic skills are challenged, while at the same time addressing his weaknesses on a daily basis. An understandable concern raised by most parents is that once their child is labeled as having "special needs" they will not be challenged enough to reach their full potential. In fact, we have found just the opposite to be true. Most of the children we have worked with in these classrooms have performed above their expected grade level because they were given the external structure and support they needed to do the work.

Another concern shared by both parents and professionals is that if the child is in a special class he will not be getting good social role models from his peers. What is important to remember here is that a reason why one may be considering this class is that the child is not picking up the subtle nuances that dominate his peers' social interactions. One would not want the child in a class for children with severe social and emotional problems or behavior problems because these children tend to have more externalizing behavior problems, providing the wrong cues which may be easy for the child with Asperger's Syndrome to read. They may also be run by staff that are not trained to work with the communication and cognitive issues that are central to understanding the behavior and learning styles of young children with AS. As always, evaluating the teacher's skills and seeing how negative behavior is handled is critical in making the decision about the fit of any particular class.

Is it beneficial for a child to have an aide in the classroom?

Another service, which is sometimes available in districts with strong resources, is a one-on-one aide for a portion of the child's day in the regular classroom. Aides who are trained to work with the unique challenges of Asperger's Syndrome can be enormously helpful in decoding social demands and verbal directions by prompting and modeling communication skills for the child within his regular setting. The aide can help the child pick up cues from both his peers and the teacher, as well as help the child modulate any anxiety that may build during unstructured times or during transitions. The aide can also play an important role in helping the child organize his work by breaking down complex assignments to tasks he can complete one step at a time.

Many aides available through a public school may not have specific training to work with Asperger's Syndrome; therefore the need for ongoing training and support is critical. Parents who have resources available can always encourage collaboration between the school team (including the aide) and other professionals working with the child. Thus, training can occur under the guise of collaboration. Parents and teachers should also refer back to earlier chapters, such as Chapter 7 (parent–child therapy), Chapter 8 (group therapy), Chapter 9 (speech and language), and Chapter 10 (sensory-motor), that outline many interventions that can be helpful for classroom teachers and aides.

As the classroom teacher, what is my role working with an aide?

The classroom teacher plays a critical role in establishing guidelines for the aide and mapping out an intervention plan to meet the needs of the child. Together, the teacher and aide should identify those times where the child needs more one-on-one attention and those times where the aide can act more as a facilitator for an activity or interaction. As the child adapts to a classroom routine and his behavior is better controlled, the aide may begin to choose times when he will pull back and work with other students or help the teacher with other activities. The classroom teacher should be the one to identify where and when the aide may redirect his attention to support the class as a whole.

Collaboration with other professionals

An essential component of any child's intervention is collaboration between the professionals involved in the child's care, his parents, and school staff, to provide an integrated and consistent approach to addressing his social, communication, and behavioral difficulties. For example, if a child is participating in a social skills group, the therapist running the group may be working on a particular approach to a behavioral issue, which he or she can share with both

---

Table 11.4 Suggestions for teacher from Steven's social skills group therapist

- Steven has difficulty following multiple verbal instructions. Multi-sensory approaches are critical for Steven. He is very attuned to visual cues and they provide a helpful guide for verbal instructions.

- A chart with visual cues and words describing the class schedule might help him organize his activities and reduce the anxiety that arises when he feels confused about what he needs to do, may do, or will be doing.

- Steven will frequently shut down when overloaded with lots of verbal instructions. When overloaded he will appear not to be listening, not focusing on his task, or he might start to act out. If he becomes overloaded, counting can help calm him. It is also important to decrease the verbal demands being made on him and provide him with clear, concrete, step by step, visual cues.

- Frequent positive feedback will help Steven best learn the rules. Feedback needs to be specific and concrete.

- If possible, allow Steven to bring a snack. When stressed, Steven frequently says he is hungry or thirsty and if he can have a few crackers or some juice he often calms down.

- Steven responds well when he has an assigned seat. If this consistency is available, and he knows where he is going to sit, he won't have to perseverate and worry as much about the transition.

- Steven responds best to an environment that provides consistency and structure in a caring and sensitive manner. Changes need to be anticipated for him and information provided to him in a concrete manner. He is easily overwhelmed by strong affect and can become oppositional and defiant if approached in an authoritarian and strong manner.

the parents and the teacher. If the child gets the same feedback in all three situations, he is much more likely to begin generalizing the skill. Similarly, outside therapists can provide consultation to classroom teachers to help them understand the inner workings of a child, and provide some suggestions as to how to handle particular behavioral or social difficulties. Written suggestions are often very helpful to teachers. In the case of Steven, the child described earlier in this chapter, he participated in a social skills group, and in preparation for a consultation with his teacher, the group therapist wrote a summary of his progress in the group to share with the school. Table 11.4 was provided to her.

Other benefits of getting help from outside clinicians have been described in earlier chapters. For services to be beneficial for the child, it is key for there to be collaboration among all professionals working with the child to ensure continuity and consistency across settings. Since the classroom teachers are often the people who spend the most time with these children, their expertise and perspective is important for other clinicians. It is important for parents to encourage clinicians working with their child (and for clinicians to remember) that consultation with teachers is a *two way dialogue*. Teachers appreciate support and suggestions but they are also a wealth of information that should be tapped into. Building connections takes time and commitment. Time is often a rare commodity in the busy life of parents, teachers, and other professionals. Sometimes it takes the persistence of a parent to demand that the professionals involved in their child's care follow up with the rest of the team. This persistence has its payoff and is in the best interest of the child.

How do I get more help for a student in my class? I don't feel the child's needs are being met by me alone!

It is not uncommon for teachers to feel that a child needs more help than they can provide. When this occurs, it is important for teachers to express their concerns to school personnel and problem solve how they may get some support. Support can come in many forms. A teacher might benefit from the school psychologist coming and observing the classroom and making suggestions regarding adaptations to the classroom. School staff may recognize that the child needs a break during a particular period of the day that is too over-stimulating for the child, and find something for the child to do in the front office during that time. The teacher, together with the family and school personnel, may revisit whether the child might qualify for additional services to address the child's developmental and behavioral issues. And sometimes, teachers just need to be reminded how much they are doing and how frustrating it is that changes in social and communication skills can take a long time.

Next year my child will be entering kindergarten. Should I be looking for different things than I looked for in a preschool setting?

In general you will want to look for all of the same qualities described earlier in the chapter about evaluating a preschool setting. The one major difference is that with kindergarten comes the formal introduction of pre-academics curriculum and performance expectations. Up until this point, the children may have been encouraged to use letters and numbers but they typically are not evaluated in these areas. Once evaluations are introduced, there often is a growing sense of pressure on both the child and the teacher to make sure that the basic skills are mastered so that the child is "prepared" for first grade. Furthermore, kindergarteners are often expected to either be or become more independent beings. Teachers may feel that children should begin resolving their own conflicts instead of turning to the teacher for help. The children may be expected to keep their materials and clothes organized. For a young child with Asperger's Syndrome, some of these expectations may be challenging and unrealistic. Once again, with good communication between home and school, there will be a dialogue about the developmental and social challenges these children face in order to make for a successful experience.

In the section below you will see that we have used the developmental framework discussed throughout this book as a guide for addressing some of the issues and intervention strategies that may be helpful for young children with Asperger's Syndrome in the kindergarten setting (Williams 1995). *Once again, we cannot stress enough that the strategies we present are broad and they must be finely attuned and tailored to meet the unique needs of an individual child.*

Common challenges for young children with Asperger's Syndrome and their teachers in the school setting

Motor and sensory issues

Children are expected to sit for longer periods of time for circle time as well as at a table or desk. This can be especially difficult for a sensory defensive child who moves around in the chair to get sensory stimulation. Children also may have difficulty with printing and writing due to fine motor and visual motor skill delays. Group sports are often introduced, a challenge for children who may not understand the rules or who have their own interpretation of the rules. Children often are expected to stand in line during many transitions of the day, which is difficult for the child who doesn't easily tolerate being bumped, poked, or pushed.

INTERVENTION STRATEGIES

- As in preschool it may help to have objects that the child can pull, squeeze, and push at with his fingers while he is expected to be sitting in his seat and listening to his teacher's or peer's presentations.

- An occupational therapist may have helpful suggestions regarding different types of pens, pencils, and writing materials that can make writing tasks easier.

- Break down tasks into parts that can be accomplished one at a time, with feedback from a teacher after each part is accomplished.

- Provide guidelines drawn on the assignment that help the child control the size and uniformity of the letters he writes.

- Prepare the child for the sport by reviewing the rules, the positions, and movements.

- Create a social story to explain how different people may play the same game different ways.

- Have the child stand first or last in line, giving him a job to do while the other children are in line, or let him sit at the table or push against a wall while he waits in line.

Communication issues

Difficulties with pragmatic language become particularly notable in kindergarten, where children are often expected to be able to sit quietly in a circle and listen to the teacher. Some children's attempts to be active participants in group activities are misunderstood as being immature, disruptive behavior. This may include speaking out of turn, talking off the topic, poor turn taking, or not picking up on others' social cues, to list a few. Because young children with Asperger's Syndrome often have their own interpretation of how an assignment should be completed, they can encounter difficulties with their peers or teacher when they refuse to do the assignment a "different" way. Remember that these children often interpret information very literally and concretely.

INTERVENTION STRATEGIES

- Create a visual guide to the type of talking (tone, volume, length, and content) that fits with different activities – for example, circle time, silent reading, and outdoor play.

- Write a social story about the specific social interactions a child finds challenging – for example, waiting his turn to talk at the morning meeting, having to listen to something that does not interest him, using a name to get someone's attention. For Social Stories to be effective they must be repeated several times during the day for several days in a row (Gray 1995).

- It may be helpful for the child's speech and language pathologist to observe the child in the classroom, provide intervention in the classroom, and give the teacher consultation on ways to help the child regulate his pragmatic language appropriately.

- Go over assignments step by step, write them down on a piece of paper using visual cues, and have the child cross out each step when it is finished since he has such a hard time organizing his work.

- Be aware of concrete interpretations and clarify for the child when he has misunderstood a situation.

Cognitive issues

As bright as many young children with Asperger's Syndrome are, many have difficulty with abstract reasoning and verbal comprehension. They are often wonderful rote learners and many have a plethora of information regarding a special interest. Finding the best way to contain and support the child's special interest can sometimes be trial and error. His unique way of seeing the world can have an impact on attention, organizational, problem-solving, and reasoning skills.

INTERVENTION STRATEGIES

- A child can be told that he can only focus on his interest in the classroom after the assigned tasks are completed and he has checked them off his visual list, or during a specific time of the day agreed upon by the child (e.g. recess).

- Another approach is to go with the child's area of special interest and use it as a source of motivation for reading, writing, art, and math. Remember that the child may not understand the facts or be able to generalize them to related areas without the teacher's help.

- Anticipate unstructured time when children are supposed to be working independently – provide the child with a visual list of activities he may do during this time.

- Similar visual guides can be used to help organize the desk.

- Provide labels for pens, pencils, paper, and crayons etc.

- Provide ongoing feedback from the teacher about the child's progress. A chart can be provided which might list each subject, with a place to stick a star for listening to the teacher, participating in the activity, and completing the work.

- Sit the child at the front of the class where he is more likely to have fewer distractions and a better chance at picking up on the teacher's instructions.

- The teacher and child can work out nonverbal cues for times the child is not attending (e.g. a pat on the back).

Play skill issues

The lack of common sense and some of the emotional challenges of young children with Asperger's Syndrome often surface in relationship to play with peers. The child's ability to engage in positive interactions with his peers impacts his ability to perform in the classroom as well. Teachers aren't always available to negotiate peer conflicts, and children often have less supervision during unstructured times such as recess. The unstructured free play times are typically some of the most challenging parts of the day. A child may pace around the borders of the playground thinking about an area of special interest, play the same game over and over again, avoiding giving others a turn, or interact with other children in an authoritarian way, telling them what they have done wrong.

INTERVENTION STRATEGIES

- Provide an aide during recess time, whose goal is to facilitate positive social interactions between the child and his peers. The aide may find ways to expand the child's interest to include others (looking for insects), set up a board game, or help the child learn how to navigate and join into a lively game of tag.

- Praise the child for simple, expected behaviors that other children do naturally.

- Identify an older peer mentor who may help facilitate the child's interactions during more unstructured times.

Social and emotional issues

Teachers often feel responsibility to prepare the children for school and thus are less tolerant of tantrums and aggressive, "silly," or disrespectful behavior, such as making bathroom sounds during circle time. Because of the difficulty reading and interpreting social cues, young children with Asperger's Syndrome frequently are misunderstood, leading to strong feelings that the children often don't know how to express. They may appear anxious or angry when things occur that are out of the ordinary, such as a change in the day's schedule, a substitute teacher, a class party, or a special assembly. The teacher will need help in understanding how confused children with Asperger's Syndrome are about their and others' feelings.

INTERVENTION STRATEGIES

- The teacher should use natural teaching opportunities to point out the emotions of others in a story, the classroom, or playground, as well as label the child's feelings. One must remember that just because a child can identify the feelings of a character in a picture, or recite the school's rules about appropriate behavior, it does not mean that he can identify his own feelings or those of others, especially when he is upset.

- Provide the child with a concrete list of what he can do when he becomes upset. Have the list readily available during class time for the child to access.

- Teachers should be aware of how disorganized a child may become by a teacher's strong affect. If possible, attempt to maintain a more neutral tone when providing feedback to a child.

- Anticipate changes in the child's schedule by both notifying his parents, who can help prepare the child, as well as discuss changes with the child using concrete visual cues.

The school environment

The elementary school is a new territory that is much larger than the preschool or childcare setting. It is very helpful to visit the school several times before you begin, draw a map of where the child enters, is picked up, the playground, the office, the bathroom, and any other places you think he should know. Knowledge of the layout of the school can help ease some of the anxiety the child may be feeling in facing a new environment. The school may have an enriched curriculum with many assemblies, school trips, visiting teachers, special art and music classes, and trips to the library. A child may find these activities to be his favorite parts of the day, but they can lead to a guaranteed melt down if the child is not prepared ahead of time about when the special activity will take place, where, what it entails, and what is expected of him in each setting. Help the child avoid unnecessary surprises by trying to know as much as possible about your child's schedule and potential changes in the schedule.

There may be other challenges that a child faces upon entering kindergarten. There certainly are many other interventions that can be implemented to address a variety of behaviors and learning challenges. Most importantly, parents need to help teachers understand how their child sees and interprets the world and social relationships and support the child's efforts at connecting. And parents must be open to feedback from their teacher and learn from the teacher's experiences as well. Kindergarten is a big step for all students and is often a year of many transitions and developmental strides.

Conclusion

Building connections between home and school is an ongoing process. It begins with teachers and parents coming to an understanding of each other's perceptions of the child – his strengths, his needs, their concerns about their ability to address these needs, and ways in which they feel they might be able to intervene in the school environment. With this mutual understanding, the best interest of the child can be the focus for building the partnership between home and school. This partnership is likely to be the most powerful intervention for a young child with Asperger's Syndrome. As we have noted, research determining specific program parameters which best support a young child with AS is sorely missing, yet we know how crucial it is to see changes in the children generalize across settings, between the home, the therapeutic setting, and the school. Therefore parents, practitioners, and teachers have to be willing to accept the challenge, confusions, and complexity of intervention as they push themselves and support each other to become creative in meeting the needs of these children.

Books that may help in navigating the school system

Bashe, P. R. and Kirby, B. (2001) *The OASIS Guide to Asperger Syndrome*. New York: Crown Publishers.

Cumine, V., Leach, J. and Stevenson, G. (1998) *Asperger Syndrome: A Practical Guide for Teachers*. London: David Fulton Publishers.

Harris, S. and Handleman, J. (2000) *Preschool Education Programs for Children with Autism*. Austin, TX: Pro-Ed.

Siegel, L. (2001) *The Complete IEP Guide: How to Advocate for your Special Ed Child*. Berkeley: Nolo Press.

Wright, P. and Wright, P. D. (2001) *From Emotions to Advocacy – The Special Education Survival Guide.*. Hartfield, VA: Harbor House Law Press.

CHAPTER 12

The Ongoing Journey

The journey that parents and professionals travel in understanding the inner world of the young child with Asperger's Syndrome is as challenging as it is encouraging. Our desire in writing this book was to provide a developmental framework for understanding these children and the interventions that will best serve them and their families. Our second goal was to provide a book that would support the professionals who work with and admire these children. Parents and professionals both have the difficult task of maintaining the essence of the whole child while at the same time clearly delineating the child's strengths and weaknesses in order to develop and implement interventions. Our understanding of what is reasonable to expect of a young child both at home and in a school setting can be somewhat subjective and culturally prescribed, yet therein lies the work for parents and professionals. They must determine when they should be concerned about a child's social development and what meaning to make of the child's behavior.

In the first five chapters we provided a framework for understanding the rich world of young children and how these children with Asperger's Syndrome may experience their developmental changes and the assessment process, and how families may cope with the diagnosis. Diagnosing young children is controversial and because of the sensitivity so many clinicians have about the varied nature of development, many clinicians hesitate to provide a diagnosis until the child is older. However, in our experience a diagnosis provides a framework for developing a shared understanding of the child's areas of developmental strength and difficulty and acts to guide and inform people *so that behavior is not misunderstood* and appropriate interventions can be obtained. Since these young children can have so many strengths, and their awkwardness in social situations may not always be obvious, teachers and clinicians not involved in the evaluation process may lose sight of the diagnosis. In this case, it often falls to the parents to help others learn how to see their child's difficulties intermingled with their strengths. As the parents describe in their poignant stories, it is a process to understand the diagnosis, advocate for your child, and accept the developmental differences.

We feel it is important to reiterate how similar this process is for other professionals working with the child. The chapter on collaborating with schools described how this also occurs with teachers. We have seen the same issues with occupational therapists, speech and language pathologists, mental health clinicians, and pediatricians. Often these clinicians only see a "snapshot" of the child's everyday functioning. Depending on the task at hand and the setting, this snapshot may capture all the strengths of a child or all of his weaknesses. If you are seeing only the child's strengths, you may wonder if you should continue treatment and wonder if the child has been misdiagnosed – this process being similar to that of the parents. Questioning and challenging one's thinking about a child is important but it is also important for all professionals to learn about the child outside of the clinical setting. The following questions can help a clinician have a feel for the child's experiences: What is the child's day like? Does the child have friends? What do they like to play together? How does the child spend his free time? Collaboration and dialogue between professionals and parents can help inform perspectives and encourage a more comprehensive understanding of the child.

In the second part of the book we examined interventions that target core areas of the young child's difficulties in communication, relating, and interacting with peers. This part also addressed the role that intervention can play in supporting parents and couples as they make the often difficult decisions regarding their child's education, and choice of interventions. Lastly, the part took a closer look at the parallel processes that both parents and teachers go through when determining what is the best school setting for a child and how to meet the child's needs in that setting. It has been our experience that the process always runs more smoothly when everyone acknowledges that they all want to help the child but they may have different ideas about what to do and how to do it.

Since most of the interventions explored in this book lack objective studies that assess the outcomes for young children with Asperger's Syndrome, it is difficult to provide very reliable measures of the effectiveness of any particular intervention. As this book goes to press, numerous researchers around the world are conducting outcome studies on different therapeutic modalities. Still, the vast majority of these projects are targeted at more homogeneous populations, such as autistic children. We hope that this book will stimulate clinicians to write about the programs they are conducting and develop both treatment process and outcome measures so that we can develop a better understanding of the populations that we serve, and offer interventions that are most appropriate and tailored for specific individuals and groups.

You may wonder what happens as these children grow and develop into young adults. Parents are likely to have questions regarding the challenges these children will face in the future. As we have emphasized throughout the book, it is important to recognize the uniqueness of every child and to be prepared for challenges that may arise as the social and academic demands increase. Parents' and professionals' roles as advocates never stop and in some ways may become more important as the child grows and his developmental challenges are less obvious. The social and emotional well-being of the children may become the greater focus as they grow and become more self-aware and recognize that they seem to view the world differently than their peers. As you can probably predict, there is no singular intervention program, education plan, or outcome that applies to all of the children.

What we have learned is that the same daily living and social skills difficulties that may have prompted an evaluation when the child was young will usually be the same areas that influence the child's adjustment to middle school, high school, and college. The child might not need help getting dressed but may forget to shower and comb his hair, or may insist on doing it several times a day! He may not have difficulty separating but may need extra help figuring out how things work at a new campus and organizing himself so that he can get from class to class on time. Just as he had to learn in preschool that he could not answer every question at circle time, as he gets older he may have to learn that no teacher or classmate appreciates a child who acts like the class "expert." He may need help in understanding why it is not always best to be totally open and honest, especially if it means insulting someone. Learning why it is important to say thank-you for something even if you do not want it and when it is O.K. to clown around and when it can get you in trouble are subtle and often-difficult social skills for the child to grasp. He may need help deciphering the social map of the school. These are all things that children with Asperger's Syndrome can learn with the support of adults who are aware of these children's strengths and social needs.

We also know that the red flags we saw in the preschool child's difficulties in organization, abstract thinking, and flexibility will continue to present academic challenges for them throughout their education. These are the children who may never bring a letter home from the teacher because they got distracted by another object or person while they were supposed to be putting it away. Thus, it will always work better if the teacher and parent communicate through other means, such as e-mail.

It is helpful to remember that all of these challenges can be addressed, as long as one keeps in mind how the child is experiencing them, and develops ways for the child to understand and assimilate the new information. With this in mind let us take a look at the children we presented in Chapter 4, realizing that we are presenting just a snapshot of the developmental strides these children have made, as well as the social challenges that may continue as new situations arise.

Many of the children who we first met and assessed while in preschool are doing very well in fourth grade. This is due to the continuous efforts of their parents to understand their children and find the services and learning environments most attuned to their evolving needs, and the work of clinicians willing to develop a collaborative, evolving relationship with their families and other service providers.

Steven (the impulsive, active child we met in Chapter 4) attends a very challenging public school. He continues to be mainstreamed, is now performing at grade level in all of his academics, and enjoys going to school. His mother reports that the one area where he still needs help is in navigating the social world of the elementary school playground. Understandably, she is concerned about his future adjustment to junior high, but she is doing all she can to make whichever school he goes to attuned to his needs and the strategies that support his functioning. He continues to love the outdoors and is ready to go for another summer at his favorite nature camp.

Ben, the shy child, loves his neighborhood school, and is greatly relieved to meet other children who enjoy learning as much as he does. The school's psychologist has moved from spending individual time with him on the playground to setting up a small lunch group with peers from his class to simply keep an eye out for him on the playground. Ben knows that he is always welcome to stop by and say hello or share a new discovery with her. Not surprisingly, his obsession with dates, numbers, and movie scripts has decreased as he has found more appropriate ways to connect with the children in his school. Ben has become friends with a girl in his class who loves books as much as he does, and they enjoy talking about their favorite books with each other.

As you will recall, Mark is the very complex little boy who at times appeared to be very active and impulsive and at other times quite withdrawn. He is becoming a very wise young boy, aware of the areas he excels in, and those which he continues to find stressful. What makes it so much easier for both him and his family is that he can now verbalize how he is feeling and come up with more adaptive ways of coping with these situations. He laughs when his mother reminds him of how he used to go to school and hide under the table when he felt overwhelmed. That seems so long ago to him. What he is grappling with now is how physically and emotionally demanding the social aspects of school can be. Both he and his family know that when he gets home he needs "down time" before he talks to anyone – including his mother! At times, it still feels to him as if his peers are speaking a different language or that he is from a different planet. Following his request, his parents have arranged for him to meet with the child psychiatrist who, in addition to pre-scribing medication to reduce his anxiety, talks with him about what it feels like to be different. Mark does not want to change everything about himself but would like help coping when he feels overwhelmed in social situations. His mother has him enrolled in a few community programs, realizing that he also needs down time to just hang out, play his favorite computer game, and play with the neighbors. Here his mother reflects on her continuing journey:

> The answering machine blinks with another message. As I listen to our therapist of five years tell me that YES, she and a colleague were writing a book on Asperger's Syndrome (AS), joy fills me, as this is our family's journey since our two oldest of three children are diagnosed with AS. As I listen, I am even more touched that they have asked me to contribute a letter giving the parent's perspective of their journey with Asperger's Syndrome. But for weeks I can't seem to "find the time" to hash out the feelings, the thoughts, the trials onto the computer. In sheer embarrassment I sit down forcing myself to write. Why do I dread this assignment and feel so over-whelmed with a simple contribution to a book? Finally I realize the magnitude of my assignment to face the hurt all over again, along with the multitude of feelings. Feelings of relief, fear, apprehension, grief, frustra-tion, apathy, and the list goes on. How do I tell a five-year journey of one child and a two-year journey of the other child in a few short paragraphs? I give up the task once again.
>
> Two weeks later the phone rings…it is the principal of our school. "You don't need to come to the school…just wanted you to know Mark lost control and hurt another child…we have dealt with it and he is remorse-ful…" trails her voice. Suddenly the pain rears its ugly head and I cry for the

first time in years over Mark's struggles, his misreading of social cues and his misreading of his emotions. A few hours later the phone rings again. This time it is our daughter's teacher wanting to know if we can have a meeting with next year's teacher to discuss possible retainment and her social difficulties. The wave of pain reverberates through me again, as all at once I want to give up and run away, yet the conflict rages in me that I CANNOT give up on these kids and must keep pressing on. In that moment it came to me that the biggest struggle throughout all these years (not just the "diagnosed" years, has been repeatedly…GUILT. It keeps me awake at night, it makes me cry, it robs me of the "gut-knowledge" to do what is best for my child (despite the "professional opinion"). It makes me avoid the gaze of on-lookers in a store, at school, at church, as I cannot face another possible judgmental and well-meaning word of "advice" or blatant reproach.

Yes, this is the hardest part. From the moment Mark wouldn't stop crying as an infant, pummeled others in preschool, ignored the "obvious" cues for play, conversation, and affection, interrupted the neighborhood basketball game with dinosaur theories of extinction, we have been inundated with guilt. Was it the pregnancy? Is it our home life? Perhaps we didn't give him enough OT, auditory therapy, herbs, diet changes, or speech therapy? And then again maybe we intervened too much and he doesn't learn on his own? And just when the answers seemed to be resolving over the first child, child number two was struggling. Perhaps she is reaching out for attention over the oldest child and now the second child is emotionally hurt. Perhaps we inadvertently did not meet her needs since we were so focused on meeting the needs of our older child? The guilt just felt, and still feels, overwhelming at times.

As a parent who wants nothing short of the best for my children socially, emotionally, spiritually, academically, and physically, how do I arrive at a balance of intervention, mainstream life, and letting go of guilt? I still have no easy answer. It is just a journey. Journeys to the place where I acknowledge two of my three children have an autistic spectrum disorder that neither they, my husband, nor myself ever asked for. It is acknowledging that because of this disorder they view the world uniquely, with microscopic lenses that I get to only glimpse at through their eyes on occasion. It is because of this disorder that Mark reads proficiently and is ready to advance the world of paleontology at the precious age of nine, that he sees people through to their heart and is confused by their words and social expertise. He knows if you are genuine. It is because of this disorder that his sister Ellen practices ballet with diligence and the perseverance only a child who perseverates on an activity can do. It is this disorder that enables her art to stream forth from inward feelings that cannot exit her mouth, only her hands, into a visual form.

It is this disorder that causes tears in my eyes as they initiate a hug from one another, share a Popsicle with their baby brother, or give up their allowance for a disadvantaged child. I know the effort they put into their world and I know these actions are pure and genuine. I do not take for granted a kiss and the comment "you're the best mom," because it took years to hear those words and I cherish the small rewards of parenthood. Perhaps because of this journey I will pause to thank God for the little miracles in life: they went to school all day AND had a good day, they made a friend, and they enjoyed a family gathering.

And perhaps through my journey I will begin to look differently at THEIR journeys. Perhaps it is not making them adapt to my world and style of thinking, making them belong in my "country" of "norm." What is needed is a strong bridge with foundations of social skills, a sensory regulated body, translations for action in the "norm" world and always a person to TRUST when confused, and for us, a lot of prayer. Then Mark and Ellen can keep their unique abilities, gifts, and pleasures inherent in the "disorder" and cross the bridge when desired or needed to function in our society, to be independent adults and even to enjoy the flavors of this world. But when it is too much they can cross back over into a more comfortable world of their own mind and body.

Finally, the writing is over and with relief I can clarify my journey and possibly other parents' journeys, as I go from guilt to balance and acceptance. To build a bridge for our children and, better yet, for me as the parent to use that bridge to cross into my children's world and enjoy life as they see it too. I suppose too, as I turn off my computer, that this is a process, a trip one will take often, and the journey is ongoing as the world of Asperger's Syndrome is explored and understood. And inwardly I thank the writers of this book for an opportunity to share this experience from a parent's perspective.

This passage very eloquently depicts the ongoing journey of parenting a child with Asperger's Syndrome and the feeling that there is so much more to be learned. Professionals working with these children are likely to experience similar feelings. We are confident that in the future our understanding of the etiology, diagnosis, and intervention for Asperger's Syndrome will greatly improve. Nonetheless, the rewards are only strengthened when partnerships between parents and professionals are built and maintained for the best interests of the child.

Questioning, advocacy, and acceptance are some of the recurring themes in the stories told by parents who are raising a child with Asperger's Syndrome. The struggles and achievements of both the children and their families have touched us very deeply, and they have taught us even more than we have been able to share in this book.

Diagnostic Criteria

Diagnostic and Statistical Criteria for Asperger's Disorder from the Diagnostic and Statistical Manual of Mental Disorders, Fourth Edition, Text Revision DSM-IV-TR (American Psychiatric Association 2000)

A. Qualitative impairment in social interaction, as manifested by at least two of the following:

(1) marked impairment in the use of multiple nonverbal behaviors such as eye-to-eye gaze, facial expression, body postures, and gestures to regulate social interaction

(2) failure to develop peer relationships appropriate to developmental level

(3) a lack of spontaneous seeking to share enjoyment, interests, or achievements with other people (e.g. by a lack of showing, bringing, or pointing out objects of interest to other people)

(4) lack of social or emotional reciprocity

B. Restricted repetitive and stereotyped patterns of behavior, interests, and activities, as manifested by at least one of the following:

(1) encompassing preoccupation with one or more stereotyped and restricted patterns of interest that is abnormal either in intensity or focus

(2) apparently inflexible adherence to specific, nonfunctional routines or rituals

(3) stereotyped and repetitive motor mannerisms (e.g. hand or finger flapping or twisting, or complex whole-body movements)

(4) persistent preoccupation with parts of objects

C. The disturbance causes clinically significant impairment in social, occupational or other important areas of functioning.

D. There is no clinically significant general delay in language (e.g. single words used by age 2 years, communicative phrases used by age 3 years).

E. There is no clinically significant delay in cognitive development or in the development of age-appropriate self-help skills, adaptive behavior, and curiosity about the environment in childhood.

F. Criteria are not met for another specific Pervasive Developmental Disorder or Schizophrenia.

Reprinted with permission from the Diagnostic and Statistical Manual of Mental Disorders, Fourth Edition, Text Revision. Copyright 2000 American Psychiatric Association.

Research Guidelines for Asperger Syndrome from the ICD-10 (World Health Organization 1993)

A. There is no clinically significant general delay in spoken or receptive language or cognitive development. Diagnosis requires that single words should have developed by 2 years of age or earlier and that communicative phrases be used by 3 years of age or earlier. Self-help skills, adaptive behavior, and curiosity about the environment during the first 3 years should be at a level consistent with normal intellectual development. However, motor milestones may be somewhat delayed and motor clumsiness is usual (although not a necessary diagnostic feature). Isolated special skills, often related to abnormal preoccupations, are common but not required for diagnosis.

B. There are qualitative abnormalities in reciprocal social interactions (criteria as for autism).

C. The individual exhibits an unusual, intense, circumscribed interest, or restricted response and stereotyped patterns of behavior interests, and activities (criteria as for autism, however it would be less usual for these to include either motor mannerisms or preoccupations with part-objects or non-functional elements of play materials).

D. The disorder is not attributable to other varieties of pervasive developmental disorders: simple schizophrenia, schizo-typal disorder, obsessive-compulsive disorder, anakastic personality disorder, reactive and disinhibited attachment disorders of childhood.

Reprinted with permission from the World Health Organization (1993).

Diagnostic Criteria of Asperger Syndrome from the ICD-10 (World Health Organization 1993)

A.   There is no clinically significant general delay in spoken or receptive language or cognitive development. Diagnosis requires that single words should have developed by 2 years of age or earlier and that communicative phrases be used by 3 years of age or earlier. Self-help skills, adaptive behavior, and curiosity about the environment during the first 3 years should be at a level consistent with normal intellectual development. However, motor milestones may be somewhat delayed and motor clumsiness is usual (although not a necessary diagnostic feature). Isolated special skills, often related to abnormal preoccupations, are common, but are not required for diagnosis.

B.   Qualitative abnormalities in reciprocal social interaction are manifest in at least two of the following areas:

(a)   failure to adequately use eye-to-eye gaze, facial expression, body posture, and gesture to regulate social interaction;

(b)   failure to develop (in a manner appropriate to mental age, and despite ample opportunities) peer relationships that involve mutual sharing of interests, activities, and emotions;

(c)   lack of socio-emotional reciprocity as shown by an impairment or deviant response to other people's emotions: or lack of modulation of behaviors according to social context: or a weak integration of social, emotional, and communicative behaviors;

(d)   lack of spontaneous seeking to share enjoyment, interests, or achievements with other people (e.g. a lack of showing, bringing, or pointing out to other people objects of interest to the individual).

C.   The individual exhibits an unusually intense, circumscribed interest or restricted, repetitive and stereotyped patterns of behavior, interests, and activities manifest in at least one of the following areas:

(a)   an encompassing preoccupation with stereotyped and restricted patterns of interest that are abnormal in content or focus: or one or more interests that are abnormal in their intensity and circumscribed nature though not in the content or focus;

(b)   apparently compulsive adherence to specific, non-functional routines or rituals;

(c) stereotyped and repetitive motor mannerisms that involve either hand/finger flapping or twisting, or complex whole body movements;

(d) preoccupations with part-objects or non-functional elements of play materials (such as their color, the feel of their surface, or the noise/vibration that they generate);

However it would be less usual for these to include either motor mannerisms or preoccupations with part-objects or non-functional elements of play materials.

D. The disorder is not attributable to the other varieties of pervasive developmental disorders: simple schizophrenia, schizo-typal disorder, obsessive-compulsive disorder, anankastic personality disorder, reactive and disinhibited attachment disorders of childhood.

Reprinted with permission from the World Health Organization (1993).

Behavioral Strategies Chart for Group Settings

Activity: Circle Time

Behavior	Issues	Strategies
Child is overly active either before or at the beginning of group.	Child not sure what to do during transition time when there is new stimulation.	Inside group, ask child to come with you to see the chart which has the schedule written on it. Show him the first activity and briefly tell or show child what they can do during that time. Show child his place to sit in room (which is ideally marked by a rug mat or chair). Help parent support child by cueing child about activities which will follow.
Child is not listening and having difficulty responding to mother's instructions.	Child is overstimulated and likely confused.	Help parent find a quieter spot to wait, and, if in group, move child to a less active area in the room or cue whole group to quiet down. Can use a noise meter/thermometer as visual cue for children to lower their voices.
	Child is preoccupied by internal distractions (problem at school, mother didn't drive to school the "correct" way).	Elicit from parent possible reasons for distraction – did something happen differently today? Label child's worry and give concrete suggestion what to do now to put worry away (e.g. let's turn off that worry button).
Child is jockeying to be in the front of line, pushing peers who get in his way.	Wants to be first and thinks first is the only good option.	Use a visual wheel which illustrates what activity child will go first at so he can anticipate his responsibilities.

Child wiggles or lays down.	Child has weak torso muscles.	Child can lean against parent or be provided with a chair which may help him feel more contained.
	Child is seeking sensory input (feel of floor on his stomach, etc.).	If out of group, help parent recognize child's anxiety and elicit their help in helping child focus on something like a book or action doll they may enjoy.
Child raises hand but responds out of context.	Discussion is overly verbal or child is internally distracted by his special "interest" and wants to participate.	Support child for talking but remind him what the question was. If child answers again off topic, repeat question, providing several choices of answers to select from. Clinician presents materials in simpler way with more visual aids. Rephrase question in simpler terms.
Child name calls or says everything is stupid.	Child misinterprets social situation and misperceives malice on part of other child or adult.	Empathize with child how confusing things may seem and then decode other child's face. Script words for child to respond with.
	Child is confused by what is expected of him or is disorganized by affect of other child.	Revisit situation with peer and help child differentiate the expressions by describing what you saw. Provide child with a script to respond back to peer with.
	Child doesn't understand what is expected of him.	Review in simple terms what is expected at that moment – provide two simple choices for child to respond to.
Child crawls into teacher's lap and doesn't want to sit in his designated spot.	Child is attempting to connect with teacher and is seeking tactile experience to feel the connection.	Tell the child how happy you are to have him in group and sitting near you. Explain how you can't show him the activities if he is in your lap. Ask him to return to his spot.

Activity: Table Time

Behavior	Issues	Strategies
Child calls project dumb.	Child may be unsure of what is expected of him.	Provide visual example of project and clarify there is *no one way* of doing things.
Child doesn't follow the directions and continues pursuing his own interests.	Child may feel threatened by the project and his inability to complete it exactly as outlined.	Reinforce there is no one way of doing things and redirect to project, breaking down the steps involved. Alternative supplies may need to be provided if child has deficit in an area like fine motor (use stickers instead of having to draw…).
Child gets disruptive, grabs materials from other child.	Child may have difficulty with one of the skills required of the project. Child is unaware of other child's needs and overly focused on completing his task.	Have child look at other child's face to see how that child feels. Provide child with words to ask for what it was he was wanting. Redirect child to his work, supporting his efforts.
Child messes up other children's projects.	Child feels insecure about how his project is going. Child feels threatened that other child's project is better than his.	Break down interpretation of why child messed up other child's work and give concrete feedback about how that makes other child feel. Encourage child to help peer rebuild or provide space for other child to redo his project.
Child insults other child's drawings.	Child feels his project isn't as good as peer's. Child feels other child didn't follow directions exactly as outlined, thus assumes child was "bad."	Reinforce how everyone's picture is nice and that you like them all.
Child ignores peer's request for materials.	Child doesn't pick up on peer's cue – doesn't always maintain eye contact, thus misses cue.	Have child look at peer who is requesting something and then prompt child to respond, providing a script if needed.
Child won't share.	Child feels unsure that other child will return the materials and is set on doing project in his precise way, thus gets anxious when asked to stop and share.	Acknowledge child's fear that he won't get materials back and then assure him that you will intervene if they aren't returned.

Activity: Floor Time

Behavior	Issues	Strategies
Child wanders and won't participate in play.	Child doesn't know how or what to do to engage peer.	Provide child with visual guides for the play (can be story, pictures). Identify role child can follow. Provide props that can help the child engage with others.
Child turns back on peer who comes near him and shouts "Get away."	Child fears that peer will disrupt his play. Doesn't process other child's feelings.	Identify how it makes other child feel when they shout. Label child's fear of disruption but comment on the positives of having a friend play. Help children distinguish what they could do together (initially will likely be side by side).
Child turns every play idea into his area of specialty (e.g. space) and doesn't follow lead of others.	Child can be confused by open ended play and resorts to what he knows well. Child not picking up on cues of others and ignores them.	Redirect child with visual cues. Assign child a role he can have and initially he may need help with scripts to use talking to his peers. Some children may initially need to use their area of special interest to break the ice with being in a room with other children – try to connect them with peers through their ideas.
Child starts humming loudly and avoiding any interaction. May even try to leave the room.	Child is becoming overstimulated and is self-stimulating himself to block out outside discomfort.	Child needs more structure – slower approach with other children – defined space to be near peers – initially may play parallel but with staff assistance, bridges to peers can be made.
Child talks nonstop at the air and isn't directing his conversation towards peers.	Child has pragmatic language difficulties but is full of ideas that he wants to express.	Stop child and ask to see his eyes. Prompt him to look at a peer's eyes and tell his friend one idea he was having. Cue child if he continues to talk nonstop and ask other child to respond.
Children become very noisy and disorganized – running about room.	Group is becoming overly stimulated and are not being provided with enough visual aids and support to combat feeling overwhelmed in unstructured play. Child feels insecure in unstructured situations.	Stop play. Turn off lights to cue children that they need to slow down. Use noise meter to visually illustrate that it was too loud. Provide more structure to play, assigning roles and using visual story aides to help organize them.

Activity: Outdoor Time

Behavior	Issues	Strategies
Child rushes out the door knocking into others, wanting to be first.	First is the only position in line that makes sense. Child thinks in black and white terms and first is it.	Provide visual wheel which defines who is first – break down the other parts of the line into parts they can understand (e.g. caboose, passenger car, food car, etc.).
Child refuses to join in activity such as tag.	Child doesn't understand the rules or may feel uncomfortable being physical with other children. May not understand or have competitive feelings towards games.	Before going outside, discuss what game is going to be played. Role-play and act out the rules and actions beforehand. Assign roles/teams for children and adult can assist child who is hesitant.
While playing tag, child crashes aggressively into peers and says, "Got you."	Child has sensory regulatory problems, making it harder for him to get sensory feedback after touching peer, unless it is a hard touch. May not have good control over his gross motor movements and is clumsy.	Model how one tags another child. Identify area in the body (e.g. the arm) that can be tagged if child is having difficulty refraining from a tackle. Label feelings of other child when he is hurt.
Child insists that he knows the rules and that others are cheating.	Child may have learned rules for same game differently in other setting. Doesn't distinguish that rules can vary depending on who you are playing with.	Ask child where he learned his rules. Talk about rules being different in different settings and role-play when necessary the rules being followed – practice run.
Child becomes aggressive when another child tries to climb on play structure near him.	Child may need some down time after a lot of interaction, thus feels invaded when peer approaches his space. Child may be engaged in his own play and feels threatened by the approach of another.	First identify how other child felt being pushed. Ask child to ask other child if he is O.K. Ask child to tell you what his ideas are – and evaluate if child has room to include other in play. If child is clearly needing space, ask him to find an area where other children are not playing where he can have some space.
Child is overly passive and uninterested in doing anything.	Child is insecure doing gross motor activities. Doesn't feel safe outside. Environment may be too unstructured or stimulating for child.	Child may need adult assistance initially to watch play – adult can talk about what other children are doing and try to find a way child can be included (e.g. score keeper, ball retriever…).

Activity: Snack Time

Behavior	Issues	Strategies
Child criticizes snack.	Child unsure of what he should say during snack.	Help child think of something he can share – e.g. a story or event that child can retell.
	Child may be a picky eater and not comfortable trying new foods.	Ask parents about foods child enjoys and try to have them available so child can relax and participate eating with friends.
Child becomes silly – playing with food or making faces.	Child doesn't know how to connect with peers but wants to get their attention. Child exhibits more extreme facial expressions because that emotion is stronger and more understandable to them.	Reflect child's efforts to get peers' attention and problem solve different ways to make friends laugh or join them. Problem solving in form of puppets or use of a social story. Reinforce efforts made that are more appropriate. Simple comment about liking the way a child got his friend's attention, pointing out how a friend responded when approached positively, helps develop child's awareness of what works.
Child falls out of chair, laughing.	Child desires attention of peers.	Help identify other ways a child can make a friend laugh – e.g. jokes or funny stories. Practice jokes and help children know why the joke is funny.
	Child may find himself physically fatigued and having harder time sitting upright.	Child may need to go early to carpet square where he can lounge on it without demands of having to sit upright.
Child talks loudly, unaware that other children are having a conversation.	Child has pragmatic language delays and isn't looking for cues from peers when it is O.K. to talk.	Provide child with a visual cue (can be a small stop sign) that you show child to deter long-winded conversation. Then prompt child to look at his friends to see who is talking and to wait until there is a break in the conversation. Then signal child to share one piece of information.
	Child has difficulty regulating his voice and doesn't hear himself speaking loudly.	If voice continues to be loud, signal child with voice meter that he is in the red or yellow.

Eligibility Criteria for Special Education Services in the United States

How do the "Education of All Handicapped" laws translate for the young child with Asperger's Syndrome? It is important to understand that, despite having a diagnosis of autism or Asperger's Syndrome, a child isn't automatically guaranteed special education services. Eligibility is determined by evaluating whether or not the child's disorder is significantly impacting the overall functioning (academic, behavioral, and social) of the child in his classroom environment. States can vary in the way they interpret the federal guidelines; however, most states look to determine a discrepancy between a child's IQ and his academic functioning. Younger children typically qualify for services when their scores on standardized assessments in language, motor, and preacademic skills fall below 7 percent in two or more areas. Thus it is common for an autistic child to qualify, as the autism does impact a variety of areas of his or her functioning. But as discussed throughout this book, young children with Asperger's Syndrome typically have average cognitive, motor, receptive, and expressive language skills, not qualifying them readily for special education services. Thus the challenge can be how to appropriately describe the deficits of a child with Asperger's Syndrome when structured testing doesn't always pick up the pragmatic language, organizational, social, and behavioral weaknesses, and they don't meet all the criteria for autistic-like behavior. A good IEP (individualized education plan) team who has experience with these children may be able to determine eligibility based on behavioral and social difficulties. But often these services aren't available until after the child has exhibited significant behavioral problems in a mainstream regular classroom where interventions have been tried and modifications made by the teacher.

More often than not, it is the parents who learn to advocate for their child's rights that end up acquiring more services. However, parents need to be prepared that in many instances, despite strong advocacy, districts may not have the resources available. Parents also should be aware that districts can vary widely in how they interpret behavior and how they view inclusion/pull-out services.

Thus, again, parents and advocates for the child need to be prepared to navigate the complex webs of the IEP process.

IEP process

Let us review the process of referring a child for an evaluation and determining eligibility for special education services. The first step is to contact your local school district's office of special education and request an evaluation in writing (sign and date your request). Legally, your school district has a time line in which they need to respond, assess, and have an IEP meeting. Once an assessment plan is established and agreed upon by the parent, the district typically has 50 school days (holidays excluded) to complete the evaluation. Previous reports can be sent to the district in order for the school district clinicians to review tests administered and supplement findings to gain their own independent understanding of the child. However, districts are legally required to do their own assessments and not depend solely on reports from an independent clinician. Districts can vary how they handle receiving previous reports; some may freely incorporate results from other examiners and try streamlining the assessment (e.g. may use results of a speech and language assessment completed by an outside source and instead do an observation), while other districts do not like to incorporate any findings from others, and do their own battery.

The assessment team is likely to consist of a school psychologist and a speech and language therapist. Although each assessment team differs, typically the following often occurs during the assessment process. Each evaluator will use standardized assessment tools; a developmental history will be taken with parents; a family interview is conducted; medical history is reviewed; and natural and structured observations in multiple settings occur. Parents may be asked to complete standardized parent questionnaires regarding their child's behavior. Once the assessment is completed, an IEP meeting (or in some districts a meeting with just the parents and the representatives from the evaluation team) will be held to discuss results and eligibility. The parent has the right to ask to include in the meeting anyone with specific expertise in the child's difficulties. For many families, having a representative from the initial assessment team/clinician outside the school system can be very helpful to both advocate for the child's needs as well as bridge the two assessment findings. If the team determines that the child does not qualify for services, an IEP will not be written and no further intervention is provided. Parents do have a right to appeal the decision to deny services and request a hearing to reconsider eligibility.

When a child does qualify for services, the team proceeds with the following:

- a statement of the child's present level of educational performance in the areas of adaptive, cognitive, communication, physical, and social and emotional development

- determination of the eligibility of the child to receive special education services

- the child's annual goals and short-term objectives

- the special education and related services to be provided

- the extent to which the child will participate in the regular education program

- the way in which the child's progress will be determined

- the date of initiation and projected duration of services

- an optional transition plan (if the IEP team finds it appropriate). (Davis *et al.* 1998)

If the child presents with significant delays in several areas of functioning, he is likely to qualify for services. The team must check a box that describes the child's handicap. They provide a classification which attempts to best describe the child's disabilities. The options that qualify a child were previously outlined in Table 11.3. Since there is no qualifying classification of Asperger's Syndrome, team members are often forced to decide what qualification best describes the impairment and most often rely on the autistic category. Qualifying under autism does not mean the child automatically is placed in a class with all autistic children or even that a child will be placed in a special day class. It just means that the child now qualifies for special education services and the primary handicaps are in the areas of social, communication, and behavior. Some children may present with such a significant split between their verbal performance and their nonverbal skills that they may qualify under Specific Learning Disability. Some may qualify for Communication Impairment due to difficulties in pragmatic language. Many children have sensory-motor issues; however, the degree of impairment is rarely severe enough for districts to provide occupational therapy (OT) services. OT is only provided as an adjunctive service; therefore, for a child to receive these services, they must be eligible under a different classification. Finally, if the behavior is viewed as significantly interfering with learning, some children with Asperger's Syndrome may qualify through Severe Emotional Disturbance (SED). Many parents, understandably, feel very threatened by this label and some might not choose services if SED is the only way the child qualifies.

The IEP team will determine the least restrictive environment in which the child's specific needs can be addressed. Follow-up discussions regarding placement generally occur after the parent has had the opportunity to go look at programs/classrooms that have been recommended.

As outlined above, if results qualify the child for special education services then the team will develop and write specific goals and objectives for the child's education. Goals tend to cover broader, more general, areas to be addressed, with objectives being specific, measurable behaviors or skills that can be addressed in the short term. For example, a goal might be to improve communication and socialization; the objective would then be to establish and maintain eye contact when speaking to teachers and peers.

All parents should know that once their child has a written IEP they have the right to call an IEP meeting at any given time. By requesting an IEP meeting, goals and objectives can be reevaluated, and placement discussed and subject to possible change at the parent's request and pending available placement options. Without the request, an IEP meeting automatically occurs annually. At the annual meeting, goals will be assessed and revised where appropriate. Placement will be reviewed and decisions for the following year made. Every three years, the assessment team is required to reevaluate all areas of functioning using standardized testing as in the initial assessment. There are many good resources available to help plan for and develop good IEPs. In particular, *The OASIS Guide to Asperger Syndrome* provides valuable information for helping parents develop IEPs for their children.

It is common for children with Asperger's Syndrome not to qualify for special education services. However, this doesn't mean that there aren't other avenues to be pursued to get help for a child. In the United States, school districts have established something called a "504 Plan," which is a legal document written and agreed upon with the parents, teacher, and a school representative (typically the school psychologist or Director of Special Education Services). This plan establishes specific interventions to be implemented by the teacher to address difficulties that have not responded to standard classroom interventions. The "504 Plan" was largely created in response to the increasing number of children with ADHD for special services. ADHD unto itself does not qualify a child for special education services, but the disorder does present with some specific challenges that often aren't accommodated by regular classroom behavioral management techniques. A "504 Plan" provides documentation of efforts being made on behalf of the school to address these difficulties. If, despite efforts to implement strategies outlined in the "504," the child continues to exhibit difficulties, both the teacher and the parent have more recourse to go back to the special education staff and evaluate eligibility. And if the "504 Plan" is working, teachers will be accommodating the individual needs of children who require a more specific intervention approach.

Asperger's Syndrome Web Sites

Asperger Syndrome Coalition of the United States
http://www.asperger.org

Asperger Syndrome Web Ring
http://www.aspie.org

Asperger's Syndrome
http://www.cmhc.com.disorders/sx68.htm

Asperger's Syndrome
http://www.human-nature.com/odmh/asperger.html

Autism Related Resources
http://quest.apana.org.au/

Center for the Study of Qautism, Asperger Syndrome
http://www.autism.org

Future Horizons
http://www.onramp.net/autism/

M.A.A.P. Services, Inc.
http://www.maapservices.org/index.html

National Autistic Society
http://www.oneworld.org/autism-uk/

Online Asperger Syndrome Information and Support (OASIS)
http://www.udel.edu/bkirby/asperger/

Pervasive Development Disabilities Web Site
http://info.med.Yale.edu/chldstdy/autism/

The Contributors

Christine Bate has had a rich career as a speech and language pathologist. She spent the last 19 years of her career at the Children's Health Council in Palo Alto, California, where she was the speech and language pathologist for the interdisciplinary team that assessed infants and young children and provided play-based speech and language intervention.

Lori Bond is a clinical psychologist at the Children's Health Council where she directs a multi-disciplinary team that assess infants and young children with developmental and behavioral problems. Her clinical interests and expertise include psychological assessment and parent-child therapy for young children with autistic spectrum disorders.

Teri Wiss, an occupational therapist, is the owner and director of Development is CHILD'S PLAY! The private agency provides occupational therapy for children, and consultation with parents and other professionals. Teri has published and lectured on the topics of sensory integration and autistic spectrum disorders and mentors numerous therapists.

References

Achenbach,T.M. (1991) *Child Behaviour Checklist.* Burlington, VT: University of Vermont.

American Psychiatric Association (1994) *Diagnostic and Statistical Manual of Mental Disorders, 4th edition.* Washington, DC: American Psychiatric Association.

Anderson, J.M. (1998) *Sensory Motor Issues in Autism.* San Antonio: Therapy Skill Builders.

Anderson-Wood, L. and Smith, B. R. (1997) *Working with Pragmatics.* Bicester: Winslow Press Limited.

Anzalone, M. E. and Murray, E. A. (2002) 'Integrating sensory integration with other approaches to intervention.' In A. C. Bundy, S. J. Lane and E. A. Murray (eds) *Sensory Integration: Theory and Practice, 2nd Edition.* Philadelphia: F. A. Davis.

Asperger, H. (1991) 'Autistic psychopathy in childhood.' In U. Frith (ed) *Autism and Asperger's Syndrome.* Cambridge: Cambridge University Press.

Aston, M. C. (2001) *The Other Half of Asperger Syndrome.* London: The National Autistic Society.

Attwood, T. (1998) *Asperger's Syndrome: A Guide for Parents and Professionals.* London: Jessica Kingsley Publishers.

Autism Society of America (1993) 'Treatment Options' http://www.autism-society.org

Autistic Disorder Observation Scale (2001) Western Psychological Services.

Ayres, A. J. (1972) *Sensory Integration and Learning Disorders.* Los Angeles: Western Psychological Services.

Ayres, A. J. (1979) *Sensory Integration and the Child.* Los Angeles: Western Psychological Services.

Ayres, A. J. and Mailloux, Z. (1981) 'Influence of sensory integration procedures on language development.' *American Journal of Occupational Therapy 35,* 383–390.

Baker, S. M. and Pangborn, J. (1999) 'Biomedical Assessment Options for Children with Autism and Related Problems.' Paper presented at the Defeat Autism Now! (DAN), Dallas, TX.

Baranek, G. T., Foster, L. G. and Berkson, G. (1997) 'Tactile defensiveness and stereotyped behaviors.' *American Journal of Occupational Therapy 35,* 91–95.

Bashe, P. R. and Kirby, B. (2001) *The OASIS Guide to Asperger Syndrome: Advice, Support, Insight, and Inspiration.* New York: Crown Publishers.

Belsky, J. (1981) 'Early human experience: A family perspective.' *Developmental Psychology 17*, 13–23.

Benbow, M. (1995) 'Principles and practices of teaching handwriting.' In A. Henderson and C. Pehoski (eds) *Hand Function in the Child: Foundations for Remediation*. St. Louis: Mosby.

Benbow, M. (1999) *Teacher Guide: Fine Motor Development: Activities to Develop Hand Skills in Young Children*. Columbus, OH: Zaner-Bloser, Inc.

Bishop, D. V. M. (1989) 'Autism, Asperger's Syndrome and semantic-pragmatic disorder. Where are the boundaries?' *British Journal of Disorders of Communications 24*, 107–121.

Bishop, D. V. M. (1998) 'Development of the Children's Communication Checklist (CCC): a method for assessing qualitative aspects of communicative impairment in children.' *Journal of Child Psychology and Psychiatry 39*, 6, 879–891.

Bissell, J., Fisher, J., Owens, C. and Polcyn, P. (1998) *Sensory Motor Handbook: A Guide for Implementing and Modifying Activities in the Classroom*. San Antonio, TX: Therapy Skill Builders.

Blanche, E. I. and Parham, L. D. (2001) 'Praxis and organization of behavior in time and space.' In S. S. Roley, E. I. Blanche and R. C. Schaaf (eds) *Understanding the Nature of Sensory Integration with Diverse Populations*. San Antonio: Therapy Skill Builders.

Bristol, M. (1987) 'Mothers of children with autism or communication disorders: Successful adaptation and the double ABCX model.' *Journal of Autism and Developmental Disorders 17*, 469–486.

Bristol, M., Gallagher, J. and Schopler, E. (1988) 'Mothers and fathers of young developmentally disabled and non-disabled boys: Adaptation and spousal support.' *Developmental Psychology 24*, 441–451.

Bundy, A. C. (1991) 'Play theory and sensory integration.' In A. G. Fisher, A. Murray and A. C. Bundy (eds) *Sensory Integration: Theory and Practice*. Philadelphia: F. A. Davis.

Burpee, J. D. (1997) 'Sensory integration and visual functions.' In M. Gentile (ed) *Functional Visual Behavior: A Therapist's Guide to Evaluation and Treatment Options*. Bethesda, MD: The American Occupational Therapy Association.

Butterfield, P. M. (2002) 'Child care is rich in routines.' *Zero to Three 22*, 4, 29–32.

Cacace, A. T. and McFarland, D. J. (1998) 'Central Auditory Processing Disorder in School-Aged Children: A Critical Review.' *Journal of Speech, Language, and Hearing Research 41*, 355–373.

Case-Smith, J. (1995) 'Grasp, release, and bimanual skills in the first two years of life.' In A. Henderson and C. Pehoski (eds) *Hand Function in the Child: Foundations for Remediation*. St. Louis: Mosby.

Case-Smith, J. (1997) 'Clinical interpretation of Factor analysis on the sensory profile from a national sample of children without disabilities.' *The American Journal of Occupational Therapy 51*, 496–499.

Case-Smith, J. and Humphry, R. (1996) 'Feeding and Oral Motor Skills.' In J. Case-Smith, A. S. Allen and P. N. Pratt (eds) *Occupational Therapy for Children, 3rd Edition*. St. Louis: Mosby.

Case-Smith, J., Heaphy, T., Marr, D., Galvin, B., Koch, V., Ellis, M. G. and Perez, I. (1998) 'Fine motor and functional performance outcomes in preschool children.' *The American Journal of Occupational Therapy 52*, 788–798.

Cumine, V., Leach, J. and Stevenson, G. (1998) *Asperger Syndrome: A Practical Guide for Teachers*. London: David Fulton Publishers.

Dalrymple, N. J. and Ruble, L. A. (1996) *Technical Assistance Manual on Autism for Kentucky Public Schools*. (Available from the Kentucky Department of Education, 500 Mero Street, Frankfurt, KY 40601.)

Davies, D. (1999) *Child Development: A Practitioner's Guide*. New York: Guilford Press.

Davis, M., Kilgo, J. and Gamel-McCormick, M. (1998) *Young Children with Special Needs*. Massachusetts: Allyn and Bacon.

Dunn, J. (1985) *Siblings*. Cambridge: Harvard University Press.

Dunn, W. (1999) *Sensory Profile*. San Antonio: The Psychological Corporation.

Dunn, W., Myles, B. S. and Orr, S. (2002) 'Sensory processing issues associated with Asperger syndrome: A preliminary investigation.' *The American Journal of Occupational Therapy 56*, 97–102.

Dunst, C. J. (1999) 'Placing parent education in conceptual and empirical context.' *Topics in Early Childhood Special Education 59*, 471–474.

Ewald, J. A. and Parham, L. D. (1997) 'Strategies to enhance play experiences of preschoolers with prenatal drug exposure.' In L. D. Parham and L. Fazio (eds) *Play in Occupational Therapy for Children*. St. Louis: Mosby.

Exner, C. E. (1995) 'Remediation of hand skill problems in children.' In A. Henderson and C. Pehoski (eds) *Hand Function in the Child: Foundations for Remediation*. St. Louis: Mosby.

Feber, J. (1996) 'A look in the mirror: self concept in preschool children.' In L. Koplow (ed) *Unsmiling Faces: How Preschools Can Heal*. New York: Teachers College Press.

Fein, G. (1981) 'Pretend play: An integrative review.' *Child Development 52*, 1085–1118.

Fertel-Daly, D., Bedell, G. and Hinojosa, J. (2001) 'Effects of a weighted vest on attention to task and self-stimulatory behaviors in preschoolers with pervasive developmental disorders.' *The American Journal of Occupational Therapy 55*, 629–640.

Fiese, B. H. (2002) 'Routines of daily living and rituals in family life: A glimpse at stability and change during the early child-raising years.' *Zero to Three 22*, 4, 10–13.

Fraiberg, S. (1980) *Clinical Studies in Infant Mental Health: The First Year of Life.* New York: Basic Books.

Fredrickson, J. M., Schwartz, D. W. and Kornhuber, H. H. (1966) 'Convergence and interaction of vestibular and deep somatic afferents upon neurons in the vestibular nuclei of the cat.' *Acta Otolaryngologica 61*, 168–188.

Frick, S. (2002) 'Therapeutic listening: An overview.' In A. C. Bundy, S. J. Lane and E. A. Murray (eds) *Sensory Integration: Theory and Practice, 2nd Edition.* Philadelphia: F. A. Davis.

Frick, S. M. and Hacker, C. (2001) *Listening with the Whole Body.* Madison, WI: Vital Links.

Frick, S., Frick, R., Oetter, P. and Richter, E. (1996) *Out of the Mouths of Babes: Discovering the Developmental Significance of the Mouth.* Hugo, MN: PDP Press.

Frith, U. (1991) *Autism and Asperger's Syndrome.* Cambridge: Cambridge University Press.

Frith, U., Morton, J. and Leslie, A. (1994) 'Autism and theory of mind in everyday life.' *Social Development 3*, 2, 108–124.

Gallagher, J. J. (1992) 'The roles of values and facts in policy development for infants and toddlers with disabilities and their families.' *Journal of Early Intervention 16*, 1–10.

Gepner, B., Mestre, D., Masson, G. and de Schonen, S. (1995) 'Postural effects of motion vision in young children with autism.' *Neuroreport 6*, 1211–1214.

Giuffrida, C. (2001) 'Praxis, motor planning and motor learning.' In S. S. Roley, E. I. Blanche and R. C. Schaaf (eds) *Understanding the Nature of Sensory Integration with Diverse Populations.* San Antonio: Therapy Skill Builders.

Glasberg, B. (2000) 'The development of siblings' understanding of autism spectrum disorders.' *Journal of Autism and Developmental Disorders 30*, 143–156.

Gowen, J. (1995) 'The early development of symbolic play.' *Young Children 50*, 3, 75–84.

Gray, C. (1995) 'Teaching Children with Autism to "Read" Social Situations' In K. Quill (ed) *Teaching Children with Autism.* New York: Delmar Publishers.

Greenspan, S. (1992) *Infancy and Early Childhood: The Practice of Clinical Assessment and Intervention with Emotional and Developmental Challenges.* Madison: International Universities Press.

Greenspan, S. and Wieder, S. (1998) *The Child With Special Needs.* Reading, MA: Perseus Books.

Henry Occupational Therapy Services, Inc. (1998) *Tool Chest: For Teachers, Parents and Students.* Youngtown, AZ: Author.

Henry Occupational Therapy Services, Inc. (2001) *Tools for Parents: A Handbook to Bring Sensory Integration into the Home.* Youngtown, AZ: Author.

Hoshino, Y., Kumashiro, H., Yashima, Y., Tachibana, R., Watanabe, M. and Furukawa, H. (1982) 'Early symptoms of autistic children and its diagnostic significance.' *Folia Psychiatrica et Neurologica Japanica 36,* 367–374.

Ireton, H. (1992) *Child Development Inventory.* Minneapolis: Behaviour Sciences Systems.

Iwanaga, R., Kawasaki, C. and Tsuchida, R. (2000) 'Brief report: Comparison of sensory-motor and cognitive function between Autism and Asperger Syndrome in preschool children.' *Journal of Autism and Developmental Disorders 30,* 2, 169–174.

Kawar, M. (2002) 'Oculomotor control: An integral part of sensory integration.' In A. C. Bundy, S. J. Lane and E. A. Murray (eds) *Sensory Integration: Theory and Practice, 2nd Edition.* Philadelphia: F. A. Davis.

Klin, A. and Shepherd, B. (1994) 'Psychological assessment of autistic children.' *Child and Adolescent Psychiatry Clinics of North America 3,* 131–148.

Klin, A. and Volkmar, F. (1996) 'The pervasive developmental disorders: Nosology and profiles of development.' In J. B. S. Luthar, D. Cicchetti and J. Wiesz (eds) *Developmental Perspectives on Risk and Psychopathology.* New York: Cambridge University Press.

Klin, A. and Volkmar, F. (2000) 'Treatment and intervention guidelines for individuals with Asperger Syndrome.' In A. Klin, F. Volkmar and S. Sparrow (eds) *Asperger Syndrome.* New York: Guilford Press.

Klin, A., Volkmar, F. and Sparrow, S. (1992) 'Autistic social dysfunction: Some limitations of the theory of mind hypothesis.' *Journal of Child Psychology and Psychiatry 3,* 861–876.

Klin, A., Volkmar, F. and Sparrow, S. (eds) (2000) *Asperger Syndrome.* New York: Guilford Press.

Koegel, R. L., Schreibman, L., Loos, L. M., Dirlich-Wilhelm, H., Dunlap, G., Robbins, F. R. and Plienis, A. J. (1992) 'Consistent stress predictors in mothers of children with autism.' *Journal of Autism and Developmental Disorders 22,* 205–216.

Kohlberg, L. and Fein, G. (1987) 'Play and constructive work as contributors in development.' In L. Kohlberg (ed) *Child Psychology and Childhood Education.* New York: Longman.

Konidaris, J. A. (1997) 'A sibling's perspective on autism.' In C. C. F. Volkmar (ed) *Handbook of Autism and Pervasive Developmental Disorders,* 2nd ed., vol. 22. New York: John Wiley and Sons.

Koplow, L. (ed) (1996) *Unsmiling Faces: How Preschool Can Heal.* New York: Teachers College Press.

Koplow, L., Abrams, S., Ferber, J. and Dennis, B. (1996) 'Helping children with pervasive developmental disorders.' In L. Koplow (eds) *Unsmiling Faces: How Preschools Can Heal.* New York: Teachers College Press.

Kopp, C. B. (1982) 'Antecedents of self-regulation: A developmental perspective.' *Developmental Psychology 18*, 199–214.

Kranowitz, C. S., Szklut, S., Blazer-Martin, L., Haber, E. and Sava, D. I. (2001) *Answers to Questions Teachers Ask About Sensory Integration: Forms, Checklists, and Practical Tools for Teachers and Parents, 2nd Edition.* Las Vegas: Sensory Resources.

Kubicek, L. F. (2002) 'Fresh perspectives on young children and family routines.' *Zero to Three 22*, 4, 4–9.

Lane, S. J. (2002) 'Structure and function of the sensory systems.' In A. C. Bundy, S. J. Lane and E. A. Murray (eds) *Sensory Integration: Theory and Practice, 2nd edition.* Philadelphia: F. A. Davis.

Larson, N., Henthorne, M. and Plum, B. (1994) *Transition Magician: Strategies for Guiding Young Children in Early Childhood Programs.* St. Paul, MN: Redleaf Press.

Leslie, A. (1987) 'Pretense and representation: The origins of "theory of mind".' *Psychological Review 94*, 4, 412–426.

Leslie, A. (1992) 'Pretense, autism, and the theory of mind module.' *Current Directions in Psychological Science 1*, 1, 18–21.

Levine, K. J. (1991) *Fine Motor Dysfunction: Therapeutic Strategies in the Classroom.* San Antonio: Therapy Skill Builders.

Linder, T. (1993) *Transdisciplinary Play-Based Assessment: A Functional Approach to Working with Young Children, Revised Edition.* Baltimore: Paul H. Brookes.

Lindquist, J. E., Mack, W. and Parham, L. D. (1982) 'A synthesis of occupational behavior and sensory integration concepts in theory and practice, Part 2: Clinical applications.' *American Journal of Occupational Therapy 36*, 433–437.

Losche, G. (1990) 'Sensorimotor and action development in autistic children from infancy to early childhood.' *Journal of Child Psychology and Psychiatry 31*, 5, 749–761.

Mailloux, Z. and Burke, J. P. (1997) 'Play and the sensory integrative approach.' In L. D. Parham and L. Fazio (eds) *Play in Occupational Therapy for Children.* St. Louis: Mosby.

Manolson, A. (1992) *It Takes Two to Talk.* Toronto: Hanen Center Publications.

Martin, A., Patzer, D. K. and Volkmar, F. (2000) 'Psychopharmacological treatment of higher-functioning pervasive developmental disorders.' In A. Klin, F. Volkmar and S. Sparrow (eds) *Asperger Syndrome.* New York: Guilford Press.

McCormick, L. and Schiefelbusch, R. L. (1990) *Early Language Intervention: An Introduction.* Columbus: Merrill Publishing Company.

McDonald, J. (1989) *Becoming Partners with Children.* Chicago, IL: Riverside Publishing.

Milgram, N. A. and Atzil, M. (1988) 'Parenting stress in raising autistic children.' *Journal of Autism and Developmental Disorders 18*, 415–424.

Miller, L. J. and Summers, C. (2001) 'Clinical applications in sensory modulation dysfunction: Assessment and intervention considerations.' In S. S. Roley, E. I. Blanche and R. C. Schaaf (eds) *Understanding the Nature of Sensory Integration with Diverse Populations*. San Antonio: Therapy Skill Builders.

Mitchell, P. (1977) *Introduction to Theory of Mind*. London: Arnold.

Morris, S. E. and Klein, M. D. (1987) *Pre-Feeding Skills: A Comprehensive Resource for Feeding Development*. San Antonio: Therapy Skill Builders.

Morris, S. E. and Klein, M. D. (1999) *Mealtime Participation Guide*. San Antonio: Therapy Skill Builders.

Mulligan, S. (2002) 'Advances in sensory integration research.' In A. C. Bundy, S. J. Lane and E. A. Murray (eds) *Sensory Integration: Theory and Practice, 2nd Edition*. Philadelphia: F. A. Davis.

Murray-Slutsky, C. (2000) 'Tactile discrimination disorders and intervention strategies.' In C. Murray-Slutsky and B. A. Paris (eds) *Exploring the Spectrum of Autism and Pervasive Developmental Disorders: Intervention Strategies*. San Antonio: Therapy Skill Builders.

Myers, C. A. (1992) 'Therapeutic Fine-Motor Activities for Preschoolers.' In J. Case-Smith and C. Pehoski (eds) *Development of Hand Skills in Children*. Rockville, MD: The American Occupational Therapy Association.

Myklebust, H. R. (1975) 'Nonverbal learning disabilities: Assessment and intervention.' In H. R. Myklebust (ed) *Progress in Learning Disabilities, vol. 3*. New York: Grunne and Stratton.

National Research Council (ed) (2001) *Educating Children with Autism*. Washington DC: National Academy Press.

Oetter, P., Richter, E. W. and Frick, S. M. (1995) *M.O.R.E.: Integrating the Mouth with Sensory and Postural Functions, 2nd Edition*. Hugo, MN: PDP Press.

Okoye, R. (1997) 'Neuromotor prerequisites of functional vision.' In M. Gentile (ed) *Functional Visual Behavior: A Therapist's Guide to Evaluation and Treatment Options*. Bethesda, MD: The American Occupational Therapy Association.

Olsen, J. Z. (1998) *Handwriting Without Tears, 7th Edition*. (Available from Jan Z. Olsen, 8802 Quiet Stream Ct., Potomac, MD 20854, 301–983–8409, www.hwtears.com.)

Ottenbacher, K. J. (1991) 'Research in sensory integration: Empirical perceptions and progress.' In A. G. Fisher, E. A. Murray and A. C. Bundy (eds) *Sensory Integration: Theory and Practice*. Philadelphia: F. A. Davis.

Ozonoff, S. and Miller, J. (1995) 'Teaching theory of mind: A new approach to social skills training for individuals with autism.' *Journal of Autism and Developmental Disorders 25*, 415–433.

Palombo, J. (2001) *Asperger's Disorder, Learning Disorders and Disorders of the Self in Children and Adolescents.* New York: W.W. Norton.

Parham, L. D. and Mailloux, Z. (1996) 'Sensory Integration.' In J. Case-Smith, A. S. Allen and P. N. Pratt (eds) *Occupational Therapy for Children, 3rd Edition.* St. Louis: Mosby.

Parham, L. D. and Primeau, L. (1997) 'Play and occupational therapy.' In L. D. Parham and L. Fazio (eds) *Play in Occupational Therapy for Children.* St. Louis: Mosby.

Parham, L. D., Mailloux, Z. and Roley, S. S. (2000) 'Sensory processing and praxis in high functioning children with autism.' Paper presented at Research 2000, Redondo Beach, CA, February.

Paris, B. (2000) 'Motor control and coordination difficulties.' In C. Murray-Slutsky and B. A. Paris (eds) *Exploring the Spectrum of Autism and Pervasive Developmental Disorders: Intervention Strategies.* San Antonio: Therapy Skill Builders.

Pehoski, C. (1995a) 'Cortical control of skilled movements of the hand.' In A. Henderson and C. Pehoski (eds) *Hand Function in the Child: Foundations for Remediation.* St. Louis: Mosby.

Pehoski, C. (1995b) 'Object manipulation in infants and children.' In A. Henderson and C. Pehoski (eds) *Hand Function in the Child: Foundations for Remediation.* St. Louis: Mosby.

Piaget, J. (1962) *Play, Dreams, and Imitation.* New York: W. Norton and Co.

Piaget, J. (1974) *The Origins of Intelligence.* New York: International Universities Press.

Riquet, B. C., Taylor, N. D. and Benaroya, S. (1981) 'Symbolic play in autistic, Down's and normal children of equivalent mental age.' *Journal of Autism and Developmental Disorders 11*, 439–448.

Rodrigue, J. R., Geffken, G. R. and Morgan, S. B. (1992) 'Psychosocial adaptation of fathers of children with autism, Down syndrome, and normal development.' *Journal of Autism and Developmental Disorders 22*, 249–263.

Rogers, S. (1998) 'Empirically supported comprehensive treatments for young children with autism.' *Journal of Clinical Child Psychology 27*, 2, 168–179.

Rosenkoetter, S. and Barton, L. R. (2002) 'Bridges to literacy: Early routines that promote later school success.' *Zero to Three 22*, 4, 33–38.

Rourke, B. P. and Tsatsanis, K. D. (2000) 'Nonverbal learning disabilities and Asperger Syndrome.' In A. Klin, F. Volkmar and S. Sparrow (eds) *Asperger Syndrome.* New York: Guildford Press.

Ruble, L. A. and Dalrymple, N. J. (2002) 'COMPASS: A parent–teacher collaborative model for students with autism.' *Focus on Autism Developmental Disabilities 17*, 76–83.

Saunders, D. (2002) 'Pre-writing skills for children under five.' *OT Now* (Canadian Association of Occupational Therapists, Ottawa, ON, Canada), May/June, 31–32.

Seligman, M. and Darling, R. B. (1997) *Ordinary Families, Special Children.* Second Edition. New York: Guilford Press.

Shonkoff, J., Hauser-Cram, P., Krauss, M. and Upshur, C. (1992) 'Development of infants with disabilities and their families – Implications for theory and service delivery.' *Monographs of the Society for Research in Child Development 57*, 6.

Sigman, M. and Ungerer, J. (1984) 'Attachment behaviors in autistic children.' *Journal of Autism and Developmental Disorders 14*, 3, 231–244.

Slater-Walker, G. and Slater-Walker, C. (2002) *An Asperger Marriage.* London: Jessica Kingsley Publishers.

Sparrow, S. (1997) 'Developmental based assessments.' In D. Cohen and F. Volkmar (eds) *Handbook of Autism and Prevasive Developmental Disorders.* New York: John Wiley and Sons.

Spitzer, S. and Roley, S. S. (2001) 'Sensory integration revisited: A philosophy of practice.' In S. S. Roley, E. I. Blanche and R. C. Schaaf (eds) *Understanding the Nature of Sensory Integration with Diverse Populations.* San Antonio: Therapy Skill Builders.

Sroufe, A. (1979) 'Socioemotional development.' In J. D. Osofsky (ed) *The Handbook of Infant Development.* New York: John Wiley and Sons.

Sroufe, A. (1995) 'Attachment: The dyadic regulation of emotion.' In A. Sroufe (ed) *Emotional Development: The Organization of Emotional Life in the Early Years.* Cambridge: Cambridge University Press.

Tobias, M. V. and Goldkopf, I. M. (1995) 'Toys and games: Their role in hand development.' In A. Henderson and C. Pehoski (eds) *Hand Function in the Child: Foundations for Remediation.* St. Louis: Mosby.

Trott, M. C. (2002) *Oh Behave! Sensory Processing and Behavioral Strategies: A Practical Guide for Clinicians, Teachers, and Parents.* San Antonio: Therapy Skill Builders.

Twatchman, D. D. (1995) 'Methods to enhance communication in verbal children.' In K. A. Quill (ed) *Teaching Children with Autism.* New York: Delmar Publishers.

Volkmar, F., Cohen, D. and Paul, R. (1986) 'An evaluation of DSM-III criteria for infantile autism.' *Journal of the American Academy of Child Psychiatry 25*, 190–197.

Warren, J. J., Bishara, S. E., Ortho, D., Steinbock, K. L., Yonezu, T. and Nowak, A. J. (2001) 'Effects of oral habits' duration on dental characteristics in the primary dentition.' *Journal of the American Dental Association 132*, 12, 1685–1693.

Weiss, R. (1981) 'INREAL intervention for language handicapped and bilingual children.' *Journal of the Division of Early Childhood 4*, 40–51.

Wilbarger, P. (1984) 'Planning an adequate sensory diet: Application of sensory processing theory during the first year of life.' *Zero to Three 5*, 7–12.

Wilbarger, P. (1995) 'The sensory diet: Activity programs based on sensory processing theory.' *Sensory Integration Special Interest Section Newsletter 18*, 2, 1–4. Rockville, MD: American Occupational Therapy Association.

Wilbarger, J. and Wilbarger, P. (1991) *Sensory Defensiveness in Children Aged 2–12*. Santa Barbara, CA: Avanti Educational Programs.

Willey, L. H. (1999) *Pretending to be Normal: Living with Asperger's Syndrome*. London: Jessica Kingsley Publishers.

Willey, L. H. (2001) *Asperger Syndrome in the Family: Redefining Normal*. London: Jessica Kingsley Publishers.

Williams, D. (1992) *Nobody Nowhere*. London: Transworld Publishers.

Williams, K. (1995) 'Understanding the student with Asperger's Syndrome: Guidelines for Teachers.' *Focus on Autistic Behavior 10*, No. 2. Austin, TX: PRO-ED.

Williams, M. S. and Shellenberger, S. (1994) *"How Does Your Engine Run?": A Leader's Guide to the Alert Program for Self-Regulation*. Albuquerque, NM: TherapyWorks.

Williamson, G. G. and Anzalone, M. E. (2001) *Sensory Integration and Self-Regulation in Infants and Toddlers: Helping Very Young Children Interact with their Environment*. Washington, DC: Zero to Three.

Williamson, G. G., Anzalone, M. E. and Hanft, B. E. (2000) 'Assessment of sensory processing, praxis, and motor performance.' In *Interdisciplinary Council on Developmental and Learning Disorders, Clinical Practice Guidelines: Redefining the Standards of Care for Infants, Children, and Families with Special Needs*. Bethesda, MD: ICDL Press.

Wolfberg, P. J., Berry, R. and Fuge, G. (2001) 'Combining integrated play groups and sensory integration: A unique approach for guiding peer interaction and play.' Paper presented at the Annual Conference of the Autism Society of America, San Diego, California, 2001.

World Health Organization (1993) *Tenth Revision of the International Classification of Diseases and Disorders*. Geneva: World Health Organization.

Wing, L., Gould, J., Yeates, S. R. and Brierly, L. M. (1977) 'Symbolic play in severely mentally retarded and in autistic children.' *Journal of Child Psychology and Psychiatry 12*, 2, 167–178.

Subject Index

advocacy 121–5
advocate
    parent as 105–10, 121–5, 134, 143,
        188, 264, 280–1
    other specialists as 60, 281
    teacher/school as 118, 239, 244–5,
        261
    therapist as 133, 145–48
aggressive behavior 10, 36, 47–9, 51, 60,
    82, 84–9, 98–101, 114–19, 161,
    182, 216–7
    interventions for 259, 278, 294
anxiety 26, 28, 30, 38, 47, 50–1, 59, 63,
    72, 74–5, 86, 96, 102, 181
    disorder 59, 71, 72–4, 167
    intervention for 140, 168, 174,
        186–7, 252–3, 259–60, 266,
        275–6
Asperger, Hans 10, 11
assessment 53–66, 87
    behavioral component 57, 60–2,
        65–6, 69–72, 79–82, 125
    cognitive 61
    cultural factors 17, 58, 66, 193
    developmental 61–6
    environmental factors 50
    family history 58–9
    learning difficulties 59, 96
    medical history 60, 66, 140, 281
    professional 55
    school observation 63, 94
    sensory motor 65–6, 77–8, 212
    speech and language 64–5, 77,
        190–2
    structured play session 56, 63
    see also diagnosis
attachment 27, 47
Attention Deficit Hyperactivity Disorder
    (ADHD) 75–6, 97–104, 135, 168,
    283
attention difficulties 42
    assessment of 62, 76
auditory defensiveness 229
auditory training 192

autism 10, 68–9, 71, 249
    diagnostic criteria 69–70, 270
    differentiated from AS 70
Autism Diagnostic Observation Schedule
    (ADOS) 67
avoidance
    of food 224
    of motor tasks 37
    of movement 218
    of other children 48
avoidant behavior 48, 75

behavioral consultant/specialist 104, 163
behavioral interventions 36, 141–2
behavioral management 7
behavioral problems in AS 60, 70, 81
behavioral strategies 181, 222, 274–9
brushing 223–4

central auditory processing (CAP) 192,
    208
clumsiness 27, 37, 218, 220
classroom aide/shadow 90, 195, 252
cognitive development 23, 25, 42–4, 67,
    102, 271–2
    see also assessment
comorbidity 78
    ADHD see Attention Deficit
        Hyperactivity Disorder
    Anxiety Disorders 72–4
    Nonverbal Learning Disorder (NLD)
        72, 76–7
    Obsessive Compulsive Disorder
        (OCD) 74–5, 135, 271
    Semantic Pragmatic Language
        Disorder 72, 77
    Sensory Integration Disorder (SID)
        72, 77–8
communication 10–11, 72
    assessment of 56, 64–5, 72, 73–4,
        77, 100, 190
    circles of 26, 39, 93, 146, 162, 191
    interventions 49, 77, 90, 96, 152,
        160, 163, 171, 175, 183, 194,
        208, 210
    discourse skills 193
    cues
        auditory 199

nonverbal 10, 40–42, 165, 171, 258,
social 10, 40, 22, 29, 32, 41, 43, 48, 52, 69, 71, 86, 160–2, 256, 259, 267
verbal 10, 53, 62, 165, 223, 258
visual 10, 62, 95, 102, 168–9, 171, 183, 185, 257–8, 260
see also nonverbal and pragmatic language and expressive and receptive language
communicative intent 150, 193
concrete thinking 25, 27, 38, 43–4, 46, 62, 75, 175, 177, 187
coping behaviors 60
cultural sensitivity 58, 193

Defeat Autism Now 142
developmental assessment 57, 61, 66
see also assessment
diagnosis 9–10, 53–80
criteria for AS 67–70
DSM-IV, Diagnostic Statistic Manual of Mental Disorders, 4th edition 270
ICD-10, International Classification of Diseases, 10th revision 271
in young children 71
sharing with others 78, 124–5
with friends 78, 124, 146
with family members 78, 146
with teacher/school 53, 79, 107–9, 121–2, 124–5, 238, 242
with the child 79
dietary interventions 141
dyadic therapy 144–159
Dysfunction in Sensory Integration (DSI) 77
see Sensory Integration Disorder

echolalia 191
egocentric thinking 24, 48
emotions

expressing 21, 28–9, 46, 89, 202, 203, 206
understanding 46, 50, 132, 203, 206, 259
empathy 28, 48, 138
environmental factors 36, 50–1, 65, 70, 212, 214–5, 219–20, 233, 240–1, 249, 260
environmental interventions 133, 152, 196, 208, 236, 238–9
expressive language 21, 23, 37, 280
assessment of 64–5, 67, 72
Interventions see communication interventions
externalizing behaviors 60, 82, 125
executive functioning 25, 61–2
eye contact 40–1, 48, 71, 75, 84, 138, 142, 161–2, 166, 191, 198, 201, 203–4, 209, 276, 283

fathers 109–12
fight or flight response 36, 215
fine motor
skills 19, 21, 37, 211, 216, 228, 255
interventions 175–6, 228, 255, 276
see also sensory motor development
flexibility 23–4, 47, 173, 216
in play 24, 43, 145, 161
in thinking 24, 62, 264
floor time 186
food intolerance 35, 119, 142, 216
freezing 149
Friend's Group 167–187
see also social skills group
friendship with peers (relationships) 26, 28–9, 44–5, 47–8, 71, 160

generalizing skills 182, 188, 254
gluten 142
gross motor
development 19, 21, 36
interventions179, 214, 232, 278
see also sensory motor development

handwriting 37, 219
Hanen Program 196
hearing evaluation 191–2
hereditary factor 58

ICD-10, International Classification of
    Diseases, 10th revision 9, 67–9, 271
IDEA PL 105–17, 249, 280-3
ideation 213, 220–1, 230–2
imaginary play 25, 44, 52, 70, 72,
    162–3
Individualized Education Plan (IEP) 250,
    261, 280, 281–3
INREAL (INter-REActive Learning)
    195–202
    strategies of 200–2
internalizing behaviors 60, 82, 91, 96,
    125
    behavioral management 180–187,
        274-9
    social skills 152, 160–89

language 10, 21–3, 37–41
    delayed vs. different 66, 68–9, 72,
        191
    observation of 64
    social language, areas of difficulty
        195–209
    standardized testing 55, 64–5, 190
    see also communication
learning difficulties 59, 96
listening skills 191, 208–9

mainstreamed 250–1, 265, 267, 280
masked grin 41
medical history 575, 60, 66, 115, 140
medication 78, 96–7, 104, 140–1, 266
mind blindness 42
modeling 163, 186, 201–2, 231, 241,
    252
motor development 19–21, 29, 35–7, 76
    see also sensory motor development
motor planning 21, 213, 220, 230, 232
muscle tone 21, 218

nonverbal behaviors 29, 150, 270
    gestures 41, 55, 64, 161, 198, 203,
        205–7, 270
    facial expression 28, 40–1, 71,
        160–1, 198, 201, 203, 205
    proximity 161
    tone of voice 39, 207
Nonverbal Learning Disorder (NLD) 72,
    76–7
    see comorbidity

OASIS (Online Asperger Syndrome
    Information and Support Web Site)
    134–5, 138, 141, 240–2, 261
Obsessive-Compulsive Disorder (OCD)
    74–5, 78, 135, 271, 273
    see also comorbidity
occupational therapy 66, 91, 211–14,
    236–7, 250, 282
    frequently asked questions 233–6
    organizations 236
oppositionality 51, 60, 113–4, 253

pain, sensitivity to 35, 215
parenting 10, 54
parents 7, 12, 17, 27, 53
    fathers 109–112, 128, 134
    history 106–8
    in the diagnostic process 53, 56–9
    ways of coping with the diagnosis
        acceptance 123–8
        advocacy 121–3
        bargaining 117–20
        denial 112–4
        depression 120–1
        frustration 114–7
parent–child relationship 26, 29–30,
    49–52
parent support 137, 163, 169
    couples therapy 135, 157
    family therapy 136–7
    online 138, 284, Appendix IV
    support groups 121, 137, 163
parent–child therapy/dyadic therapy
    definition of 144
    questions on 157–8
    role of therapist 146–50

role of therapy 144, 156, 169
  strategies 152
pedantic speech 22
peptides 142
perfectionism 82
perseverative 43, 173, 253
play
  development of 25–8, 40, 44
  parallel 28, 33–5, 84, 92, 103
  rigid 10, 42, 88–9, 92, 103, 294
  social 28–9, 48, 67, 84, 90, 92, 100
  symbolic (pretend/imaginary) 25–8,
    44–6, 52, 71–2, 89, 92–4,
    99–101, 103
play-based therapy
  dyadic 144–6
    see also parent–child therapy
  group 173–80, 184–7
  individual 131
  sensory motor 213, 223, 225–6,
    231, 235
  speech and language 72–3, 195–7
pragmatic language 2–3, 39–41
  assessment of 64, 77, 132, 280, 282
  intervention of 77, 96, 160–2, 169,
    188, 203, 251, 256–7, 280, 282
  see also communication
praxis
  assistance of 213, 230, 232
  definition of 66, 220
  see also motor planning
preschool 21, 161
  consultation to 246
  selecting 239–40
private speech 22
propioceptive processing 66, 217–19
  assistance for 225–7
psychiatrist 55, 98, 104, 131, 140, 145,
  170, 266
psychologist 55, 61, 145, 236, 254, 265,
  281, 283
  assessment 61–4
  role of 61, 63, 254
psychotherapy 132, 135, 144
  family 133–7
  group 164–87
  individual child 131–3
  parent 138–9
  parent–child 144

see also dyadic therapy

rigidity 50, 152, 220
  in behavior 10, 50, 82, 216, 220,
    222, 232
  in play 50–2, 103, 145–6, 231
  in thinking 10, 51, 208
routines 63, 71, 74, 148, 221, 230, 231–2

scaffolding 163
schools 124, 173, 238–61
  building rapport 149, 243–6
  role of consultant 246–9
  see also preschool
school-based intervention 166, 255–60
  see also sensory motor and
    communication
secretin 143
selective hearing 199, 208–9
sensory motor development 19–21,
  35–7, 50, 54, 211–15
  assessment of 65–6
  interventions for 213–14, 235
  treatment of 212–13
sensory integration 55, 212–15, 229,
  236–7
  definition of 19–21, 77, 214
sensory strategies 222–3, 233
  brushing 223–24
sensory diet 232–5
shadow 195
  see also classroom aide
siblings 58, 133, 136
social skills 152, 160–89, 202, 214,
  235–6, 253, 264
SOUL (silence,
  observation, understanding, and
  language) 200–2
special education 69, 118, 249–51
  mainstreaming 250
  qualification for in US 250, 280–3
special interests 71, 80, 88
stress and coping 30–1, 51, 54, 137

tactile defensiveness 66, 216, 222–3,
  229

tactile processing 66, 215–24
    assistance for 222–4
teacher 48, 114, 121, 181, 183, 184,
    197
    assessing skills of 240–2
    relationship with collaborators 133,
        148, 253–4
    relationship with parent 53,
        118,143, 243
    role of 56–57, 165 183, 197,
        239–49, 252
    sharing diagnosis with 124–5,
        242–3
    support for 195, 245, 246–7, 252,
        254–5
Theory of Mind 24, 25, 42
turn-taking 39, 43, 150, 151, 191, 202,
    208, 209, 256
treatment *see* interventions

vestibular processing 217–20
    assistance for 228–9
visual–motor planning 21, 102, 219,
    255–6
    assistance for 175, 256
visual thinking 45, 89
vitamins and minerals 142–3

web sites 138, 284
Wilbarger Protocal 224
w-sitting 218, 228
World Health Organization *see* ICD-10

Author Index

Achenbach, T. 86
American Psychiatric Association 9, 67, 270
Anderson, J. 222
Anderson-Wood, L. and Smith, B. R. 196
Anzalone, M. E. and Murray, E. A. 65, 227
Asperger, H. 10, 11
Aston, M. C. 135
Attwood, T. 44, 67, 182, 203, 221, 239
Ayres, A. J. 213, 214, 220
Ayres, A. J. and Mailloux, Z. 220

Baker, S. and Pangborn, J. 142
Baranek, G. T., Foster, L. G. and Berkson, G. 216
Basche, P. R. and Kirby, B. 135, 141, 208, 240
Belsky, J. 26
Benbow, M. 228
Bishop, D. V. M. 77
Bissell, J., Fisher, J., Owens, C. and Polcyn, P. 228
Blanche, E. I. and Parham, L. D. 220
Bristol, M. 58
Bristol, M., Gallagher, J. and Gallagher, E. 134
Bundy, A. C. 213
Burpee, J. D. 219
Butterfield, P. M. 231

Cacace, A.T. and McFarland, D. J. 192
Campbell, S. B.
Case-Smith, J. 213, 228, 235
Case-Smith, J., Heaphy, T., Marr, D., Galvin, B., Koch, V., Ellis, M. G. and Perez, I. 228
Case-Smith, J. and Humphry, R. 224
Cumine,V., Leach, J, and Stevenson, G. 261

Dalrymple, N. and Ruble, L. 241
Davies, D. 21, 22, 23
Davis, M., Kilgo, J. and Gamel-McCormick, M. 282
Dunn, J. 26
Dunn, W. 35, 211
Dunn, W., Myles, B. S. and Orr, S. 211, 215, 219
Dunst, C. J. 134

Ewald, J. A. and Parham, L. D. 213
Exner, C. E. 228

Fein, G. 26, 153
Fertel-Daly, D., Bedell, G. and Hinojosa, J. 225
Fiese, B. 231
Fraiberg, S. 138
Fredrickson, J. M., Schwartz, D. W. and Kornhuber, H. H. 227
Frick, S. 220, 229
Frick, S. M. and Hacker, C. 220, 229
Frick, S., Frick, R., Oetter, P., and Richter, E. 220, 222, 233
Frith, U. 10, 42
Frith, U., Morton, J. and Leslie, A. 10, 42

Gallagher, J. J. 134
Gepner, B., Mestre, D., Masson, G. and de Schonen, S. 36
Giuffrida, C. 230
Glasberg, B. 136
Gowen, J. 26
Gray, C. 147, 257
Greenspan, S. 26, 39, 43, 196
Greenspan, S., Wieder, S. and Simons, R. 146, 153

Hoshino, Y., Kumashiro, H., Yashima, Y., Tachibana, R., Watanabe M. and Furukawa, H. 35

Ireton, H. 86

301

Iwanaga, R., Kawasaki, C. and Tsuchida, R. 221

Kawar, M. 219
Klin, A. and Shepherd, B. 45
Klin, A. and Volkmar, F. 69, 132, 160, 161
Klin, A., Volkmar, F., and Sparrow, S. 9, 10, 42, 68, 69, 182
Koegel, R., L. Schreibman, Loos, L., Dirlich-Wilhelm, H., Dunlap, G., Robbins, F. and Plienis, A. 134
Kohlberg, L. and Fein, G. 153
Konidaris, J. A. 136
Koplow, L. 27, 47
Koplow, L., Abrams, S., Ferber, J. and Dennis, B. 44
Kopp, C. B. 20
Kranowitz, C.S., Szklut, S., Blazer-Martin, L., Haber, E. and Sava, D. 222, 237
Kubicek, L. F. 231

Lane, S. J. 220
Larson, N., Henthorne, M. and Plum, B. 232
Leslie, A. 42
Levine, K. J. 228
Linder, T. 20, 21, 23, 28, 37, 40, 78
Lindquist, J. E., Mack, W. and Parham, L. D. 37, 40, 78, 213
Losche, G. 45

Mailloux, Z. and Burke, J. P. 213
Manolson, A. 196
Martin, A., Patzer, D. and Volkmar, F., 141
McCormick, L and Schiefelbusch, R.L. 202
McDonald, J. 153
Milgram, N.A. and Atzil, M. 134
Miller, L. J. and Summers, C. 215, 222
Mitchell, P. 24
Morris, S. E. and Klein, M. D. 224
Mulligan, S. 237

Murray-Slutsky, C. 224
Myers, C. A. 228
Myklebust, H. R. 76

Oetter, P., Richter, E. W. and Frick, S. M. 222, 233
Okoye, R. 219
Olsen, J. Z. 229
Ottenbacher, K. J. 237
Ozonoff, S. and Miller, J. 182

Palombo, J. 132
Parham, L.D. and Mailloux, Z. 213
Parham, L.D., Mailloux, Z., and Roley, S. S. 220
Parham, L.D. and Primeau, L. 213
Paris, B. 216, 219
Pehoski, C. 228
Piaget, J. 24, 25, 145

Riquet, C., Taylor, N. and Benaroya, S. 44
Rodrigue, J. R., G.R. Geffken, and Morgan, S.B. 134
Rogers, S. 44
Rosenkoetter, S. and Barton, L. R. 231
Rourke, B. and Tsatsanis, K. 77
Ruble, L. and Dalrymple, N. 241

Saunders, D. 228
Seligman, M. and Darling, R.B. 134
Shonkoff, J., Hauser-Cram, P., Krauss M. and Upshur, C. 137
Sigman, M. and Ungerer, J. 44
Slater-Walker, G. and Slater-Walker, C. 135
Spitzer, S. and Roley, S. S. 237
Sroufe, A. 27, 28

Tobias, M. V. and Goldkopf, I. M. 228
Trott, M. C. 222
Twatchman, D. D. 196

Volkmar, F., Cohen, D., and Paul, R. 35

Warren, J., Bishara, S., Ortho, D.,
    Steinbock, K., Yonezu, T. and Nowak,
    A. 224
Weiss, R. 195
Wilbarger, J. and Wilbarger, P. 224
Wilbarger, P. 232, 233
Willey, L. H. 135
Williams, D. 221, 255
Williams, M. S. and Shellenberger, S. 222
Williamson, G. G. and Anzalone, M. E.
    65, 221
Williamson, G. G., Anzalone, M. E. and
    Hanft, B. E. 65, 221
Wolfberg, P. J., Berry, R. and Fuge, G.
    231
Wing, L., Gould, J., Yeates, S. and Brierly,
    L. 10, 44